Zombies and Sexuality

Essays on Desire and the Living Dead

Edited by SHAKA MCGLOTTEN
and STEVE JONES

CONTRIBUTIONS TO ZOMBIE STUDIES

McFarland & Company, Inc., Publishers
Jefferson, North Carolina

LIBRARY OF CONGRESS CATALOGUING-IN-PUBLICATION DATA

Zombies and sexuality : essays on desire and the living dead / edited by Shaka McGlotten and Steve Jones.
  p.   cm.
Includes bibliographical references and index.

ISBN 978-0-7864-7907-8 (softcover : acid free paper) ∞
ISBN 978-1-4766-1738-1 (ebook)

1. Zombies—Social aspects.   2. Sex in literature.
3. Zombies in literature.   4. Queer theory.
5. Zombie films.   I. McGlotten, Shaka, 1975–
editor.   II. Jones, Steve, 1979– editor.

GR581.Z65 2014
398.21—dc23   2014030916

BRITISH LIBRARY CATALOGUING DATA ARE AVAILABLE

On the cover: poster art, *Return of the Living Dead: Rave to the Grave*, 2005 (Denholm Trading Inc./Photofest)

Printed in the United States of America

McFarland & Company, Inc., Publishers
  Box 611, Jefferson, North Carolina 28640
    www.mcfarlandpub.com

Table of Contents

Introduction

Zombie Sex

STEVE JONES AND SHAKA McGLOTTEN

How would you respond to the onset of a zombie apocalypse? Given only moments to live and faced with the prospect of shambling endlessly through the world as one of the mindless undead, what activity would top your "bucket list"? Luckily for the unimaginative procrastinators among us, zombie narratives offer various helpful suggestions. For example, in *Zombies vs. Strippers* (2012), ecdysiast Jasmine elects to give infected strip-club bouncer Marvin a final lapdance. Whether or not this sounds appealing, *Zombies vs. Strippers* also presents a warning: our desires are worth reflecting on in detail, since they might not play out exactly as we hope they might. Moreover, as we move into undeath, our desires may also mutate in unbidden and unforeseen ways. Marvin and Jasmine's misinterpreted exchanges exemplify such slippage. When Marvin moans about his bodily failure ("I can barely see. I'm so stiff"), Jasmine thinks that he is "talk[ing] dirty." As Marvin posits that he is "so close" (to death), Jasmine assures him, "It's okay baby, you can come." Amorousness and mortality meld. That amalgam finds its fullest expression when Marvin finally turns. Jasmine thinks it is "sweet" when Marvin declares that he values Jasmine for her "braaaaains" rather than her looks, but she does not bargain on Marvin proving it by immediately biting her face off. The next time the couple are depicted, Jasmine (now faceless and topless) continues to dry-hump the fully zombified Marvin. In this instance, living sexual desire and the zombie's carnal longings are indistinguishable from one another. The motto of this particular story may be that love transcends even death. Maybe Jasmine and Mar-

1

vin's tryst signals that once enflamed, our passions are unstoppable forces. Alternatively, these gyrating sacs of viscera might underscore that even grotesque ghouls need a little lovin'.

Whatever conclusion one reaches, the unpalatable combination of zombies and sex is provocative, triggering a multitude of questions about the nature of desire, sex, sexuality, and the politics of our sexual behaviors. Colleagues' and friends' varied responses to our proposal for this volume attest to how stimulating (intellectually or otherwise) the idea of zombie sex is. Their reactions ranged from polite curiosity to surprise, from disgust to shock. Yes, zombies and sex. Is the juxtaposition really so surprising? Zombies are increasingly ubiquitous cultural figures most commonly associated with a decaying half-life and a mindless appetite for human flesh (and/or brains). Sex is even more ubiquitous, manifesting as erotic attachments and practices that are variously reproductive, fun, banal, troubling, and carnal. Whatever form sex takes, it is central to virtually every human life and form of sociality. What is perhaps more shocking than the combination of "zombies and sex" is how infrequently this juxtaposition has been addressed in extant scholarship, not least since our book proposal resonated with so many: we received nearly 50 abstracts in response to our call for papers. We were surprised by the range of cultural texts—pornographic, straight, and queer—that our contributors drew upon, by the multifarious ways in which zombies and sex have been brought together in zombie texts, and by the latent sexual themes zombie narratives explore. Zombies crystallize fears and desires related to contagion and consumption, to the body and sociality, to autonomy and enslavement. They represent a rarified drive that underpins our conscious desires: to consume. In zombie narratives, this drive impels contagious forms of contact, sweeping up new bodies as it builds. The result is that human sociality is fundamentally altered, taking form as a collective comprised of individuals seeking connection with one another, or a swarm of bodies devoid of individual subjectivity, for example. The essays in this book explore what happens in the wake of these encounters, when sex and undeath are brought together.

The Zombies Are Coming

Since the early 2000s, zombies have become an increasingly significant presence in the landscape of popular culture. They have flourished in their customary locale: the horror film (*28 Weeks Later* [2007];

Survival of the Dead [2009]), and they have also found success in genre mashups, where horror merges with comedy (*Zombieland* [2009]; *Juan of the Dead* [2011]; *Cockneys vs. Zombies* [2012]). Zombies even make appearances in family fare like 2012's animated *ParaNorman*. They have spread beyond film into stage musicals (*Fleshed Out* [2012]; *Musical of the Living Dead* [2012]); videogames (*Dead Island* [2011]; *Left 4 Dead* [2008–2009]); and comics (*Chaos Campus* [2007–present]; *Marvel Zombies* [2005–present]). That same ethos of amalgamation is evident in transmedia manifestations of the zombie myth, such as videogame/film adaptations (*Resident Evil* [1996–present/2002–present]; *House of the Dead* [1997/2003]), literature/film crossovers (*Warm Bodies* [2012/2013]); *World War Z* [2006/2013]), and television/graphic novel adaptations (*The Walking Dead* [2003–present/2010–present]). The mixed-media remake *Night of the Living Dead: Reanimated* (2009) and the literary mash-up *Pride and Prejudice and Zombies* (2009) further exemplify the zombie's transmedia circulation. Indeed, as Max Thornton observes in his contribution to this volume, the zombie offers a bridge between an iconic object of print media (the Christian Bible) and contemporary Internet meme culture.

The zombie's ubiquity also underscores its theoretical applications. As monsters that straddle the gulf between life and death, zombies disturb established ontological and epistemological categories, as well as hegemonic norms. Those disruptions are frequently associated with an assortment of social anxieties: about viral contagion, biological warfare, neoliberal and totalitarian securitization, environmental collapse, and capitalist end-times. Unsurprisingly, our contributors evoke some of these themes, either implicitly or explicitly; Emma Vossen's analysis of *The Walking Dead* concentrates on the apprehension and anticipation that follow in the wake of global economic crisis. In this regard, Vossen's essay reiterates that in the horror genre zombies commonly symbolize apprehension over social precariousness and radical change. Zombies expose the abject physiology beneath human skin, either because they rip into living tissue, or because their flesh is falling apart. Zombies also reveal what bodies are capable of, and what they can endure. Yet the zombie's presence outside of horror signals that the undead are not limited to reflecting collective *fears*. As Vossen's essay elucidates, the zombie renaissance offers a multitude of new insights into the zombie's capacity to reflect our erotic and even political desires. Contemporary zombie narratives also expose an array of truths about our shared global present, especially those that are tied to automation, disposability, and new collectivities.

The zombie boom is a mass culture trend that is fueling a diverse body of new scholarly work. As Steve Jones observes in his contribution to this volume, although the zombie is foremost a movie-monster, the living dead's significance has been contemplated outside of film studies, particularly in the philosophy of consciousness (see Heil; Kirk; Locke). Additionally, since the early 2000s zombies have become increasingly visible in a wider variety of scholarly disciplines. Neuropsychologists have drawn on the zombie in discussions of automated bodily functions (Rossetti and Revonsuo; Aquilina and Hughes; Behuniak). The zombie appears in computer scientists' deliberations over artificial intelligences and hacks (Gray and Wegner; Kari Larsen). Posthumanists have evoked the zombie when debating the failures and possibilities of impersonal or pre-personal subjectivity (Christie and Lauro). Marxists have utilized the living dead in metaphors regarding the deadening effects of late capitalism and the turmoil and violence that results from ongoing global economic crises (Giroux; Harman; McNally).

Necro-Sociality

Importantly these various approaches are all rooted in concepts of sociality—the relationships and forms of reproduction that organize associations between people, social systems, and non-human others. Zombies are social monsters, and their monstrosity is a reflection of our own. Lone zombies are ineffective, comical rather than frightening. En masse, however, the zombie swarm is terrifying. Zombies reproduce sociality itself as a kind of latent zymotic disease that threatens humanity's existence. This trait, what we might call the zombie's necro-sociality, illustrates ways in which zombies metaphorically capture anxieties about identity, embodiment, and agency that resonate with contemporary and historical social contexts. As Marcus Harmes observes in his contribution to this volume, one important context that has been largely under-theorized in zombie scholarship to date is Victorian social attitudes towards dead bodies. Drawing on the quasi-necrophilic imagery of European zombie-horror set in the nineteenth century, Harmes exposes the fetishistic, sexual overtones of cultic Victorian mourning practices.

A tandem socio-historical context has received far more attention in zombie studies; numerous thinkers have drawn upon the zombie's origins in Haitian folklore to understand histories of racism and racialized labor (Moreman and Rushton; Castronovo). Many cinematic depictions of zombies are overtly racialized. For instance, zombies have been treated as somnambulistic slave figures in *White Zombie* (1932) and *I Walked with a Zombie* (1943), or monstrous cannibals pitched against white westerners in *Zombie Flesheaters* (1979), *Zombie Holocaust* (1980), and *Zombie Creeping Flesh* (1980). These texts illustrate specific anxieties (and fantasies) about race and colonialism. *White Zombie* and *I Walked with a Zombie* make these links explicit via their Gothic postcolonial Caribbean settings, anxious miscegenation fantasies,[1] and zombie laborers. In African traditions, zombies are not undead creatures hungering after the flesh of the living, but ordinary people who have been victimized by a witch or sorcerer who then forces them to work against their will. As Lars Bang Larsen observes, "The origin of the zombie in Haitian *vodoun* has an explicit relationship to labor, as a repetition or reenactment of slavery. The person who receives the zombie spell 'dies,' is buried, excavated, and put to work, usually as a field hand." These themes were explored, as Larsen points out, by Wade Davis in his controversial book *The Serpent and the Rainbow*, in which the ethnobotanist sought a pharmacological explanation for zombies. Davis's social analysis is more compelling than his pharmacological insights, however; for people of African descent in the post-colony, zombies represent "the loss of physical liberty that is slavery, and the sacrifice of personal autonomy implied by the loss of identity" (qtd. in Lars Bang Larsen; see also Thomas). In these traditions, zombies are terrifying not because they are consumptive or contagious, but because they evoke enslavement to the will of another. More recently, thinkers have drawn upon the zombie to comprehend the apparently magical accumulation of wealth under postcolonial neoliberalism (Comaroff and Comaroff) and widespread experiences of social precariousness.

Although it is now largely forgotten, the paradigmatic image of the zombie as a looming, murderous horde also derives from the Caribbean, and especially the Haitian revolution, which was perceived by the West as mindless, rapacious destruction (Sibylle 2). The contemporary zombie likewise almost always appears as a horde that threatens existence as we know it. The zombie swarm is an inverted fantasy. Like contemporary capitalism, it represents destruction through voracious, insatiable consumption. Simultaneously, zombies represent that which could deliver us from that self-same death drive. Thus, zombies might appear as a revolutionary multitude—faceless, inexorable, forcing a global transformation toward a genocidal absolute war—or they might catalyze a permanent détente, in which humans band together regardless of ethno-national and religious differences. By dwelling on themes of collective power and revolution, zombie narratives typically reduce the social world to its day zero, providing opportunities to re-envisage society. However, a number of our contributors point out that in some narratives zombie futures bear a striking resemblance to our political present. Moreover, as Sasha Cocarla argues in relation to *Warm Bodies* and both Cathy Hannabach and Vossen argue in relation to different iterations of *The Walking Dead*, many zombie narratives reproduce or even celebrate norms tied to romance, gender, ability, and heterosexuality.

The Promise of a Zombie Future

The leveling of social difference, and of society itself, is paradoxically facilitated by the zombie's lack of subjective agency. The zombie represents humanity in a pre-conscious state. Thus, the zombie's revolution is not only social: it also represents day zero for human identity, and the imbricated experiences of individuality and interdependence on which sociality is founded (see also Lauro and Embry). As Sheets-Johnstone observes, animate corporeality is the foundation of lived experience. In this view, our bodies tie us to the world prior to the formation of identity. In Mel Chen's recent articulations of "animacies," the liveliness of an identity, body, or idea depends on its place within ordered hierarchies and specifically its relationship to forms of matter considered dead or insensate. Chen argues that these hierarchies are profoundly relational. What makes one body appear dead or alive has to do with how it affects or is affected by others. The zombie—animated flesh evacuated of identity and agency—enlivens concepts of life or of humanity in which the human is unconstrained by social or cultural limits. Zombies are freed of any obligations, other than to their own hunger. As Trevor Grizzell explores in his analysis of *The Walking Dead* television series in this volume, the displacement of excess onto zombies underscores human efforts to exercise forms of purity and control—to erect animate hierarchies that guard humanity from forms of consumption or violence that are deemed beyond the pale. To draw upon a famous example, that unconstrained drive to excess leads zombies to return to the suburban mall where they once shopped in George A. Romero's *Dawn of the Dead* (1978). Although driven by a quest for comforting familiarity, the zombies are disoriented in the mall's terrain: they fail to find peace, because their new state is incompatible with their previous existence. Romero's interests in social politics are explicitly critical, as is elucidated by the ways the "normal" human social world of conspicuous consumption is echoed in the zombie's insistent, insatiable hunger. For the audience and the living protagonists, the zombie's presence in the mall is disquieting, not only because they are incongruous with the setting. Firstly, the wastage involved in consumer capitalism is personified by the zombies, who are humans-as-waste. Secondly, the zombie's fruitless desire and resultant confusion replicate the emptiness of living human desires. Zombies are evacuated of self, but they also reveal that for the living, autonomous will is empty. In his essay, Steve Jones examines the gradual erosion of the human will and rationality in zombie transition narratives. Zombie metamorphoses, Jones suggests, highlight the tenuousness of our claims to rationality, as well as illustrating tensions in different philosophies of the self and sociality. The zombie's body is post-mortal excess, standing in for the ugly, blind needs that are left after our jobs, relationships, life-plans, and cherished personalities are excised. Since the zombies reveal that our needs are aimed towards false, unsatisfying goals (the mall, consumption), those needs are not constituted by anything substantial. *We* are insubstantial, animated by powerful but opaque desires.

This is Romero's most significant contribution to zombie lore, and one that is developed by allowing the zombie to explicitly evolve into consciousness from *Day of the Dead* (1985) onwards. Also in 1985, *Return of the Living Dead* transformed the zombie inasmuch as it employed post-modern humor to develop the evolution of zombie-consciousness. In this instance, zombies are relatively articulate. They are also able to mobilize and plan their cannibalistic assaults; "send more paramedics," one zombie requests, in preparation for an ambush. These changes mean that the zombie clearly attains subjective existence, far removed from the lumbering, irrational beings offered in many earlier entries into the zombie canon. The prospect of zombie consciousness is of concern because the paradoxes of the oxymoron "living-dead" and "motorized instinct" (as the doctor phrases it in *Dawn of the Dead*) unhinge foundational ontological suppositions. The monsters are uncomfortably akin to their apparently rational, living human brethren. As Webb and Byrnand note, "there is always something 'nearly me' about the monster" (84). The social horror at hand is exacerbated precisely by the human-zombie parallel offered in these films; these monsters are uncanny doppelgängers.

Zombie Love

Not all undead beings were treated as mindless entities prior to the 1970s; *The Mummy* (1932), *Dracula* (1931), and *Frankenstein* (1931) all feature central "living dead" figures that display conscious motivation. Interestingly, these monsters are driven by explicitly human concerns— in particular, the quest for sexual companionship (although Frankenstein's creation does not find his partner until *Bride of Frankenstein* [1935]). These films pivotally present living dead beings not as mechanized husks, but as individuals who lay claim to sexual identity (even if that identity is impersonal, distasteful or disaffected).

What is at once central and strangely absent from current debates about the zombie is any detailed consideration of sex and sexuality. This oversight is startling, not least since sex is arguably the most intimate form of social engagement, and is a profound aspect of human social identity. What makes the omission even more remarkable is how appositely the zombie reflects socio-sexual desires and fears. Zombies are fundamentally reproductive, attaining power through violent, interpersonal and contagious contact. In tandem, zombie texts typically feature a band of survivors, families or their analogues, who must struggle to endure the zombie apocalypse, and presumably repopulate the world. In zombie narratives, human sex is symbolically powerful: it is an anxious reprieve to dystopian threat, and a promise that future generations of the living will still inherit the earth. In one sense, sex might be envisaged as buttressing heteronormative fantasies, then. Allegorically, the nuclear family closes ranks and is arrayed against an encroaching horde (of foreigners or queers), and heterosexual propagation is presented as the ultimate goal that might save humanity. On the other hand, zombie procreation represents a powerful alternative to heterosexual breeding, one that de-naturalizes the relationship between heterosexual intercourse and propagation. In the zombie narrative, heterosexual reproduction is superseded, and what Lee Edelman dubs "reproductive futurism" is upended. In his essay here, Grizzell argues that such upendings, and especially the failures represented by zombie propagation, offer useful queer re-conceptualizations of culture.

Where the zombie-film's sexual politics have been addressed by academics, feminist methodologies have typically been used to examine the living characters' gendered relationships (Grant 200–212; Greenberg 86; Paffenroth 59–66; Patterson 103–118). Subsequently, there are two major oversights in the body of existing literature. First, sex and love play crucial roles in numerous zombie narratives. That is, sex is important to the plots and meanings of many zombie films, and manifests in a multitude of ways. For example, *Shaun of the Dead*'s (2004) zombie plague is a backdrop for a romantic narrative that drives towards lead protagonist Shaun being happily reunited with his lover Liz. However, the film's pivotal relationship is a "bromance" between Shaun and his best friend Ed, who is more pertinently Shaun's partner in the narrative. Although Ed becomes infected, the film closes not with a heterosexual coupling, but with a merging between heterosexual and homosocial, between living and dead: Shaun, Liz, and the now undead Ed live together in a "happily ever after" union. In the Japanese film *Wild Zero* (1999), lead protagonist and wannabe rocker Ace is initially distressed to discover that his "damsel in distress" beau (Tomoe) is male. However, the zombie plague is the film's only crisis: Ace's momentary confusion is swiftly overturned when Ace has a vision of his rock'n'roll hero Guitar Wolf, who proclaims, "Love has no borders, nationalities, or genders! DO IT!!!" The romance unfolds in accordance with Guitar Wolf's enthusiastic assertion. Further indications that zombie-narratives are not exclusively focused on heterosexuality are exemplified by Noble Romance's "Zombies versus Lesbians" novellas, such as Amber Green's *Dead Kitties Don't Purr*. The series uses zombie outbreaks as complications in gay romance stories. Given that sex and love are driving forces in so many zombie narratives, it is surprising that they have been disregarded by scholars in favor of other less prominent themes. In her essay for this volume, Sasha Cocarla explores the queered normativity of R, the zombie protagonist of Isaac Marion's novel, *Warm Bodies*. R engages in a three way relationship with Perry, whose brain he has devoured and whose feelings he subsequently experiences, and Julie, Perry's former love interest. Cocarla links R's quest toward greater liveliness to the affective aspirations interpellated by neoliberal notions of freedom, rationality, and the salvific couple form.[2]

The second element overlooked in current academic discussion is zombie sexuality: the fact that the undead have sex with each other and with humans in many contemporary zombie narratives. Since the late 1990s, zombies have been increasingly represented as sexual figures. Frequently, the results have seemingly reiterated normative sexual hierarchies, in which certain bodies and modes of existence are subordinated to others. Denise N. Cook's contribution to this volume evokes precisely these problems. Critiquing Giddens' "plastic sexuality" paradigm, Cook's dissection of short-stories about undead sex-work demonstrates that although zombie sexuality represents versatility and freedom on one hand, such imaginings are typically anchored by restrictive norms that fetter sexual liberty.

Dead Straight/Dire Straights

In an extension of the associations made between zombies and racialized identities then, it may appear that sexual zombies are utilized to support the notion that male heterosexuality, for example, is the dominant standard against which other forms of sexual expression, identities or genders are judged. It is clear why one might reach this conclusion. In the case of *Lesbian Zombies from Outer Space* (2013), for example, female homosexuality is tallied with zombidom, and therefore implied to be monstrous. Indeed, lesbianism is presented as an object of heterosexual desire rather than as an autonomous identity within this context. As the film's trailer proposes, a world of lesbians is "one man's fantasy" which "becomes a nightmare" only because the women in question are undead. The audience is interpellated into that presumed position of heterosexual privilege via the tagline: "They want *you*, but not in a sexual way ... hang on to *your* Johnson."[3]

The trend of sexualizing zombies is largely aimed at straight men. Both the Adult Swim Flash Game *Zombie Hooker Nightmare* (2009) and Edward Lee's comic book *Grubgirl* (1997) depict only female zombie prostitutes and heterosexual male patrons. Since 2000, the website zombiepinups.com, for instance, has drolly exhibited portraits of "undead vixens" as gruesome sex symbols. Playfully evoking the iconography of 1950s pinup modeling as a "dead" form of pornography, these images make light of the incongruity between cadavers and erotic photography. More recently, the marketing for Nintendo's Wii game *ZombiU* (2012) utilized the same discrepancy in relation to contemporary glamour modeling. The print advertisement presents a model stripping off her bra, accompanied by the leading question, "She's got a body to die for ... wanna see?" On turning the page, the viewer is greeted with an undead version of the model ("We did warn you"). In both cases, humor arises from a presumed incompatibility between rotting, animated corpses and erotic desire. However, this maneuver involves treating zombies as sex objects by placing them in contexts typically associated with the sexual objectification of women. Zombies become a logical extension of the visual tropes and practices of looking that render women's bodies as fragmented objects of male desire. *Zombie Strippers!* (2008), for instance, presents the undead in a context synonymous with heterosexual male voyeuristic desire.[4] In this case, the living clients respond to the zombie dancers with greater enthusiasm than they do the living ecdysiasts. In this case, the zombies are treated as sex symbols in their own right, being dubbed "beautiful" by the customers who summarily reject the living strippers.

Such interchanges between sexual voyeurism and zombies throw doubt over the presumed lines between "disgusting" and "desirable." The decaying corpse epitomizes disgust (Menninghaus 1).[5] In usurping living bodies that are indicative of conventional sexiness and debunking the structures that institutionalize those conventions, the apparently dichotomous division between desire and disgust becomes blurry at best. This ideological collapse is not just concerned with why some bodies are deemed un/desirable, but also the desirer's motives. In some recent films such as *Doghouse* (2009), gender difference is hypostatized as a binary opposition: all females are transformed into flesh hungry ghouls who attack the living (men). In *Stripperland* (2011) a similar division is created, with an added degree of sexualization: women are transformed into undead strippers. What is notable in these cases is not male heterosexual dominance, however. These films depict sexual objectification as both oppressive and absurd. The notion that heterosexual men might see all women as mindless strippers is a damning indictment of the former rather than the latter. In these cases—particularly in *Doghouse*—men that stubbornly stick to sexual stereotyping are painted as laughable. At best, such men are ill-equipped to survive the onset of change. At worst, such men are limned as more monstrous than the anthropophagic cadavers that threaten them.

Numerous films take the logic of objectification further by depicting human heterosexual men using female zombies as sexual receptacles. The film *Deadgirl* (2008), for instance, portrays a group of ordinary young heterosexual men who become fixated on sexually violating an imprisoned female zombie (see Jones, "Gender Monstrosity"). Such fantasies are stark reflections of prevalent desires and fears at the outset of the 21st century: an era in which consumption is deeply tied to sexualized desires for control, and in which necrophilic "extreme" pornography has been the subject of legal enquiry (see Aggrawal 180; Attwood and Smith 178). In cases such as *Deadgirl*, however, the zombie is not a monster: the undead's blankness evokes powerlessness. In contrast, the human males are ghoulish abusers. Being associated with sexual deviancy (Downing 168; Canter and Wentink 491; Gutierrez and Giner-Sorolla 854–55), necrophilia underscores how morally disgusting the males' actions are. Harmes' and Cook's essays in this volume offer nuanced dissections of this necrophilic dynamic. It should also be noted that zombies are not always *victims* of sexual violence. In *The Necro Files* (1997) and its sequel (2003), and *Rape Zombie: Lust of the Dead* (2012), for example, zombies rape the living. In these cases, zombies are portrayed as sexually active beings whose cravings for living flesh are not limited to anthropophagy.

Queer Eye for the Dead Guy

Even when it is straight, then, sex between zombies and humans is inherently queer. Elsewhere, the figures involved are queer. Queer interventions in zombie lore allegorize gay male sexuality run amok (often humorously), but they also underscore the political potential represented by zombie sexuality. A few examples include VidKid Timo's parody *At Twilight Come the Flesh-Eaters* (1998), Michael Simon's *Gay Zombie* (2007), and Chris Diani's campy homage to 1960s horror films, *Creatures from the Pink Lagoon* (2006). These films all play with the idea that gay male sex and mindless zombie hunger have something in common. In *Creatures*, for example, a group of gay men at a beach house fight off a group of undead gay men, who had become infected by radioactive mosquitos at a cruisy rest stop. *Gay Zombie* follows a gay zombie through the difficulties of dating in the clonish West Hollywood scene. In both, gay male sexuality is represented as comically repetitive, and a little dumb. *Creatures* plays with stereotypes of gay "man-eaters," while *Gay Zombie* suggests that with the right attitude even the dead can fit in among Los Angeles' clones.

Bruce LaBruce's queer interventions offer other, more politically engaged, perspectives, which are probed at length by Darren Elliott-Smith in this volume (see also McGlotten; McGlotten and VanGundy). In *Otto; Or, Up with Dead People* (2008) and *L.A. Zombie* (2008), the Canadian independent filmmaker upends the zombie mythos. In these films, the zombies are gay outsiders for whom their zombie difference is figured as a queerness that is at once enlivening and deadening. In *Otto*, the titular character is a young amnesiac zombie, who is new to his undeath. His existential quest for an identity brings him into contact with Medea Yarn, an experimental filmmaker who is completing a political-pornographic film about gay zombies called *Up with Dead People*. Yarn is intrigued by Otto's authenticity—although she (like the viewer) is unsure whether he really is a zombie or just a messed up kid—and decides to make a documentary about him, a study of alienated queer difference. In Yarn's film, an explicitly gay zombie army rises up to combat the banalities of late capitalism and deadened living. Otto's own quest is less revolutionary or dramatic, however. Rather than discovering his will-to-power, Otto models forms of impersonal subjectivity that refuse the lure of a destructive jouissance or the revolutionary multitude. All living beings seem like the same person to him, a person he "doesn't like very much." In the end, Otto opts out, enacting what Halberstam (*The Queer Art of Failure*) and others have dubbed a queer politics of refusal, leaving Berlin to head north, hoping to discover a "whole new way of death." In Darren Elliott-Smith's reading, *Otto* provides LaBruce with a means to critique both the violence of homophobia and the bourgeois homonormativity of contemporary gay cultures. Otto himself is a fundamentally ambivalent character, and one who serves to satirize gay male sexual politics of top/bottom—he is both an object and a reluctant consumer.

L.A. Zombie (2010) likewise presents a gay zombie protagonist, although this film is explicitly sexual, co-produced by porn companies Wurstfilm and Dark Alley Media. In *L.A. Zombie,* an alien zombie rises from the Pacific Ocean and then roams through Los Angeles' violent sexual underworld. Again, LaBruce upends zombie conventions. In this film, the zombie is a lone wanderer who re-animates rather than devours his objects of desire. He seems less motivated by a consuming hunger (for sex or brains) than by a melancholic and compassionate desire to undo the effects of violence. When he encounters a dead young man, their sexual congress and specifically his black, oil-like ejaculate brings him back to life. In *L.A. Zombie,* LaBruce extends his critique of gay culture as dead or boring, and he also ambivalently offers sex as both effect and remedy to what queer critics like Lisa Duggan have called the new homonormativity (*The Twilight of Equality?*), a gay culture rooted in an assimilationist ethos and oriented toward consumption and domesticity. Sex, LaBruce suggests, is one possible route toward an aesthetic and political reanimation of gay culture. Yet Elliott-Smith also underlines the film's critique of gay male sexual publics, which values hypermasculine forms as yet another capitalist "meat" byproduct. The sexual politics of gay zombies may be as alienating as they are empowering.

In her essay for this book, Cathy Hannabach likewise offers a skeptical queer reading of zombies. Bringing a queer disability studies approach to *The Walking Dead*, Hannabach argues that the show consistently presents ableist and heteronormative views of embodiment, sex, and sociality. Yet she also takes pleasure in one of its characters; indeed, she identifies a radical queer crip potentiality in Michonne, a butch black woman, who destabilizes the shows otherwise conservative moralizing. Max Thornton finds equally radical potential in an alternative and unlikely figure: Jesus Christ. Drawing on contemporary secular meme culture, Thornton explores the queer potential arising from evoking Christ in potentially blasphemous ways, beginning with comparison between Christ's miraculous resurrection into immortality and zombie undeadness. This comparison has been underlined elsewhere by several filmmakers, including Daniel Heisel (*Jesus H. Zombie* [2006]), Christopher Bryan (*The Zombie Christ* [2012]), and self-proclaimed "King of the B-Movies" Bill Zebub (*Zombiechrist* [2010]), who depicts a skeletal Christ engaging in sexual activity. The latter revels in offensiveness, but Zebub's comparison between Christ and zombie affronts because it queers constructed reverential hierarchies. The undead are especially apt as a conduit for such deconstruction precisely because they disturb the presumed life-death dichotomy.

Necrosexuality

Death is the great leveler of socio-political differences. The zombie is the leveler of desires. It is not that humans who objectify zombies are singled-out as perverts in these films, but that all human desires are aberrant. Just as there is no line between living and dead in zombie texts, the constructed lines between "normal" and deviant desires fail.

The result is a kind of sexual freedom that manifests in two ways. First, zombies invade locales associated with sexual license: for example, in *Zombies! Zombies! Zombies!* (2008), the living dead attack a strip-club. In this case, the strip-club is transformed into a sanctuary from the zombie-outbreak. Once the zombies invade, the location is devoid of sex: that is, it is free from the constructed (and limited) anthropocentric vision of sex it previously stood for. Second, the zombies' carnal hedonism is not limited to specific locations or even body parts. During the zombie invasion, all spaces and all flesh are subject to the zombie's passion. The implication is that zombie's cravings are not bound by the restrictions placed on human sexual freedom, be they fears regarding

STIs, or the limitations of one's sexual identity. Zombie sexuality incites dystopian destruction of civilization *as we know it*, but that means opening up a sexual world that is distinctly utopian: of sexual citizenship *as it could be*.

Given these thematic strands, it is little wonder that the logical home for zombie sexuality is in the realm of pornography, the "separated utopia" of sexual pleasure as Linda Williams famously termed it (*Hard Core* 164). For Williams, harm is not part of porn's lexis because all action contributes to sexual pleasure within porn's diegesis, even if the acts depicted would be considered harmful outside of that context. In zombie-themed porn, living participants' (performed) pain does not inhibit the undead in their quest for carnal satisfaction. Indeed, in the porn context, their counterparts' suffering is of no concern; either the living find pleasure in the violence inflicted on them, or their pain is swiftly passed over (and thereby negated) in these texts. For example, porn texts such as *Night of the Giving Head* (2008) include (contrived) genital mastication sequences, but the zombies' destructive behaviors do not halt the text's flow. Zombie porn amplifies both the hedonism and harm (real and imagined) that characterizes much contemporary pornography. In doing so, a post-human, necrosexual space is created, one in which sexual fantasy (as we understand it) is made stranger, and in which agency and pleasure are radically reconfigured.

The zombie-porn crossover manifests in numerous ways. First, various horror films such as *Horno* (2009) and *Porn Star Zombies* (2009) depict sexually active zombies performing within the porn industry, but do so without offering genitally explicit images. Second, several zombie-horror films feature performers who are primarily associated with hardcore porn filmmaking. *Bloodlust Zombies* (2011, starring Alexis Texas) and *Swamp Zombies* (2005, starring Jasmine St. Claire) are just two examples. These films also do not contain explicit sex. Third, a number of hardcore porn films offer genitally explicit images of zombies engaging in sex, either with the living, or with other zombies. Although Jamie Russell (134) pegs zombie porn as being rooted in Joe D'Amato's early 1980s films, there has been a significant boom in zombie porn since the *fin de siècle*, represented by films such as *Dawna of the Dead* (2008) and the 2005 film adaptation of Edward Lee's comicbook *GrubGirl*. In these cases, the zombies are not just sex objects: they clearly express their own forms of sexual desire. Moreover, since humans and zombies frequently engage in sexual congress with one another in these films, the living are "infected" by the zombies' necrosexuality.

In her essay, Laura Helen Marks offers a detailed examination of the zombie's incursion into hardcore porn. Comparing two types of undeadness—vampirism and zombidom—Marks observes that the zombie's physical abjectness does not disturb pornographic desire as we might initially presume; bodily fluids, for example, are prevalent in hardcore movies. Rather, porno-zombies have the potential to queer in the hardcore context because they highlight that porn's female subjects are not passive in the way that zombies are, and that female porn performers are *reputed* to be. As Marks argues, hetero-hardcore customarily centralizes highly ritualized performances of female sexual agency. Moreover, porn's female zombies offer an alternative to the routine performances of sexuality typically offered in hardcore movies. Even in their passiveness then, porno-zombies have a unique kind of sexual identity. Subsequently, they offer new forms of sexual fantasy for audiences.

That same trend towards zombies attaining sexual identity is evident in non-pornographic horror films, as part of the zombie's broader blossoming into subjectivity since the mid–1980s. Just as zombie porn has blurred the lines between human desire and the zombie's sexual freedom, zombie horror has portrayed sex as a transition point. Several films depict sex as a bridge between life (constructed, constricted) and death (free). For instance, in *Dance of the Dead* (2008), nerdy protagonist Steven is infected by popular cheerleader Gwen, who bites him as they kiss. Posthumously, the pair pursue their assignation, biting and scratching each other. As the last act they engage in while alive and the first they engage in post-death, sex is the bridge that frees these characters from life's limiting social structures. The hierarchy that separated them—the difference between cheerleader and nerd—is divested of meaning, attesting to their freedom. An extra-diegetic pop-rock love song confirms that their newfound desire is cause for celebration. The soundtrack legitimates Steven and Gwen's zombie-loving by evoking the euphonic crescendos of conventional romantic films. Although arguably that juxtaposition of romantic convention and unconventional (grotesque) love may be humorous, it stems from powerfully destabilizing established expectations.

All of these forms of necrosexuality provide a hideous mirror via which to perceive humanity. Having once been alive, the undead are similar enough to the living to be reflective of human desire. Simultaneously, because they are different to the living—being alive yet dead—the zombie is divergent enough to render those desires strange. Zombie sexuality is akin to human experience of sex because it is of the body, although the zombie-body has a different set of capacities and limitations compared with human embodiment. The zombie body is incapable of sustaining sexuality "as *we* know it." That is most clear in films where the living dead seek to engage in the same sexual activities they enacted while alive, but are incapable of doing so because their rotting bodies fail. For example, *I, Zombie: The Chronicles of Pain* (1998) reveals one reason why there are so few instances of zombie-masturbation in the history of cinema: the undead protagonist's penis falls off while he pleasures himself.

The creative and frequently disturbing inversions of the zombie mythos offered in portrayals of zombie sexuality are an important point of departure for the subgenre. The visions of zombidom discussed above and in the rest of this volume all re-envisage the zombie as lively rather than lifeless. In its various manifestations, the zombie queers notions of agency, identity, and sex acts themselves, productively troubling the ways in which gender, race, and ability constellate around animate hierarchies (Chen). Sex is no longer, if it ever was, a measure of one's vitality, while death does not bring carnal desire to an end.

NOTES

1. On zombie liminality, miscegenation, and interracial identity, see Ponder.

2. In a similar vein, both *Zombie Honeymoon* (2004) and *Zombie Marriage Counseling: I'm a Lesbian* (2009) question the validity of marriage as a "'til death do us part" union.

3. There are some notable foils to this trend. For example, *Cupcake: A Zombie Lesbian Musical* (2010) features songs such as "My Girlfriend Ate My Pussy, Literally" and "No Penis Between Us," which counter the heterosexual bias found elsewhere in the zombie canon.

4. For a detailed discussion of various recent zombie films set in and around stripclubs, see Jones "XXXombies."

5. For an extended discussion on zombie sexuality and disgust, see Jones, "XXXombies."

Take, Eat,
These Are My Brains

Queer Zombie Jesus

Max Thornton

In 2013, I received a Facebook invitation to a "Zombie BBQ": "This Sunday is Easter, which is basically a day where we celebrate the existence of zombies. Celebrate by eating meat that isn't braaaaaains at my house." San Francisco's Sisters of Perpetual Indulgence held a "Zombie Christ Haunted House" fundraiser for Easter weekend 2013, inviting visitors to "travel through the disco inferno where flaming queers practice their delightful sinning; Survive the ghastly church with its soul-consuming pope; Feast with disciples at the zombie last supper!" (Faetopia Crew). Meanwhile, a quick Google search for "Zombie Jesus" yields a robust 15 million results, including "Zombie Jesus Lives!" (zombiejesus.com), ZombieJesusDay.org, and Ira Hunter's short film *Corpus Delecti* (*The Passion of Zombie Jesus*, 2009)—all these on the first page alone.

The Internet phenomenon of Zombie Jesus is largely a joke, propelled by social media users enjoying the cheeky blasphemy of wishing each other a "happy Zombie Jesus Day" on Easter Sunday. But could there be wider social and theological implications? I suggest that, when viewed through a queer theology lens, Zombie Jesus can be seen as a queer religious figure who bridges between secular Internet culture and Christianity.

Queer theology is a relatively young discipline, but queer figurations of Jesus have abounded for most of Christian history. The fourteenth-century mystic Julian of Norwich wrote passionately about Jesus as Mother, endlessly giving birth to us. Renaissance artwork depicting Jesus' body is fairly bursting with homoeroticism: Michelangelo's *Cristo della Minerva*, Maratti's *Flagellation of Christ*, and Signorelli's *Resurrection of the Flesh* are but three artworks that exemplify the exquisitely detailed male nudity offered by artists of the period. Early twentieth-century attempts to portray Jesus as a ruggedly masculine figure of physical toughness and sharp business acumen were a direct reaction to a nineteenth-century Christ popularly associated with traditionally feminine characteristics such as tenderness and sentimentality (see Prothero).

What is new in queer theology is not the act of queering Jesus as such, but the conscious employment of analytical tools taken from secular queer theory: a deconstructionist methodology, a critical focus on subjectivity and embodiment, and a dedication to problematizing the gender binary (Cornwall 27). By using these three analytical tools in relation to Zombie Jesus, we can construct the figure of Queer Zombie Jesus as a site for theological engagement with embodiment, gender, and sexuality in a contemporary context. Queer Zombie Jesus is an example of what Marcella Althaus-Reid calls "indecent theology": the intersection of queer theory and sexuality with the social and economic justice movement of liberation theology. In particular, it is an "obscene Jesus," an image that shocks the sensibilities of mainstream Christological discourse by uncovering what has long been suppressed through the use of familiar images of Jesus (Althaus-Reid 110–124). This is an obscene Christ for an Internet age, crossing discourses to provide a stimulus to critical thought and liberatory action in both Christian and secular circles.

The first part of this essay will summarize three key areas of Christian theology which are relevant to the popular conception of the zombie: resurrection immortality, the Eucharistic consumption of flesh, and the corporate identity of the Church. The second part will consider the nature of the Zombie Jesus meme, and will proceed to examine how Zombie Jesus queers each of these theological fields. Finally, I will suggest that Queer Zombie Jesus bridges between the meta/physical worlds of Christianity and the web, acting as both exemplar of equality and stimulus toward justice, especially for sexual minorities.

Theological Backgrounds

In 1968, George A. Romero and John Russo codified the zombie as we currently understand it. Prior to the release of *Night of the Living Dead*, the zombie was a footnote in movie monster lore, an oddity of racist colonial fears of Haitian witchery. In films such as *White Zombie* (1932) and *I Walked with a Zombie* (1941), zombies were mindless slaves, controlled by drugs and/or voodoo, with no autonomy or will. Such zombies were alive, but appeared to be the walking dead. Romero and Russo's script took this one step further: their zombies really were the walking dead, but what drove their actions was not a voodoo master but the primal, cannibalistic urge to feast on human flesh. With 1985's *Return of the Living Dead*, the zombie's tastes were narrowed to the human brain specifically, which is often the meal of choice for today's zombies. By the time of the twenty-first century's pop-culture zombie boom, which was launched in large part by Capcom's wildly popular videogame series *Resident Evil* and Zack Snyder's 2004 *Dawn of the Dead* remake, the zombie had been cemented in the public imagination according to Romero's specifications: a walking corpse that eats human flesh and has no will or mind of its own (see Russell).

Romero's Catholic upbringing (Tony Williams 90) may have stimulated his creation of the flesh-eating zombie (and Christian imagery is certainly heavily pervasive in the European zombie movies of the 1970s made by Lucio Fulci, Amando de Ossorio, and others). The three core characteristics of the Romero/Russo zombie represent nightmarish inversions of three central theological tenets of Christian faith, which manifest in practices drawn from the life and death (and undeath) of Jesus. Each of these three tenets carries within it an undercurrent of profoundly embodied fleshliness, which is important to the graphically physical figure of Queer Zombie Jesus. Fleshliness denotes a fundamental, ineradicable tie to material reality and the physical bodies through which our entire perception thereof is mediated, as Merleau-Ponty pointed out and queer theory continues to emphasize. The spiritualizing tendency of Christian theological history has often belied this fleshliness, but it is inescapable in a religion that stresses God's bodily incarnation, bodily death, bodily resurrection, and bodily continuity through the Church. After all, the metaphysical need not be the non-physical, but rather the physical-and-also-beyond-physical (the meta/physical). A compelling analogy to this meta/physical nature of Christian fleshliness is found in the increasingly virtual lives of our Internet age, which I will discuss more fully at the end of this essay. The zombie, and especially Queer Zombie Jesus recovers strains of fleshliness for the contemporary meta/physical world.

Resurrection Immortality

The Nicene Creed of 325 CE, still one of the foundational declarations of Christian faith and still recited in some churches every Sunday, states: "We look for the resurrection of the dead, and the life of the world to come" (Episcopal Church 327). This resurrection is associated with eschatological transformation, with a "world to come" which will be different from this one and yet have continuity with it. Just as the "new earth" of John's vision in Revelation (21:1) is a world transformed—a world that has some recognizable similarities with the "old earth" but which arises out of the latter's passing away—so the resurrected dead of Christian eschatological hope are revolutionized re-creations of their old selves.

The pattern for this balance of continuity and dramatic change is, of course, the resurrected Christ himself. Examples of the continuities between the pre- and post-resurrection Jesus include the ability to eat, tangible materiality, visibility, audibility, and some form of physical continuity enabling him to be recognized as the same person. However, Jesus' resurrection is qualitatively different from the miracles he performed in the raising of Jairus' daughter (Luke 8:40–56 and parallels) or Lazarus (John 11). These resuscitations restore the deceased to their former state, whereas the revived Jesus is somehow new.

For example, although it is possible for Jesus to be recognized, this does not happen immediately. Both Luke and John report first encounters with the risen Christ wherein his closest friends are unable to recognize him until Jesus himself takes a decisive action (giving the disciples bread in Luke 24:30; addressing Mary by name in John 20:16). Christ's resurrected body is both like and unlike his pre-resurrection body. He is not a ghost: he can be touched (Luke 24:39), he can eat (Luke 24:42), he bears the physical marks of his painful and ignominious death (John 20:20). And yet he can vanish and reappear at will (Luke 24:31, 36), and he can pass through locked doors (John 20:19, 26).

Of course, the Gospel accounts are distinctly lacking in concrete physical descriptions of the resurrected (or, indeed, the pre-resurrection) Christ, and as such the writings of the church fathers on resurrection bodies are rife with the wildest speculation. The few New Testament passages addressing this topic are vague enough to be interpreted in almost any way one might choose: there is a much-debated contrast in 1 Corinthians 15:42–45 between psuchikon and pneumatikon bodies[1]; there is some confused imagery of tents and clothing in 2 Corinthians 5:1–4; there is the famous line in Galatians 3:28, "There is no longer Jew or Greek, there is no longer slave or free, there is no longer male and female"; there is Jesus' assertion in Mark 12:25 that "when they rise from the dead, they neither marry nor are given in marriage, but are like angels in heaven."[2]

On this slender basis, Augustine, for one, proposed that the resurrected bodies of believers would be perfected: all scars and blemishes would be removed, and everyone would be beautiful, whole, and in their absolute physical prime (Augustine 22.18.20).[3] Augustine's deep concerns around such questions as whether an aborted fetus will be raised (Augustine 22.13) might seem quaintly ridiculous to us now, but it is relevant to the forthcoming discussion of Queer Zombie Jesus that he also addresses "the problem that seems most difficult of all, the question to whom a body will be restored at the resurrection when it has become part of the body of another living man[, who] under compulsion of the last straits of starvation eats human corpses" (Augustine 22.20). Happily, Augustine reports that all flesh will ultimately be restored to its rightful owner in its original condition.

The consumption of another person's flesh might be forgiven and restored in the eternal life of the resurrection, but there is one person's flesh that must be consumed in order to attain resurrection immortality. This is, of course, the flesh of Jesus in the form of the Eucharistic bread.

The Eucharistic Consumption of Flesh

"Jesus said to them, 'Very truly, I tell you, unless you eat the flesh of the Son of Man and drink his blood, you have no life in you. Those who eat my flesh and drink my blood have eternal life, and I will raise them up on the last day; for my flesh is true food and my blood is true drink'" (John 6:53–55). The challenging nature of this instruction does not escape comment in the Bible: "When many of his disciples heard it, they said, 'This teaching is difficult; who can accept it?'" (John 6:60). Those Roman contemporaries who accused early Christians of cannibalism clearly found the practice wholly unacceptable (MacCulloch 159).

The Christian practice of Eucharist (Communion, the Lord's Supper) is instituted by Jesus in the Synoptic Gospels—those of Matthew, Mark, and Luke—with some slight variations on the familiar words:

"Take[, eat]; this is my body" (Matt. 26:26; Mark 14:22; Luke 22:19); "This cup that is poured out for you is the new covenant in my blood" (Matt. 26:28; Mark 14:24; Luke 22:20). John's Gospel, while lacking an explicit narrative of Eucharistic institution, features an extended theological discourse, commonly referred to as the "Bread of Life" discourse, in chapter 6, as well as employing the imagery of "ingesting Jesus" throughout (see Webster). Eucharistic liturgies draw directly from Paul's words in 1 Corinthians 11:23–25: "the Lord Jesus, on the night when he was betrayed, took a loaf of bread, and when he had given thanks, he broke it and said, 'This is my body that is for you. Do this in remembrance of me.' In the same way he took the cup also, after supper, saying, 'This cup is the new covenant in my blood. Do this, as often as you drink it, in remembrance of me.'" As a common thread running through all four Gospels, the Pauline epistles, and nearly two millennia of Christian liturgy, this idea of eating Jesus' flesh in the bread of the Eucharist is a powerful, lasting, and singular aspect of Christian theology.[4]

In John particularly, eating Jesus' flesh is directly linked with life, eternal life, and resurrection into immortality. Like the undead zombie who must eat the flesh of the living, the Christian believer must eat the flesh of Jesus in order to be resurrected to eternal life. It is noteworthy that, whereas the first Romero zombie to rise bestows the immortality of the undead upon others by eating their flesh, the resurrected Jesus bestows immortality on his followers through *their* consumption of *his* flesh. This important difference will become apparent in the discussion of Queer Zombie Jesus later in this essay. For now, though, I wish to consider in more detail the meaning of eating Jesus' flesh.

The different grades of understanding Christ's presence in the Eucharist are well-known: transubstantiation, the Catholic understanding whereby the substance of the bread and wine are changed into the body and blood of Christ; consubstantiation, the Lutheran notion of the coexistence of bread and wine with body and blood; memorialism, associated with Zwingli, in which the Lord's Supper functions solely as a memorial of Jesus (see McKim). For much of Christian history, the two "higher" theologies of the Eucharist have tended to prevail, and for many believers the sacrament of the Eucharist has conveyed the real presence of Jesus in one form or another.

For many medieval Christians, in fact, the Eucharist was imbued with an assortment of mystical properties. Miraculous stories circulated of pious women whose nutritional needs were completely sated by the weekly Eucharistic host. The bread transformed into the body of Christ was considered to be the site of immense power, where "the heavenly and the demonic could explode into a war of conflicting powers" (Camporesi 225). The Eucharist is the locus of permeability between the realms of the mundane and the supernal, a site of preternatural potentiality, instantiated in what Graham Ward calls the "ontological scandal" of the "is" in Jesus' statement, "This is my body" (see Ward). The identification of bread with body is the first scandal; the intake of God's holy body into the digestive tract is another scandal, perhaps even a "real trauma" (Camporesi 228) for the believer who must accept the reality of the divine flesh into the graphically physical human stomach and bowels.

There is even a sexual resonance to the Eucharist. Food and sex are generally connected in the sense that both are associated with satisfying bodily cravings (see Norman Brown 162–75). However, the specific language of the liturgy carries other sexual connotations; the intake of the sacramental bread and wine unites believers into the corporate (communal) identity of Christ's body, the Church.

The Corporate Identity of the Church

The sexual element of the Eucharistic liturgy lies in the allusive language around the ideas of *union* and *flesh* or *body*. Genesis 2:24 states that "a man leaves his father and his mother and clings to his wife, and they become one flesh." Paul quotes this verse in 1 Corinthians 6:16–17, to compare the sexual union of two individuals into "one flesh" with the spiritual union of God and believer into "one spirit." The spiritual union does not exclude but encompasses the fleshly or bodily dimension: Paul exhorts believers to "glorify God in your body" (1 Corinthians 6:20).

It is not only God with whom the believer is physically, almost sexually, united, but also the Church as a whole, in all of its members. Like the couple who in sexual union "become one flesh," the members of the Church "who are many are one body, for we all partake of the one bread" (1 Corinthians 10:17). In the Eucharistic consumption of Christ's flesh, which leads to eternal life in the resurrection, all believing individuals are united into the corporate identity of the Church as a common body.

This communal identity is described in remarkably physical, fleshly terms. 1 Corinthians 12:12–31 develops an extended image of the Church as the body of Christ, stressing in particular the many and varied parts that make up a human body, as well as the "interdependence of all the parts of the body" (Ciampa and Rosner 589). C.K. Barrett notes that, while "[t]he metaphor of the body, used to describe a group of men [sic] who have common interests and activities, was not infrequent in antiquity," Paul's innovation lies in "the description of the Church as the body *of Christ*" (Barrett 236). The Church is identified with the specific, physical body of Christ—the same body that is consumed in the Eucharist. In this way there is an element of autophagy, a self-cannibalization that takes place in the Eucharistic action of the Church. Yet this is not destructive cannibalization, but a productive and life-giving ritual, more fertile than any sexual union.

The image of the Church as the body of Christ, with the individuals as the various body parts and Christ himself as the head, is not a direct one-to-one analogy; for the analogy breaks down both as the body consumes itself in the Eucharist and as the Church recognizes the *absence* of the physical body of Christ in the eschatological hope of the parousia or Second Coming. The Church both is and is not the actual body of Christ. Neo-orthodox theologian Karl Barth stresses that the individuals who comprise the Church do *not* do so in the same way as "so many cells are united into one living organism" (Barth 441), but rather as a kind of ontological oneness in which believers participate in the unity of God without sacrificing their individuality: "They are not a mass of individuals, nor even a corporation, a personified society, or a 'totality,' but The Individual, The One, The New Man (1 Cor. Xii.12, 13)" (Barth 443).

In the same way that the spiritual union of God and believer does not oppose physical union but encompasses it, the oneness of corporate identity in the Church does not contrast with individuality but embraces and includes it. The community of the Church "does not swallow up the individual, nor obscure his or her uniqueness and unique contribution, nor take away individual freedom by assimilating it to the collective will" (LaCugna 229). This is, of course, exactly the opposite of the mindless zombie, enslaved to its basest instincts. Sadly, all too often the members of the Church succumb to uncritical dogmatism and enforced conformity to a narrow set of norms, condemning and erasing the diversity of individuals—especially sex and gender diversity. Perhaps by recognizing the similarities between the unthinking singleminded focus of zombies and the oneness of the Church, Christians can gain a heightened self-critical awareness and seek to maximize the contrast between the diverse-yet-united body the Church is supposed to be and the mindlessly assimilated brain-eating zombie it too often resembles.

Zombie Jesus

In Christian faith, then, the themes of resurrection immortality, the consumption of flesh, and corporate identity play important roles. These themes are also crucial in defining contemporary movie zombies. Despite manifesting in very different ways both zombie movie and faith-based articulations of these themes have similarly wide-reaching social and theological implications.

The zombies of *Night of the Living Dead* rise from their graves for no readily apparent reason. News channel speculation about radiation is kept in the film's background, and zombie filmmakers following in *Night of the Living Dead*'s footsteps have rarely been interested in detailed or even remotely plausible explanations for the presence of undead ghouls. The ultimate cause of reanimation is of little consequence to the embattled characters who are simply trying to survive in the face of unrelenting threat. Unlike other popular monsters such as vampires or werewolves, zombies are uninhibited by sunlight or lunar phases. Their immortality is not a state actively achieved so much as a failure to give in to physical decay (a fear increasingly relevant in a world where human lifespans are being extended beyond the capacity of the human body to remain healthy and whole). Zombies' resurrection is no divine gift of eternal life, but a nightmarish twist—like that of the ever-aging, never-dying Tithonus in Greek mythology—or perhaps even divine punishment: as the televangelist says in Snyder's *Dawn of the Dead*, "When there's no more room in hell, the dead will walk the earth." Their cannibalism is similarly monstrous, a multivalent symbol for all the ways in which humans turn on one another, such as the bitter infighting that beleaguers most every group of survivors in a zombie film. It is this same unthinking participation in social structures that is made monstrous in the corporate identity of the zombies, whose individual wills are subsumed to an irresistible hunger, offer a neat metaphor for the mob mentality that can sweep people into group hysteria, and can lead to non-reflexive participation in social (even systemic) injustices.

A queer-theory analysis of Zombie Jesus illuminates such systemic social and psychological issues. Horror film's ability to tap into the unrestricted id has made it a fruitful target for queer, feminist, and disability theorists (for example see Benshoff; Clover; Angela Smith), and Queer Zombie Jesus can unite these social critiques of popular culture and entertainment with social critiques of religion.

My Queer Zombie Jesus paradigm is not based on any one specific incarnation of Zombie Jesus out of the many found online, but rather an amalgam of various iterations that elucidate how Jesus differs from established norms of contemporary zombidom. One example is an argument that appears to have begun circulating in this specific form around Easter 2012, suggesting that Jesus was not a zombie but a lich (a type of undead creature popularized by the role-playing game *Dungeons & Dragons*). Another is a picture of "Good Guy Jesus," which plays on the popular meme "Good Guy Greg." "Good Guy Greg" is an image macro of a smiling, smoking man, accompanied by captions describing acts of kindness or generosity. "Good Guy Jesus" replaces the man's face with a popular depiction of Jesus, captioned: "Is a zombie; lets you eat his flesh."

In what follows, I analyze various ways in which Queer Zombie Jesus problematizes the three social and theological fields of resurrection immortality, the consumption of flesh, and corporate identity. Queer Zombie Jesus deconstructs binaries imposed on these three fields by Western philosophical categories—particularly mind/body dualism—in order to recover and redeem the fleshliness at their core. Transgressing and inverting the norms serves to constantly challenge our understanding of them. Such destabilization allows us to probe and query identity categories, particularly gender and sexuality, and the boundaries of identity. Zombie narratives conventionally caution against human greed and selfishness, which is hypostatized as monstrous Otherness. Queer Zombie Jesus instead invites us to see the divine in the monstrous Other and to join ourselves with it in embodied, fleshly, sexual consumption, in a redemptive tale of love and self-giving.

Queering Resurrection Immortality

Jesus and zombies have in common the most basic ideas of resurrection (rising from the dead; often literally from the grave) and immortality (indefinite or eternal life). However, the details and implications of these shared tropes are wildly divergent. After all, eternal life in Christ is consistently presented as good and desirable, whereas the eternal undeath of a zombie—unlike the vampire's more seductive existence— is invariably portrayed as unpleasant and undesirable. Zombies are subject to defeat through their physical dismemberment, but Christians believe that Jesus and his resurrected followers cannot die a second time. The bodies of zombies rot and fall apart even as they keep shuffling onward; the risen Christ not only retains his bodily integrity, but obtains some new physical abilities.

Zombie Jesus deconstructs the sharp distinctions between undeadness and Christian resurrection by drawing them together into a single figure. Zombie Jesus is the zombie that does not rot and the Jesus that does. The simultaneous *is* and *is not* of Zombie Jesus recalls the practice of negative theology, most famously practiced by medieval mystic Meister Eckhart, which seeks to radicalize one's understanding of characteristics attributed to God by negating them. For the one who believes that God is good, the statement "God is not good" means that God is so radically, cosmically, surpassingly good that the human definition of "good," bounded as it is by the limits of human understanding, cannot apply to the Supreme Being (see Eckhart). In the same way, Zombie Jesus defies and expands human understandings of what it means to be immortal and incorruptible (1 Corinthians 15:53). Excessive focus on the afterlife can reduce Christian faith to a Pascal's Wager, a get-out-of-jail-free card for death, a basely transactional conception of salvation that diminishes the whole notion of divinity and transcendence. Imagining oneself and one's savior as shambling rotting corpses can enable Christians to interrogate their own motivations in having faith, and perhaps to recalibrate the transactional soteriology that ultimately underpins our present global economy in all of its injustices (see Grau).

Moreover, Queer Zombie Jesus challenges and rejects Cartesian mind-body dualism and the sex- and body-negativity that results. Following Hegel, for whom the resurrection was not bodily but representative of a translation to spiritual presence (Hodgson 175), Christians sometimes have a tendency to spiritualize or allegorize resurrection. Unlike the airily disembodied Jesus found in metaphorical readings of faith, zombies are gruesomely physical. Thanks to special effects wizard Tom Savini, the gore and fleshy filth of decaying corpses are graphically presented onscreen in *Dawn of the Dead* and *Day of the Dead*. Meanwhile some subsequent filmmakers positively revel in upping the ante for zombie grotesquery; Peter Jackson's magnificent 1992 splatterfest *Braindead* (*Dead Alive* in North America) is one superlative example. Zombie Jesus depicts an embodied Christ with a vividness matched only by Julian of Norwich's gross-out descriptions of her bloodiest visions: "the fair skin was very deeply broken, down into the tender flesh, sharply slashed all over the dear body; the hot blood ran out so abundantly that no skin or wound could be seen, it seemed to be all blood." However, whereas Julian describes Christ's crucifixion, Zombie Jesus radically embodies the post-resurrection Christ. Even the most conservative sex- and body-negative Christian audiences today still have an appetite for gore, as testified to by some evangelical leaders' enthusiasm for Mel Gibson's notorious 2004 *The Passion of the Christ* (see Robinson). By transferring the obsessive focus on Christ's body from his tortured death to his resurrection, Zombie Jesus provides a more life-oriented, more productive, much less macabre outlet for this apparent psychological need.

Body-negative attitudes are often associated with the maintenance of patriarchal, heterosexist norms, whereby the masculine, spiritual or mental, heterosexual, cisgender, and so on are linked together and elevated over against the feminine, physical, queer, trans*, and other terms in hierarchical binary oppositions. By rehabilitating the fleshly physicality of the body within the context of Christian salvation and resurrection immortality, Zombie Jesus offers a doorway to the rehabilitation of all the suppressed and denigrated aspects of bodily human existence. Linking the object of Christian faith and devotion with the repulsive, rotting monster provides a dramatic shock to the cultural categories of sacred and secular. Rather than rejecting him in kneejerk horror, Christians who spend time considering Zombie Jesus could have their entire sense of what is right or appropriate recalibrated, just as Jesus shocked the religious sensibilities of faithful Jews in his own lifetime by spending time with lepers and healing on the Sabbath. Queer Zombie Jesus makes explicit the connection between Jesus' acceptance of "inappropriate" persons, and the need for contemporary religious institutions to accept gender and sexual minorities.

Queering the Eucharistic Consumption of Flesh

The Eucharistic consumption of flesh is perhaps the most complex field in terms of relating zombies with Jesus, as here—unlike resurrection immortality and corporate identity—the role of Jesus and the role of his followers differ. Only the followers eat Jesus' flesh; Jesus himself does not eat anybody's flesh, but he gives his flesh to be eaten by others. All zombies, on the other hand, eat human flesh. In this instance, Christians have more in common with zombies than Jesus himself does. After all, zombies do not eat other zombies, only humans; so Christians do not eat other Christians, only Jesus. To some extent, then, Christians are in this case the monstrous Other. Zombie Jesus unites the self and the monstrous Other, deconstructing the binary opposition that enables oppression and hatred of the Other, including gender and sexual minorities.

Another nuance that constitutes a difference between zombies' cannibalism and Christians' Eucharist is the fact that eating flesh appears to be an ongoing necessity for zombies. Many Christian denominations repeat the sacrament of the Eucharist on a weekly or monthly basis, following Jesus' instruction to "do this as often as you drink it" (1 Corinthians 11:25), but this is not necessary for salvation. Ingesting Jesus in the sense of receiving his word, represented in the sacrament of baptism, has a one-time salvific efficacy that does not need to be repeated. In addition to this difference, the zombies' anthropophagism is driven by mindless instinct, but the Eucharist is—or is supposed to be—the site of powerful holy meaning for Christians.

The shocking juxtaposition of sacred and profane, zombie and Jesus, consumer and consumed, drives home the radical nature of the Eucharist, revivifying this "dead metaphor"—Ricoeur's term for an image that has been so thoroughly absorbed into common usage that it can no longer surprise (Ricoeur 52)—for renewed appreciation and understanding. The central ideas of Christianity are so culturally pervasive in majority–Christian cultures that they no longer seem shocking, but the Eucharist presents a rather astonishing idea: that people are brought into union with God through cannibalism. We are made holy through an abhorrent act of profound transgression; a transgression, moreover, with strong sexual overtones. To eat another's flesh is to dissolve the boundary between self and other, to interiorize the other so completely that they become a part of oneself. Queer Zombie Jesus reclaims that sexual resonance through his strongly embodied nature, and calls for a dramatic rethinking of that which is considered abhorrent, transgressive or profane. For if holiness is found in deepest profanity, as life is found in death, we are driven to ask where else we might find holiness in places the Church has traditionally considered profane?

In particular, Queer Zombie Jesus asks us to rehabilitate gender and sexual minorities into the Church. Bodies that dissolve established boundaries, bodies that transgress societal norms, bodies that consume and are consumed in radical acts of self-giving love, are the very locus of divine activity in Queer Zombie Jesus. We might dare to imagine Queer Zombie Jesus as akin to the grotesquely copulating zombies of *Braindead* and the zombie baby they create. Bringing forth life out of death is, after all, what Christians claim that Jesus does. It seems absurd to claim that sex and procreation should be inextricable, and to exclude sexual minorities from Christianity on this basis, when the Christian God disconnects procreation from sex by bringing forth life out of death. If religion is to be of any use in the lives of those who cannot try, do not want, and should not have to "rise above" the demands of fleshly reality, those who fight for liberation and justice in this life—then it must change. "Indecent theology" represents the ongoing striving of some religious believers for equality, despite centuries of attempts on the part of the powerful to hinder the progress of liberal attitudes within organized religion. Trying to sever Christianity from secular, and particularly queer, society does a disservice to both. If engaged mutually, secular and Christian outlooks can cast light on one another's failings and lead to self-critical transformation: of secularism in the direction of transcendence, of Christianity in the direction of contemporary relevance and justice.

Queering the Corporate Identity of the Church

In Romero's 1985 film *Day of the Dead*, as Tony Williams observes, "[t]he advanced process of decay exhibited by the zombies in this film blurs every distinguishing boundary between male and female, black and white, adult and child" (Tony Williams 136). His words recall Paul's statement in Galatians 3:28: "There is no longer Jew or Greek, there is no longer slave or free, there is no longer male and female; for all of you are one in Christ Jesus." For both zombies and Christians, earthly distinctions and identity categories fall away, replaced by an overriding common identity and the pursuit of a common goal. The zombie loses all personality, characteristics, skills, wills, and desires, their place taken by the overpowering hunger for human flesh. Similarly, Paul's proclamation regarding the inclusive, equalizing power of Jesus' love might suggest that one's identity as a Christian takes priority over all other identity attributes.

Contrary to this reading of Galatians, Christians retain all aspects of their individuality, sometimes overwhelmingly. Zombie Jesus serves as a potent reminder that no one is "more" or a "better" Christian than another, no matter how talented or prominent they might be: as all are equal in the face of death, all are equal in the eyes of God. Zombie Jesus also presents the challenge that, if all the identity categories in which we invest ourselves are finite and temporal, we might have to be prepared to let them go. Identity politics too often reifies the categories that it recognizes as social constructs; by deconstructing these categories, Zombie Jesus offers a way of thinking through the contradiction. Meanwhile, some Christians utilize the freedom of identity in Christ as an argument against individual identities of which they disapprove. This freedom is conceptualized solely as "freedom *from*," erasing identities which nonetheless continue to exist in social reality. A female Christian might be free from any gender bias before God, but she is still subject to sexism in a misogynistic society. Erasing her identity as a woman in order to emphasize her equality before God might have its theological uses, but socially it is dangerous. The challenge, not to say impossibility, of living "in the world but not of it," is reified in Zombie Jesus, who is an inherently contradictory figure.

Zombie Jesus is by definition a special zombie. He is identified as a specific individual, which zombies by definition are not. He deconstructs this distinction, and he deconstructs exactly the zombification that some forms of Christianity would seem to demand from his followers. Zombie Jesus is part of a corporate identity, but by definition he has not lost his individuality as true zombies do. This is the model and the challenge for faithful Christians, and more broadly for anyone living in the world but trying to fight against the systems of oppression and injustice.

Acknowledging difference without making it insurmountable is one of the great challenges of our era. Any person who belongs to a gender or sexual (or racial or ethnic or disabled or other) minority can testify to the frustration of both extremes; of either being treated as though one's identity is entirely defined by difference, or as though one's minority status can be ignored or elided over completely. Queer Zombie Jesus is a figure that transcends the two extremes. As a zombie, he is part of an inherently communal identity in which his individuality disappears; as Jesus, he remains an identifiable individual with his own specific subjectivity. Queer Zombie Jesus exemplifies community life in diversity and difference, and so calls and challenges us to seek an end to the systemic injustices that suppress or exaggerate minority identities.

Gregory A. Waller suggests that Romero's zombies "are the projection of our desire to destroy, to challenge the fundamental values of America, and to bring the institutions of our modern society to a halt" (Waller 280). The systemic racism of the prison-industrial complex; the exclusion of people of certain genders and sexualities from full participation in social institutions; the suppression of developing countries' economic growth by transnational corporations operating in the interests of developed nations; drone strikes on foreign soil—all of these and other injustices of the world suggest that perhaps the fundamental values of America should be challenged, perhaps modern social institutions need to be impeded. Queer Zombie Jesus is an obscene figure situated at the intersection of queer radicalism, popular secular culture, and religious sensibility, uniting these fields into a call for dramatic change.

Queer Zombie Jesus

The foregoing recommendations for the role of Queer Zombie Jesus as a figure to challenge and change Christians should not obscure the fact that Zombie Jesus is primarily a construct of secular Internet culture. What can Queer Zombie Jesus offer the non–Christians who are perhaps more likely to encounter him? Any theology that hopes to be useful or relevant in the twenty-first century must avail itself of secular culture and expect to have a mutual relationship with it. The role of Queer Zombie Jesus among Christians is to present institutional Christianity with some of the wisdom and even Godliness that is to be found outside of the Church—what Tom Beaudoin terms the *"sensus infidelium."* The role of Queer Zombie Jesus among secular culture is to rehabilitate Jesus among those who are not Christians, recovering him from those who claim to speak for him.

Further, Queer Zombie Jesus hints at the Internet's meta/physical potential as a tool for liberation, self-actualization, and change. Though often described and conceptualized as purely virtual, even as the opposite of "real life," the online world is both physical and beyond-physical, meta/physical. Individually, our digital lives are mediated and defined by our physical bodies: fingers on the keyboard, eyes straining over a backlit screen, repetitive strain injury and back problems resulting from hours spent hunched and typing. Systemically, web access is dependent on physical resources: computer, modem, Internet connection, education in computer literacy, and of course money to pay for all of the above. Much like Christian faith, virtual worlds online are accessible only through the physical reality of human bodies and material resources. Queer Zombie Jesus reveals the overlap between Christianity and the web: meta/physical worlds of immense power, which can be and have been used for great good or great evil, and which can be harnessed and directed toward radical change for the better with the help of the focal point of the reimagined Jesus.

During Jesus' lifetime, some of those who claimed religious authority were opposed to the message of true love and acceptance that he preached. Jesus reclaimed God for the outcast, the oppressed, the subaltern, by using radical new imagery. Queer theology seeks to find in Jesus once more the face of the outcast and the subaltern, to make him the space where "difference and diversity are written and overwritten" (Cornwall 103) to rediscover not the triumphant king but the criminal dying on the cross.

Many who are not Christian find inspiration in the life and teachings of Jesus, exploring and rewriting him in pursuit of their own concerns. Perhaps Queer Zombie Jesus can be a place for Christians and non–Christians alike to explore a shared interest in the pursuit of a radical, embodied justice and love.

NOTES

1. *Psuchikon* and *pneumatikon* are usually translated as "natural/physical" and "spiritual," respectively, but their precise meaning is unclear. Certainly the first describes the body in life; the second, the post-resurrection body.

2. All biblical quotations are NRSV.

3. Of course, the average physical peak for humans is considered to be around 30: *the same age as Jesus at the time of his death.*

4. The practice of drinking Christ's blood is less prominent, since laypeople were not always given wine.

Victorian Values

Necrophilia and the Nineteenth Century in Zombie Films

MARCUS HARMES

Many zombie films, including the most commercially and critically successful examples within the genre, from *Night of the Living Dead* (1968) to *28 Days Later* (2002), are set in the present day. The quantity of films set more or less in the present day (according to the date of production) overshadows the fact that numerous zombie films, from *White Zombie* (1932) onwards, place the undead in historical settings. *White Zombie*, for example, was set in nineteenth-century Haiti. Other examples include the Italian *The Terrible Secret of Dr Hichcock* (*L'orrible Segreto del Dr Hichcock*, 1962), Hammer's *Plague of the Zombies* (1965) and *The Orgy of the Dead* (*La Orgia de los Muertos*, 1973), a Spanish horror. These films share in common a nineteenth-century setting. *Hichcock* is set in 1885. *Plague* is set a little earlier, in 1860. *Orgy* is not so chronologically precise but costumes and trappings locate the film sometime towards the end of Queen Victoria's reign (she died in 1901) and thus in the later-nineteenth century.

If many zombie films share in common a setting that is more or less the present day, another genre characteristic is that zombies were until recently distinctively non-sexual. Functioning as an allusive device, the zombies of Romero's *Night of the Living Dead* speak to nuclear rather than sexual anxieties, as talk of the radioactive satellite by scientists in the film would suggest. Romero's mall-set sequel *Dawn of the Dead* overtly satirizes consumerism (Wood 213). Zombies in later films are ravenous creatures; perhaps metaphorically their hunger may suggest fleshly lust, but only perhaps. It is not until more recent genre efforts such as *Warm Bodies* (2013), *Otto, or Up with Dead People* (2008) or exploitation film such as *Zombie Strippers!* (2008) or even *Dellamorte Dellamore* (1994), where a visit to the ossuary provoked feelings of high sexual arousal in a young woman (Keesey 106), that we encounter sexualized zombies and an erotic zombie aesthetic. But these films are rarities and as Steve Jones points out, zombies are traditionally asexual and gender traits are sublimated by their undead state ("Porn of the Dead" 41).

The nineteenth century-set films listed above are distinctive not only because of their historical backdrop, but also because emphasis is placed on undead sexuality in these movies. These zombies predate and are distinct from the conventional flesh eaters we are now familiar with. In these films the zombies are often sensual and male characters find them sexually attractive. In nineteenth century Britain, Europe and America, the undead were fetishized via various cultic practices. These cultic practices reached an apotheosis of sorts with the mourning at the royal court for Albert the Prince Consort, husband of Queen Victoria, who died from typhoid in 1860. Victoria's efforts were the most lavish of the period, although the immense nation-wide obsequies for the assassinated Abraham Lincoln in America come a close second (Schwartz 347), she was not alone in memorializing the dead to the point of fetish. Depending on what a bereaved family could afford, nineteenth century mourners perpetuated the memory of the dead through ceremony, sculpture, clothing and other media designed to promote the idea that the dead had not gone very far, but could easily be recalled to the mind's eye.[1]

This essay examines the perverse twist on these ornate mourning rituals offered by zombie films set in the nineteenth century. In actual Victorian society, ornate mourning rituals kept the memories of the dead alive. In these historically set zombie films, the dead themselves come back to life. This essay examines those few but notable films that locate zombies in the nineteenth century and proposes a number of theses about them. Zombie films set in the nineteenth century create a Victorian world where the dead have a clear ontological status: although they are elaborately mourned, the reanimated dead also become objects of sexual lust. That lust has further historical implications. Female bodies were subject to masculine control in Victorian society. Such exertions are iterated in these films via male characters' attempts to subjugate undead female sexuality. The fact that these women are both undead and desired opens up a liminal space that explores popular understandings of Victorian sexuality. This is most apparent in the Italian-made but British-set *Hichcock*, in which sex with the undead women takes place in surroundings which emulate the elaborate mourning ornamentation of the nineteenth century.

These European horror films permit broader perspectives on the cultural transmission of Victorian mores into twentieth century popular culture and allow for the wide-ranging analysis of questions relating to life, death and sexuality. In the introduction to *The Politics of Everyday Fear* Brian Massumi suggested that "there is always horror at the body as a pleasure site" (vii). The films under analysis here can be understood with this thought in mind. These works are both erotic and horrific. At the very heart of that horror are the deceased female bodies that men gain pleasure from. In these films, sexuality is emphatically heterosexual and oriented around male pleasure. Simultaneously, because it is expressed as lust for the undead, male lust is also perverse.

Nineteenth-Century Zombies

Taken together, *Hichcock*, *Plague* and *Orgy* present a coherent evocation of nineteenth-century England. Although only *Plague* was actually made in Britain, all three share the same British setting. An opening caption (superimposed over an image of the Big Ben clock tower of the Houses of Parliament) in the first scene of *Hichcock* establishes that the film, while made in Italy, takes place in London in 1885. *Orgy*, while made in Spain and in locations that actually seem to evoke middle Europe in terms of their appearance, is set in nineteenth-century Scotland.[2] Neither of these films' settings should, however, surprise us. The phenomenal success of Hammer's gothic horrors in Europe prompted European film makers to emulate the company's signature themes, styling and settings.[3] *Hichcock*'s producers Luigi Carpentieri and Ermanno Donati and scriptwriter Ernesto Gastaldi set out to create a gothic horror in the Hammer vein, and critical commentary on Italian horror in particular has stressed that directors within the genre are significantly indebted to British cinema (Bertellini 214). This creative debt is even signaled by the movie's credits. In an attempt to suggest the British consonances of their films the creative personnel all worked under anglicized pseudonyms.[4] *Orgy* is also clearly modeled after British horror film; the detective in the film even smokes a meerschaum pipe and is overtly likened to Sherlock Holmes, a landmark British cultural figure.

Another way these films harmonize is in their treatment of sexuality. Of the three, the Italian-made *Hichcock* is perhaps the most lurid in its themes, even if *Orgy* is most explicit in its imagery and its amount of on-screen nudity. Having faced the British Board of Film Censorship's scrutiny, Hammer's *Plague* shows the least in physical terms, but suggests a great deal in terms of potential sexual activity and violence. All three films are infused with strongly erotic currents. *Orgy*, while not quite living up to the sensational promise of its title, portrays the seduction of several women including the lady of the house and her servant by the film's protagonist. *Plague*, as noted, is less explicit in terms of nudity, but contains a powerfully suggestive scene in which a number of so-called "young bloods" attempt to gang rape Sylvia (Diane Claire), daughter of the film's hero Sir James Forbes (Andre Morrell). The rakes are dressed in hunting pinks and the *mise-en-scène* and costume design make great play of the analogue between hunting foxes and the pursuit and attempted rape of the young woman.[5] The titular "terrible secret" of Dr. Hichcock is his necrophilia, which the film's director of photography highlights by flashing lurid red lights over Hichcock (Robert Flemyng) when he is consumed by necrotic lust in a mortuary.

Dr. Hichcock's aberrant secret is indicative of a further correspondence; the sexual undercurrents of these films harmonize around perverse human sexual activity. To draw out this point, it is necessary to further extrapolate the major plot points of these films. Set in London in 1885, *Hichcock* bases its narrative around Dr. Bernard Hichcock's first and second marriages. While in public life Dr. Hichcock is a respected surgeon, noted particularly for his groundbreaking research into anesthetics, in private his skills with drugs are turned to darker ends. He drugs his first wife in order to have intercourse while she is in a death-like state. It is only while she is in this simulated death-like state (and actually near to death in physiological terms) that Hichcock can experience sexual arousal. Unfortunately, his first wife dies from the anesthetic that Hichcock uses for his quasi-necrophilic sex, and he remarries. As we learn at the end of the film however, his first wife returns from the dead to torment wife number two (Barbara Steele). More disturbingly, Dr. Hichcock's sexual attraction for his first wife endured beyond her death: together they conspire against the second wife. Coherent plotting is not one of the strengths of this film and it is never made entirely clear why Hichcock has remarried, since the reanimated first wife is still on the scene. But the remarriage plays an important dramatic function. The second wife provides Hichcock with a respectable front. The film thereby characterizes Victorian sexuality as simultaneously covert and repressive.

Necrophilia also features in *Orgy*. Set in nineteenth-century Scotland, a number of mysterious deaths attract the attention of both the young hero Serge Rosi (Stelvio Rossi, aka Stan Cooper) and the Holmes-like detective (Pasquale Basile). Woven into this narrative of the police investigation is a lurid subplot involving the gravedigger and necrophiliac Igor (Paul Naschy), who appropriates bodies from tombs in order to caress them, speak to them tenderly and make love to them. Again, the dead return to life. In this case, the living dead include the former mistress of the house, whose cadaver wanders naked through the countryside, retaining something of the attraction she aroused in men during life. While her brain is dead, her body is intact and on display and her status as object of lust and desire continues seamlessly from her living to being undead.

Both *Orgy* and *Hichcock* rationalize the cause of zombification; in the latter, it is Dr. Hichcock's potent anesthesia, and in the former it is caused by the implantation of electrical devices in corpses which allow the film's villain Professor Leon Droila (Gérard Tichy) to control the brains of the dead. *Plague* also provided explanation within its diegesis for the zombification of young Cornish men. In this instance, zombification is caused by voodoo magic which the local squire Mr Hamilton (John Carson) mastered while visiting Haiti. On his return to Cornwall he used his skill to turn the corpses from the local churchyard into slave workers in his tin mine. Not only is he the local squire, magistrate and coroner, Hamilton is also a zombie master akin to Murder Legendre (Bela Lugosi) in *White Zombie*.

The consonances between *Plague* and *White Zombie* do not end there. In the 1932 film the titular "white zombie" is Madeleine Short Parker (Madge Bellamy). After rejecting the advances of millionaire Charles Beaumont (Robert Frazer), Madeline is drugged, dies and is reanimated as the "white zombie" (her skin color is offset by the black zombie slaves toiling in Legendre's mill). In the living dead state, she can no longer reject the millionaire. However the relationship fails to bring Beaumont much sexual or emotional satisfaction, as the reanimated Madeline can do little more than sit in a catatonic state. In *Plague*, Sylvia (and before her, her old school friend Alice [Jacqueline Pearce]) falls victim to the Squire's voodoo skills and sexual associations are bound up with the practice of zombie magic. Strapped to a voodoo altar, mesmerized by ritual, and undergoing zombification, Sylvia is the object of the Squire's lust; he leans in to kiss her as the zombie magic takes hold of her. Although Sylvia is saved, the rescue itself only emphasizes the peril she had been in of becoming a sexually exploited zombie. Cumulatively, these texts illustrate a nexus between love or lust and the undead. The form of domineering male sexuality depicted in these films is contingent on depicting women as passive and sexually accessible.

Nineteenth-Century Society

The nineteenth century setting is compelling because the Victorian milieu highlights the horrors evoked by reanimation and necrophilia. The nineteenth century is richly suggestive in terms of how its inhabitants treated and regarded the dead. Victorian society created, developed and cherished mourning rituals that kept the dead immanent in relation to the living. Earlier I alluded to the death of Prince Albert in 1860. His bereft widow Queen Victoria was thought of both at the time and later as the "Widow of Windsor." Far from being prostrate, she mourned the dead Prince Consort energetically. Victoria built mausolea and monuments, and preserved his rooms as he had left them. Her entire family (especially her daughters) and the royal household participated in an immense pattern of mourning that endured until Victoria's own death in 1901. As early as 1864 Charles Dickens wrote in satiric exasperation: "If you should meet with an inaccessible cave anywhere in that neighborhood, to which a hermit could retire from the memory of Prince Albert and testimonials to the same, pray let me know of it. We have nothing solitary and deep enough in this part of England" (cited in Read 95). The cumulative impact of Victoria's efforts was to keep alive more than the memory of Prince Albert. It was possible to walk into his room and have the impression that he had just walked out and would return in a moment. His desk looked as though he had just stood up from it. His wardrobe was kept at ready as though he would require clothes and valets to perform his toilet. Busts, portraits and statues served as pervasive reminders of his appearance and physicality. In essence, Prince Albert was not allowed to die. The erotic implications of Victoria's mourning are often overlooked. When still alive, the rather prudish and repressed Prince Albert was the object of Queen Victoria's strong erotic attachment. Victoria was the product of the Hanoverian world—more robust than the conservative Coburg court where Albert was brought up—and she is now recognized by historians as having openly enjoyed sex (Pearsall 12). When she mourned Albert, she did not simply express a sense of loss for her husband but her lover as well, and the perpetuation of his memory through objects is fetishistic in tone.

Queen Victoria's protracted and attention-grabbing widowhood is one of the best remembered aspects of her life and reign. Many twentieth-century filmmakers who set their work in her lifetime incorporate the cues of conduct and fixation with the dead that define the Victorian era. *Orgy*, *Plague* and *Hichcock* are steeped in the very iconography of death. Much of the action in the Hammer film –including nocturnal body snatching and a much-imitated sequence of the undead breaking out of their graves—takes place in the village's cemetery. Both *Orgy* and *Hichcock* locate much of the action in catacombs and graveyards. In the climax of *Hichcock*, the first Mrs. Hichcock, risen from her tomb, chases the second Mrs. Hichcock through underground passages. *Orgy* meanwhile concludes with an attack of zombies in a large and lavish sepulcher. All films revolve around sites and rituals that are not simply associated with death but with its ornate commemoration.

The nineteenth century setting of these three films is significant and suggestive in terms of the Victorian period's preoccupation with the sumptuous public mourning of the dead, which carried over into the sexualization of the undead. It is also significant insofar as it illustrates the private scandal that various cultural historians presume to have existed beneath public practice in the nineteenth century. Dr. Hichcock exemplifies both the disjunction and the linkages between public practice and private perversion. The film delineates Hichcock's mourning for his (apparently) dead first wife, including scenes of black clad mourners, funerary appurtenances and rain drenched cemeteries, all on a scale to compare with the most impressive obsequies from the nineteenth century. But the film also shows the concealed scandal of his necrophilia, which takes place in a secret chamber in the Hichcock mansion. The chamber is decorated with trappings such as black crepe and feathers that render it as much a boudoir as a tomb. As such, Dr. Hichcock's dark secret epitomizes the concealed, scandalous and erotic fascination with death lurking beneath the respectable veneer of Victorian England. Among the later interpreters of Victorian sexuality, Michel Foucault has accounted for a full taxonomy of perversions that Victorian sexologists such as Krafft-Ebing and Rohleder categorized, including (besides necrophiliacs) zoophiles, zooerasts, auto-monosexualists, gynecomasts, presbyophiles, sexoesthetic inverts and dyspareunists (*The History of Sexuality* 43). But Foucault, diverging significantly from other thinkers in this field, suggests that there was a clear disjunction between perverse behaviors and those actions and practices considered normal. Rather medicalizing, etymologizing and taxonomizing these perversions simply clarified their status as non-normative behaviors (Harmes 4). The center of interest in these films, then, lies in the way any apparent disjunction is blurred, and it is blurred because of the presence of zombies in the plots. Without them, the dignified public mourning of the Victorian world—certainly a normative and respectable practice in that period even if in the twenty-first century it seems outlandish—would remain separate from perversity. The presence of zombies turns respectability back against itself; mourning the dead modulates into sexual desire for the undead, and the practices for mourning become sites of perverse sexuality.

Being Dead in the Nineteenth Century

The dead in *Orgy*, *Hichcock* and *Plague* are not allowed to rest in peace; similarly many deceased people in the actual rather than the cinematic nineteenth century enjoyed active afterlives. On one level, a degree of morbid preoccupation is not surprising. Victorian society was afflicted by appallingly high mortality statistics, and the fact of most deaths taking place in a home (with only the very poor likely to die institutionalized and then in a workhouse and not a hospital) ensured that death punctuated daily lived experiences. Long before she embarked on her protracted mourning for Prince Albert, the very young Queen Victoria was fascinated by the "painfully interesting details" of King William IV's death (Reed 156). The interest transposed to the fiction of the period, in which death bed scenes proliferate (Reed 163). But as the art historian Angus Trumble points out, death is not just a looming threat; it can also be thought of as beautiful (18). Paintings of the period testify to this aesthetic appreciation of death, as do neo–Victorian re-imaginings of the period. These three zombie films illustrate that dead women can still be captivatingly beautiful and certainly became objects of forbidden love. The first Mrs. Hichcock, who stalks catacombs wreathed in fine white fabric, embodies these associations between *l'amore* and *l'morte*.

The interest in mortality and the mortuary was also evident in the streetscapes and daily experiences of Victorian citizens. As Dickens's novels in particular suggest, large funerals and extensive mourning periods were not confined to the rich. Famously, Pip in *Great Expectations* sees "two dismally absurd persons, each ostentatiously exhibiting a crutch done up in a black bandage": in other words, the mutes at Mrs. Gargery's funeral (Poole 252). Oliver Twist found employment as a mute, and little Paul Dombey in *Dombey and Son* is conveyed to his final resting place by a cortege lead by four black horses with "feathers on their heads; and [whose] feathers tremble on the carriage that they draw" (Poole 252). Although Dickens's satire was not the only negative social comment on the ostentation of Victorian mourning, such grandiose displays endured through the nineteenth century. The cost of crepe and other fabrics, coffins and men to carry them, pageboys to accompany it, palls to cover it and horses to pull it could put the cost of mourning as high as £1,500, at a time when, as Trumble points out, a domestic servant would have earned about £11 a week (46).

Crepe, trinkets, and mourning furniture are among the tangible paraphernalia of bereavement. Freud's discussion of mourning illuminates the symbolic, intangible connotations of those concrete trappings, forging important links between desire, objects and death that are salient to zombie horror. Freud suggested the analogue between boredom and mourning, with both being a kind of paralysis (Phillip 71). Importantly, Freud also suggested that such paralysis impacts on sexual desire. As Kate Brown contends, Freud implies that if a person's loved one is dead and is mourned, then the mourner is left with both someone and no one to desire (407). Freud resolves this tension between longing and absence by pointing to the practice of mourning, in which, as Brown suggests, there took place the "deferring to reality and severing identification with the lost loved one, replacing absence with the felt presence of representation" (407). Studying one particular set of nineteenth-century texts, namely the literary output of the Brontë sisters, Brown further suggests that these works stand in contrast to Freud's understanding of mourning as paralysis and death as absence. By contrast, Brown points out how the Brontës across various works "preserve 'the dead among us,'" because they insist upon the importance of mourning as comprising objects and items that "[restore] creativity, family connection, and an image of the body as capable of fulfilling desires" (407–408).

Brown's sense of a body still being present and still provoking desire marries with the nineteenth century ethos of mourning as filling a space (rather than accentuating absence) in a way that is especially useful to understanding Victorian-set zombie films, which portray sex with the dead and the sexualization of women after they have died. The dead in *Orgy*, *Hichcock* and *Plague* are not allowed to rest in peace. Actual deceased persons also had active afterlives in the nineteenth century. If their mourning family could afford it, dark clothing was worn for months or even years as a reminder of a person's death. Tolling bells, grave monuments and even sepulchers drew attention to a person's demise. Portraits, lockets of a dead person's hair and other types of paraphernalia also kept memories alive.

Yet some sectors of Victorian society also feared another type of active afterlife, in that people may have been buried alive (Behlmer 207). Of course, fears of premature burial and the return of the dead as zombies are different horror tropes. Yet such terror highlights a liminal space: when a person's biology is thrown into doubt, so too are their social functions and position. As Behlmer points out, Victorian doctors and undertakers, as well as interested observers, had a diverse and conflicting vocabulary to account for the different stages moving from being unquestionably alive to definitely dead. Somewhere on the spectrum between these two states a person could be in a trance, cataleptic, in suspended animation or anaesthetized (as was the first Mrs. Hichcock). These different terms and their proliferation in nineteenth-century discourses on living and dying testify to the anxiety of the period that the border between living and death was not clear. Actual Victorian society feared the possibility of premature burial; figures as exalted as Lord Lytton, the Viceroy of India, feared the possibility and many stipulated that clear signs of decay needed to be waited on before final internment (Trumble 20). It is in this uncertain space that Dr. Hichcock's perverse sexuality expresses itself. He makes love to a woman who has been medically treated to appear dead, until the night he gets the dose wrong and Hichcock ends up sleeping with a woman he has killed. In *Plague*, Sylvia is tied down, groped and kissed by the Squire as she undergoes the process of zombification. Again her ontological status is uncertain.

The zombie films set in the nineteenth century exploit and promote this uncertainty. Clearly the first Mrs. Hichcock became a sexualized entity in her husband's eyes only when simulating death and therefore when she was released from the constraints of normative female conduct. Mrs. Hichcock is passive and powerless as well as vulnerable, three tropes stereotypically associated with normative Victorian female conduct. But the consequence of this conduct—that Mrs. Hichcock becomes a participant, even a passive one, in abnormal sexual practices—challenge and complicate the idea that her passivity is normative. These films also reflect a current of both Victorian theological and scientific thought that was open to ontological speculation: whether death was actually a fixed state. Giovanni Aldini's galvanic experiments were among the early nineteenth century scientific tests that seemed to reanimate the dead. In one instance a dead man's muscles began to move and "the left eye actually opened" (Behlmer 213). Experiments of this nature prompted speculations as to whether death was a permanent or a mutable condition. These three zombie films contain their own analogues to these speculations. *Orgy* actually contains a kind of "mad scientist" figure, who has been experimenting with the dead and implanting transceivers in them that allow them to be reanimated and controlled. Dr. Hichcock's chemical experiments that induce a deathlike state and ultimately kill her reflect actual Victorian scientific speculations such as Sir James Simpson's experiments with self-administered chloroform dosages, which sought to discover its properties and effects (Gordon 108). While *Plague*'s explanation for the zombies—the voodoo magic— is more traditional and not at all scientific (Sir James Forbes, Professor of Medicine at University College London, has to overcome his scientific skepticism to accept the reality and power of voodoo), it still casts into doubt the idea that death is ontologically absolute.

It is nonetheless equally clear that undead women can still be objects of desire. The key denominator between the women in *Orgy*, *Hichcock* and *Plague* is their accessibility. They occupy an uncertain space; they are neither dead nor alive but undead, and certainly passive. It is at this point that the creative decision to set these narratives in the Victorian period becomes most salient. Gary Farnell, thinking of nineteenth-century fictional women including Miss Havisham from Dickens's *Great Expectations* refers to the "eroticized and forbidden girl-woman" at the heart of many Victorian accounts of female sexuality (14). But set against this fictional construction is the very real accessibility of women's bodies to men. The 1857 Divorce Act, while making escape from a violent marriage possible for some women (albeit fraught with potential for scandal and disgrace) did not particularly mitigate legal circumstances which left Victorian women essentially as the possessions of their husbands. Nor did the Married Women's Property Act (1870) alleviate this legal reality (Combs 1028–1057). Instead the legal status of Victorian women facilitated male possessiveness. Victorian-set zombie films reflect these legal contexts. Here, possessiveness extends to posthumous control. The zombified women are sexually subordinated.

Being undead they have no voice and offer no resistance. In *Orgy* the control is explicit: the doctor has implanted devices that allow him to control the mind and actions of the deceased lady of the house. In *Hichcock* control is more oblique: Hichcock's "dead" first wife remains in his house and at his bidding, although his possession of her is not as obvious as the scientific explanation provided in *Orgy*. Both these European horror films reflect the sexual status of Victorian women, where loosely defined legislation about sexual consent provided little protection and failed to protect women who suffered unwanted sexual contact (Trumble 32). The films distil ideas on both anxieties about women's sexuality and the fears of women themselves. Women's agency is suppressed by various means—drugs, electrical implants, voodoo magic. But women's fears are also depicted; the second Mrs. Hichcock flees in terror through the catacombs and Sylvia is strapped down and unable to resist the Squire.

Being enslaved by Haitian voodoo, the zombies of *Plague* are positioned within the diegesis more as pitiful and exploited creatures than as threat; in common with the voodoo zombies of *White Zombie* these are not rampaging flesh eaters, but downtrodden manual slaves. The two women in *Plague*, Alice and Sylvia, both succumb to the powers of the zombie master Squire Franklin and both become passive victims of sexual violence. The passivity of the living dead in *Plague* was prefigured by *Hichcock* and repeated in *Orgy*. The first Mrs. Hichcock, while a willing participant in her husband's macabre sex games and consenting to the stupefying injections, does not actively participate in the lovemaking. To all intents and purposes she is dead, just as her husband likes it: she is the object of his sexuality rather than a participant in lovemaking. The two women of *Orgy*, the maidservant and the mistress, are the lovers of the hero Serge in life, but their lovemaking is shot through with suggestions of exploitation. Serge insists the maidservant strip in front of him and subjects her naked body to his gaze and evaluation, causing her humiliation. The mistress of the house meanwhile suffers her own sexual humiliation, having to share Serge's sexual favors with her servant. Tellingly, the impression of sexual exploitation continues once the mistress of the house is dead and zombified. When she has become a zombie, she moves naked and vulnerable through the "Scottish" countryside, her body on display to the men pursuing her. Her brain is dead and she no longer alert to their gaze. While this state may mean she is free from the humiliation she would have felt when alive and objectified by Serge, she nonetheless remains a sexual object. Sylvia is the least powerful of all; she is strapped down as the Squire moves in to kiss her. Actual Victorian writings on sexuality, such as "Walter's" record of sexual transgression *My Secret Life*,[6] suggest that women were mostly unwilling participants in male scopophilic gratification. The women in "Walter's" sexual memoirs are mostly remembered as assemblages of body parts whom he observed through keyholes, with the aid of mirrors, or during sex itself (Harmes and Harmes 24). Importantly, this point of view resonates with the women in these zombie horror films; once their minds have died, they too are purely assemblages of body parts, nothing more than animated corpses. This point of view also finds a natural counterpart in the funerary and mortuary rituals of the period which these three horror films evoke. Victorian mourning reduced the deceased individual to a dispersed collection of artifacts. Hair was encased in lockets and other trinkets. Such mementos of a person's physicality were handed out among friends and relatives of the deceased.

The themes iterated in these films—of funereal intercourse, of female sexual bondage that continues beyond the grave and the uncertain space that undead women occupy—evoke actual Victorian practices. The deathly fixations, including the tombs, sepulchers and mourning practices that the films showcase, were normative Victorian practices. As we have seen, a range of voices from Dickens onwards testify to the preoccupation of nineteenth-century people with mourning. While zombies did not actually roam Victorian England, intensely observed and elaborately practiced mourning rituals kept the dead alive and their status ontologically uncertain. Such rituals did not so much commemorate the dead but keep their physical presence close by. But within this normative practice, the films show non-normative types of sexuality taking place: the Squire in *Plague* is leader of a pack of gang rapists; the women in *Orgy* are adulterous; and most deviant of all is the necrophilic Dr. Hichcock. The films illustrate the productive potential of the nineteenth century setting; the period's distinctive mourning rituals are the inspiration for films that move beyond commemorating the dead to having the undead walk again.

But allied to this creative potential is the inversion of a society's sexual morality. The dead in these films transcend the mourning practices of Victorian society; returning as the undead they need no longer be mourned, but they will become objects of sexual desire and lust. Figures such as Dr. Hichcock adhere to the iconography of public mourning but repudiate the normalizing sexuality of the Victorian period. The disjunction between public practice and a private liminal space is developed across these three films. Tellingly, none of the male characters are the married *patres familias* that epitomizes Victorian respectability. Hichcock is married, but his perverse sex games do not led to "healthy" procreation. Both Serge and the Squire are bachelors. The anxious and distorted sexual realms they occupy in the films echo nineteenth century warnings against sexual deviance. The 1870 iatric text *Chronic Diseases, especially the Nervous Diseases of Women* by the German physician D. Rosch warned that "[p]unishments follow transgression, and if sins are committed against the laws of nature, the offenders are driven through abjection and affliction out of the paradise of a happy matrimonial life" (25–6). While this tract was issuing a warning, Freud made a similar point, claiming that "the essence of perversion lies ... solely in the exclusiveness with which these deviations are carried out and as a result of which the sexual act serving the purpose of reproduction is put on one side" (*Introductory Lectures on Psychoanalysis* 364). The sexual acts of these films are not reproductive. Neither the Squire nor Dr. Hichcock nor any of the male characters in *Orgy* are interested in producing children. In these three films, the purpose of reproduction is put aside in favor of sexually exploiting undead women who were unable to resist, who are objects of desire, and cannot possibly be fecund. They are bodies and nothing more.

Conclusion

These films pursue the complex linkage between private sexual perversion and the public spaces, including those where people publicly exhibited their grief. One factor above others that defines the world of Victorian mourning, mortality and commemoration is its sheer physicality. Prince Albert is the apotheosis of this idea. With his living quarters and office left as they were when he died, Albert remained a prominent posthumous physical presence in the Victorian royal household. It is neither a long nor a difficult jump from the physical proximity of the Victorian dead to a zombie. A mindless creature of instinct, a zombie is the quintessence of sheer posthumous physicality. The films under analysis in this essay as much as the more familiar zombies from American cinema bear this point out. The Cornish men zombified in *Plague* are nothing more than physical laborers in the Squire's mine, while the women in all three films become objects of sexual gratification for men. The sites and iconography of Victorian mourning became major sites of private transgressive sexuality.

But we should remember these are not primary texts; they are set in the Victorian period, but were not products of it. Rather they are 1960s and 1970s examples of European exploitation horror cinema and they raise challenging and disturbing questions about twentieth-century sexual attitudes and their bridges back to the nineteenth century. These films significantly problematize female sexuality. I suggested above that the undead women were "bodies and nothing more." The women are undead (or narrowly rescued from that state) and the films situate female sexuality and sexual action in deeply disturbing, perverse contexts. These women are not fecund, for fertility would restore them to a living realm of "normative" female sexuality, where bearing a man's children and perpetuating a family name were prime female duties, from Queen Victoria downwards.[7] But these films problematize female sexuality by severely limiting their options. In these films women are expected to become child bearers to respectable *pater familias*. The alternative is being reduced to mindless receptacles for sexual gratification. As examples of exploitation cinema, these films revel in their transgression. They do not resolve the dilemmas they pose about female roles as undead objects or fecund child bearers. They certainly make robust and dramatic use of various Victorian social mores, extrapolating to a horrific extent the mourning rituals so that they modulate into the ritualized fetishes of undead sexuality. Likewise they play with popular perceptions of the status of Victorian women, who in these films are the helpless playthings of men. But in their eagerness to exploit rather than challenge, these films bring these attitudes into the twentieth century largely intact. The films use types of secret perversity to expose the cruelty and exploitation that Victorian women were subjected to and to demonstrate that the perverse men are the real monsters here, rather than the zombie women they exploit. But as products of 20th century film making, not the Victorian era itself, the films also suggest that that these values are perhaps not as distant from the 20th (and maybe even the and 21st) century as we might imagine. Perhaps these values are, like the Victorian deceased, still all too uncomfortably present.

NOTES

1. The development of photography contributed to this discourse, creating photographic mementoes including post-mortem photographs of the deceased people, to which were added religious icons and symbols and which record the full pageantry of funerals. The spirit photographs of the Victorian period are one manifestation of this trend, but the works reproduced in *The Harlem Book of the Dead* taken by James van der Zee of corpses, caskets and mourning apparatus are its apotheosis.

2. Spanish horror films were frequently set elsewhere than Spain; many were European co-productions with other countries including Germany and Italy and used generic European settings, and sometimes more exotic settings as well, including the Tibetan setting of *Fury of the Wolfman* (*La Furia del Hombre Lobo* 1970) and *Night of the Howling Beast* (*La Maldicion de la Bestia* 1974). Other Spanish horrors of the 1970s horror boom in that country used British settings, such as *Seven Murders for Scotland Yard* (*Jack el Destripador de Londres* 1971).

3. An influence also clearly at work in other national contexts, such as the period horrors made by Roger Corman for American International Pictures, which were a series very loosely based on Edgar Allen Poe's writings, starting with *The Fall of the House of Usher* (1960), and including *The Pit and the Pendulum* (1961), *The Masque of the Red Death* (1964), and *The Tomb of Ligeia* (1964).

4. Carpentieri and Donati as Louis Mann and Gastaldi as Julyan (or Julian) Berry. Cast members in *Orgy* also acted under English names. For example, Stelvio Rossi appeared as Stan Cooper.

5. The 1966 theatrical trailer also invites such comparisons, promising cinema patrons a view of a "place dominated by men without morals, where blood lusts are excited by hunting a human quarry."

6. "Walter" is the nom-de-plume of an anonymous Victorian author, famed for his volumes of sexual odyssey.

7. Victoria herself was remarkably fecund and was pregnant for much of her married life. She gave birth to princes and princesses who married into almost all European royal families including the Prussian, Danish and Greek.

A Love Worth Un-Undying For

Neoliberalism and Queered Sexuality in Warm Bodies

Sasha Cocarla

Popular culture has long been both a key resource for knowledge on and a cultural creator of social insecurities, doubts, and fears. While enjoyment, discussion, and catharsis are perhaps the most encouraged outcomes and benefits of popular culture consumption, in moments of particular social unrest and cultural change/upheaval, popular culture avenues also become even further saturated with storylines and characters that not only assist in social understanding, but also, and perhaps even more aggressively, instill a sense a normalcy and moral righteousness in relation to outside threats and apparent indecency.

This threat to personal, social, and national security, normalcy, and life is most often portrayed as an outsider—an *Other*—who, either ideologically or literally, fails to (or perhaps chooses not to) adapt to mainstream (read: "normative") understandings and general ways of being. Whether in reference to criminal outsiders, sexual "deviants," or international "terrorist" threats, the representation of this other is always-already made monstrous. And in popular culture, this is blatantly obvious in horror and supernatural examples, where the dangerous external threat literally becomes the monster of your nightmares.

Like many fictional zombie narratives, Isaac Marion's 2011 best-selling novel *Warm Bodies* describes a post-apocalyptic landscape where the living dead scavenge for remnants of their previous lives. Uniquely diverting from more traditional rotting corpse plotlines, *Warm Bodies* (narrated by the protagonist, R, a zombie) positions heteronormative desire and romance at the forefront of the story. Hidden within this novel (and the recent film adaptation) is an unconventional reading of queerness that is, arguably, steeped within wider social consequences and commentary that rearticulate neoliberal, hetero- and queerly-normative ideals in an era that threatens to wreak havoc on traditional American values. This essay will provide a queered[1] reading of *Warm Bodies* by situating it within discussions of neoliberal ideologies and monstrous sexuality. Although this storyline allows for the possible reading of a queered, monstrous politic of desire, radical in its potential to subsume heteronormative understandings of sex, desire, and romance, it instead resituates hetero- and queer-normativity as being the only possible solution to maintaining "life."

While my queered reading of *Warm Bodies'* will weave itself throughout this essay, in order to better situate this zombie romance within a broader understanding of queerness and neoliberalism, I will first provide a brief overview of the role of zombies in current popular culture. Following this, I will move into a discussion of homonormativity and homonationalism (Duggan *The Twilight of Equality?* and "The New Homonormativity"; Puar), two theories that have highlighted the homogenizing effects of neoliberalism and American nationalism on LGBTQ identities and romantic, domestic, and sexual relationships. Drawing from these theories, "queer normativity" will be used to illustrate the homonormative-like elements that are present within many of the key themes in *Warm Bodies*, including romantic norms, understandings of life and death, ideas of progress and personal/collective growth for the betterment of society, and fear of non-complying others/tolerance of complying-others, while also making space for the monstrous, living dead, *queered* sexual desire. More specifically, queer normativity will help us make sense of the ways queered/monstrous desire and sexuality perpetuate and maintain neoliberal domestic ideals.[2] Finally, these theories will assist me in underscoring the ways that *Warm Bodies* facilitates a reading that is both extraordinary and ordinary, transgressive and uniform, and queered and normative.

Bump in the Night

The Other-as-monster[3] serves many purposes—on its most basic level, it allows for a more creative, and oftentimes, playful, way of sorting through general social anxieties and fears. On a more insidious level, however, the Other-as-monster works to perpetuate hegemonic ideals by melding together the figure of the monster and its horrific qualities/actions with the ideological myths and prejudices often ascribed to racial, sexual, gender, and dis/ability minority groups. In other words, the filmic monster lurking in the closet or eating your neighbor's brain is imbued with traits that are already deemed culturally deviant/strange/excessive/unnecessary. In this respect, this symbolic representation further vilifies, marginalizes, and ostracizes real people and experiences, while at the same time it further perpetuates mainstream, hegemonic ideals.

The joining together of monsters with real social fears and anxieties over a perceived threatening other has become a cultural mainstay in both popular literature and film, with perhaps the most popular monstrous figure being the vampire, who has represented deviant sexuality, fears of contagion, foreign outsiders, and aging and death (to name but a few).[4] While the figure of the vampire has undoubtedly portrayed such social insecurities, this monster has also manifested as less threatening, and especially recently, as domesticated and romantic (*Twilight, Vampire Diaries, True Blood*). As the vampire's less suave, unintelligible, even-more-dead dead relative, the figure of the zombie has also been no stranger to representing cultural fears and anxieties. However, unlike vampires, zombies' rotting flesh and general lack of composure has left them neutered and asexual. Until recently, that is.[5]

Since their filmic inception in *White Zombie* (1932), zombies have most often stood in as metaphors for deep cultural fears and tensions, including racism and enslavement of racial minorities, cannibalism, bioterrorism and disease outbreaks, the fall of rationality and independence to instinct-motivated herd mentality, and the complete numbing of humanity, to name but a few examples (Dendle "The Zombie as Barometer of Cultural Anxiety"; McIntosh; Drezner). Zombies have also been used to illustrate our discomfort with the abject, death, and decay. Finally, in a capitalist economy fueled by the pathological need for continual growth, consumption and expansion, it becomes clear that the zombie of modern storytelling often acts as metaphor for mass consumption under capitalism, abandoning ideals of rationality and moderation, and instead consuming without question (Dendle "The Zombie as Barometer of Cultural Anxiety" 51).

As previously mentioned, the monsters of the horror film genre have been steadily used to demonstrate social upheavals and uncertainties. Following the events of September 11th, 2001, in the United States' cultural imaginary, the zombie became one of the primary figures that social anxieties became inscribed upon. In this context, zombies have been used to both symbolically work through and reproduce uncertainties surrounding terrorism, immigration, contagious diseases, and apocalyptic events (Saunders 81). While not all are as obvious as *Call of Duty: Modern Warfare 2* (2009), which features the Taliban as literal zombies under attack by the "hero" first-person shooter, and, *Osombie*, a 2012 film that finds Osama Bin Laden as a living dead monster who is working on creating an army of zombie terrorists, the popularity of zombies in popular culture is deeply symptomatic of cultural upheaval and fear over maintaining the status quo—a sense of "normalcy."

Within popular culture, zombie storylines generally culminate in one of two ways—mass defeat of all the living dead (either through physical elimination, quarantine, or subjugation) or the slow eradication of all of humanity (Drezner 8). Unlike vampires, who are often depicted in popular culture as not only coexisting with humans but also romancing them, such narratives for zombies are few and far between.[6] In this climate, the conflation of monster/monstrosity with readings of the threatening and/or sexually perverse other become highlighted.

Within post–9/11 zombie fiction, it is clear that the very presence of a zombie-other conjures up ideas of risk and transmission, social dissent and upheaval. This contagion that the threatening other/terrorist other/monstrous other risks spreading to the masses is threatening because of its very undoing of norms. For the zombie of modern fiction, the threat seems obvious; contagion of the zombie virus and movement from living to the undead. On a symbolic level, this contagious threat (again, especially within a post–9/11 context) intersects with political and social fears about the complete destabilization of national and domestic norms, values, and ideals. Here, patriotism and nostalgic strongholds of "traditional" values become seen as the antidote to ward off the contagion of terrorism, which is feared as seeping into the cracks of society and undoing political, social, and ideological norms (through political dissent and activism, as well as "progressive" politics, lifestyles, and sexualities more generally). These fears of contagion and disease are palpable in zombie narratives—"the transmission of the zombie infection is a symbolic form of radical brainwashing, where anyone can become infected and be turned into the zombie other/an ideological threat" (Bishop *American Zombie Gothic* 29). It becomes necessary, then, in both the zombie film/story as well as in a post–9/11 society, to make every effort to protect one's self from the monstrous, sexually perverse threatening other.

Musings of a Neoliberal Corpse

The book *Warm Bodies* (2011) seems to be one exception to the zombie's general role in popular culture—not only do zombies coexist with humans from nearly the beginning of the story (albeit, on separate ends of the city), the entire storyline is premised upon an unlikely romance between a zombie and a human. The story is narrated by R, our zombie protagonist, who leads us through the monotony of his life up until he meets his romantic interest, Julie. Detailing his un-life of un-living in an airport with other zombies, occasional wanderings into the city for food (humans), and the boredom that results from not being able to talk, feel, and emote, readers are encouraged to see R as simply going through a series of motions, which he has no rational control over. What R does seem to have control over, though, are his philosophical musings. It becomes clear through his ramblings that R is not like the other zombies he exists with. He does not enjoy eating other humans and he is constantly frustrated by his inability to remember what his life was like before he became undead (Marion 7). Although R does not take pleasure in the act of eating other humans—there is no thrill behind his hunt—he does take immense pleasure in the effect that consuming human brains has on him. When zombies eat human brains, they are momentarily flooded with intense images and emotions—the memories of the brain's owner (Marion 7). These images are short-lived, but the effects are long-lasting on R. Those moments allow him to feel "less dead" and closer to life (Marion 7).

Within *Warm Bodies* it is R's quest to feel "less dead" and closer to life that propels this zombie narrative into a romantic storyline. R's quest to be alive, to resemble humanity—to be normal—are deeply steeped within neoliberal ideals. At perhaps its most basic understanding, "neoliberalism" is most often equated (at least economically) with a radically free market (Wendy Brown 38). Key to this understanding—and to understanding neoliberalism more broadly—is the term "free." Free choice, free market, and free enterprise (Harvey *A Brief History* 2). The guise of freedom and personal agency is an active myth within neoliberal policies as well as general social conditions and ideals. However, this "freedom" cannot be separated from the creation/perpetuation of an ideal "rational" actor—a citizen whose ability to invoke neoliberal agency is intrinsically tied to their classification as rational, sound, and "normal." And, perhaps most importantly, these classifications—rational, sound, normal—are themselves key markers/creations of a neoliberal ideology.

A key part to the regulation and perpetuation of neoliberal ideologies is the creation and maintenance of structures and functions that facilitate in making these ideals the norm/status quo. The military, law, politics, and other social institutions such as health care and education, are all needed to create the neoliberal cultural climate. However, state intervention must appear to be limited, as the founding characteristics of neoliberalism are freedom and independence (Harvey 2). In order for the guise of freedom to best operate within a neoliberal agenda, various processes of governmentality—governmental intervention, power, and discipline that is not related to state politics alone—must fix themselves within various bodies and institutions of power, including the body of the "free-acting" citizen (Foucault *The Government of Self and Others*). Within this space, "free" subjects internalize state power and modes of governing and they self-surveil all their actions and choices, as they increasingly become aware that they will bear the responsibility for the outcomes of *any* choice they make. After all, the rational, neoliberal subject's freedom and positionality is entirely contingent upon their very ability to make rational, neoliberal choices.

Of course, there are other positionalities within a neoliberal project. In order for there to be a "rational," "normal" subject, there equally needs to be an irrational, abnormal object—or zombie, in this case—who deviates from the path of hegemonic ideals. Under this neoliberal agenda, this deviation is most often understood as a literal failure to subscribe to the norm. It is a failure to make the right choices, failure to self-regulate and follow social rules. If one is unable to attain status and privilege within a neoliberal framework, then "it was because they failed for personal and cultural reasons to enhance their own human capital through education, the acquisition of a protestant work ethic, and submission to work discipline and flexibility"—not because the system itself flourishes on such failure (Harvey "Neoliberalism" 34).

Here, those that fail to subscribe to the neoliberal project become simultaneously seen as deviant through their inability to "choose" correctly, and, deviant through their literal inability to ever be read as a "rational" subject. The project is then cyclical. This other must make the correct choices in order to properly fulfill neoliberal ideals, and yet their choices are never—can never—be understood as being "rational" because of their very other-ness. Even more so, the neoliberal project benefits from and is maintained by both the presence of the other and their inherent inability to comply with neoliberal norms, with key sites of power (including global warfare, neo-imperialism, the prison industrial complex, to name a few) being based on racist, sexist, queerphobic, and abelist agendas and ideals.

With this in mind, it would seem that the neoliberal project should simply implode on itself due to the fact that fewer bodies are able to be read as "rational" and "normal." Within the ideal neoliberal space, the proper neoliberal subject is white, male, able-bodied, and heteronormative—meaning, they are able to subscribe to values associated with heterosexuality (the proper sexuality), including marriage, raising a family, and participating in conspicuous consumption practices. In order to perpetuate the myth of free choice and rationality, then, the neoliberal project cannot focus entirely on economic and legal reform, but must also immerse itself within identity politics, and in doing so, alter some of its membership policies for sake of a neoliberal legacy. Of course, this does not mean that, for example, queer individuals or women of color are automatically deemed "rational" citizens, with full access to the free market and all other social and political advantages. Instead, some minority groups are granted certain accesses only when they subscribe to some of the preordained characteristics that the proper, rational neoliberal subject projects, namely, mass consumption practices, unfaltering national allegiance, and normative (or as close as you can get) domestic partnerships.

But what does this look like for zombies in *Warm Bodies*? R details numerous ways that he and the other zombies try to hold onto some semblance of rationality and normal life, even if they cannot actually remember what their lives were like before they became the undead. The zombies have all congregated in an airport on the outskirts of a city. Within this airport, there are specific moments of regularity that symbolically allude to the zombies' inherent humanity and capacity to change. They meet in airport bars with their zombie friends (although these meetings are fairly uneventful since zombies can only speak a few syllables at a time). There is a zombie place of worship, where all interested zombies congregate and wave their arms towards the sky. There are marriages between male and female zombies. Zombie couples bump their bodies together in an attempt to sexually engage with one another, and unions between married zombies and parentless zombie children (who attend zombie school) form domesticated zombie families. The relevance of these activities to neoliberalism cannot be overlooked. Subscribing to social norms without question and "going through the motions" (the zombies do not know why they are doing these things) allows for the understanding that "this is simply the way things are" to go unquestioned—a key tenet of neoliberalism. This ideology simultaneously allows for the negation/ignorance of systemic inequalities, and, the apparent inevitability of this "natural" order of things. For R, there appears to be no interest in finding out why he is a zombie, why they are segregated from the humans, or why they cling to the activities of their prior human states. Instead, they go through these motions because there is some sort of understanding that that is simply what they are supposed to do in order to retain some sense of normalcy, value, and purpose.

Interestingly, while R longs to regain a sense of normalcy that he had when he was human (although he cannot remember what that normalcy looked like) sex does not figure in his longing, and in fact R is glad to be rid of his human sexual urges and is bored by bumping bodies with other zombies.

> Maybe it's a kind of death throe. A distant echo of that great motivator that once started wars and inspired symphonies, that drove human history out of the caves and into space.... Sex, once a law as undisputed as gravity, has been disproved. The equation is erased, the blackboard broken. Sometimes it's a relief. I remember the need, the insatiable hunger that ruled my life and the lives of everyone around me. Sometimes I'm glad to be free of it. There's less trouble now [Marion 18].

R bumps his body with other female zombie bodies because he feels like that is something he faintly remembers doing; he seeks normalcy through these actions simply because they are what living humans do, not because they bring him any enjoyment. As the story progresses, R's relationship to neoliberal values becomes more and more apparent, and in doing so, the possibility of him moving closer to life and humanity become tangible. However, while R's monstrosity forever denies him the possibility of attaining normalcy (read: neoliberal status quo), his ability to change and evolve exists both due to his belief in neoliberal ideologies as signifying "life" and "the norm"[7] and his differentiation from the other undead who do not show his same resolve and dedication.

The Undead Exception to the Rule

As an attempt to differentiate between "rational," neoliberal subjects and "deviant," marginalized others, a gesture of symbolic national inclusion is extended to a small group of people who have the possibility of subscribing to some of the core tenants of neoliberalism. In Jasbir Puar's discussion of homonationalism, she articulates the ways in which the proper, neoliberal, white, homosexual has become the newest addition to the nationalist project of assimilation (namely, the United States, but many other Western nation states invoke similar agendas). Within this space, "proper" homosexual bodies lose their "queerness"—their previously perceived deviance and otherness—in an attempt to not only perpetuate neoliberal free choice and market ideologies, but also, and perhaps more importantly, to encourage a national sense of belonging in the face of an always-present external threat. For Puar the temporality of these moments, sentiments, actions, and reactions create assemblages of dominant societal schemas; in other words, the neoliberal case for individuality, rationality, and freedom articulate with key historical moments, like the "war on terror," gay marriage, immigration, and so on. These assemblages create new anxieties and tensions surrounding notions of "belonging" and "not belonging," "status quo" and "abnormality," and "compliant citizen" and "terrorist other."

Within this context, certain bodies—white, male homosexuals with adequate spending power and appropriate consumption practices—are given admission into neoliberal, heteronormative sites of access.[8] However, this membership is not without a strict set of guidelines, as LGBTQ bodies that are most easily read as "normative" (primarily mainstreaming gay and lesbian individuals) must subscribe to a new sexual politics that readily hinges upon the neoliberal "possibility of demobilized gay constituency and a privatized depoliticized gay culture anchored in domesticity and consumption" (Duggan "The New Homonormativity" 175). In other words, a heteronormative approach to gay identity and experience needs to be invoked—*homonormativity*.

In *Warm Bodies*, this membership is visible through the differentiations between R and the other undead, namely, the Boneys. While R belongs to the group of zombies who, to varying degrees, have their flesh, physically resemble humans, and, as in R's case, long to regain their humanity, the Boneys are virtual skeletons who actively detest humans and strive for an undead takeover (Marion 46). In other words, even in the land of the undead, social norms, propriety, and neoliberal values still reverberate—there are "good," proper zombies, who still manage to partake in civilizing activities without knowing why they are doing so, and the inherently broken Boneys, who are too far past saving. One might assume that due to their shared undead-ness that R would hold some sort of allegiance to the Boneys. On the contrary, R's very determination to save Julie from the Boneys, positions humanity, rationality, and freedom at the forefront, even at the cost of the undead's demise (Marion 54).

It is here where homonormativity is evoked, which does not threaten dominant heteronormative ideals, assumptions, and institutions, but instead upholds and further solidifies them (Duggan *The Twilight of Equality?* 50). The effects of this are threefold, allowing for: (1) the legitimization of a depoliticized gay culture within the larger cultural imaginary ("we are just like you!"); (2) "rational" gays' access to neoliberal avenues previously hidden from them, including the free market, state recognition and acceptance of their domesticity, and patriotism; and (3) the neoliberal project to both expand its followers (who will continuously work to uphold its values) and to further differentiate themselves from monstrous others.

Returning again to Puar, this new homonormative body holds an incredible amount of power. Especially since the attacks in the United States on September 11, 2001, and the subsequent "War on Terror," national (American) allegiance is more necessary than ever in order to gain access to neoliberal norms as well as to maintain readiness against terrorist threats. The proper, neoliberal, gay citizen, who is no longer queered, perverse, and sexually deviant, becomes enveloped within this national cause, to rid the state of perceived threats—that is, the racialized "terrorist" and the queered, sexual and gendered other (Puar 3–4). Yes, the neoliberal gay citizen can still be read as sexually other through their same-sex attraction and sexual relations. But what becomes more pressing within the context of safe-guarding against monstrous others is that the American white, gay individual still enacts proper neoliberal and nationalist ideals: the spending habits, familial values, and political interests of their hetero, rational counterpart. Within homonationalism, a sexually deviant threat needs to constantly exist (or at least needs to be believed to exist) in order to best mobilize citizens to their utmost potential.

In the process of perpetuating the myth of America as an all-forgiving and accepting nation that is a safe-haven to persecuted outsiders, the racialized, queer, perverse, and "other" bodies that are perpetually deemed "monstrous" and "irrational" remain as the core ideological threats to the neoliberal project and national undoing. In other words, even though R is a literal monster himself (and thereby queered in relation to the human norm), he clings to the dominant notion of normalcy and the neoliberal mantra of achievement ("if you work hard enough, you will be successful"), implying that he has more in common with living humans than he does with the Boneys. Through a homonationalist understanding, in relation to the Boneys, R is the undead exception to the rule—the undead/homo-par excellence.

Key to the forging of a proper homonormative/homonationalist project is the distancing of gay subjects from their historically radical sexual politics, the sexual ethics and practices that in large part constituted their queerness, their difference and ostracism from the norm. This severing acts as not only a separation from more "deviant" queers, but also serves to facilitate the reproduction of classed, gendered, and racialized norms. Through this intricate relationship, the threatening, ideological other becomes inscribed with neoliberalism's disaffections, namely queerness, non-nationality, poverty, and the perversely racialized (Puar 37). In *Warm Bodies*, R is only seen as non-threatening through his desire for neoliberal values, including romance and heteronormative desire. Without the relationships described at length below, R's ability to transcend his inherent otherness would become impossible. It is therefore through his disgust of his own monstrosity, his queerness, that neoliberalism is able to grab hold. At the same time, R can never become un-undead, and so neoliberal success is tentative. The story of R and his relationships with Perry and Julie are then steeped with complexity, allowing for both impossibility and possibility, monstrosity and humanity, and queerness and normativity.

Zombie Romance: Worth Undying For

While we are first introduced to R's neoliberal yearnings through his internal musings, it is the romance between R and Julie that is the catalyst towards obtaining these ideals. On a voyage into the city to scavenge for humans, R kills and eats the brain of a young man named Perry Kelvin while ambushing a group of late teens/young adults who are also scavenging for food and resources of their own. As he begins to consume Perry's brain, R becomes affected by the human memories in a way he has never before experienced. As he is flooded with these images, for the first time since his death, R feels pain and intense emotion, to the point that he is not able to comprehend what is happening to him (Marion 15). At the same time that R is trying to process Perry's memories and their effects, he hears a woman scream. As he turns towards the noise he recognizes her as Perry's girlfriend, Julie, and is overcome with an intense desire to not only save her from the other zombies but to disguise her as a zombie and take her back to the airport with him (Marion 16).

It is at this moment that the zombie romance begins to unfold. Within the story, a queered sexuality or romance can be read in multiple ways—through the relationship between Perry and R, through the relationship between Perry, R, and Julie, and through the relationship between R and Julie. At their most basic level, all of these relationships are queered because they involve the living dead. Unlike the vampires in many current romantic storylines, the zombies in *Warm Bodies* are not attractive beings. While they may be rotting at varying stages, they are still undoubtedly decaying corpses (Marion 4). Therefore, any romantic yearning and sexual undertone evident throughout the story is always-already deeply imbued with a sexual taboo: necrophilia. It is important to note that I am not conflating queerness with necrophilia or vice versa. Instead, through an understanding of the rational neoliberal sexual subject, any "othered" sexual act, identity, and desire instantly becomes monstrous, and, through an understanding of the neoliberal subject as displaying hetero- and homonormative values, this then translates into queer monstrosity.

Perry and R

While for the most part *Warm Bodies* subscribes to a conventionally heteronormative plot (boy meets girl, boy saves girl, boy and girl fall in love), there are queer elements throughout (perhaps most notably being the fact that said lover-boy is dead). In addition to this zombie romance storyline, which I will later argue is an example of a queer normativity, there are other relationships with R that are inscribed with queerness (again, due to R's undead state), with the relationship between Perry and R being perhaps the most interesting in its queer possibility. The relationship between Perry and R opens itself up to a radical queer reading that provides a hopeful alternative to the queerly-normative pair that is R and Julie.

After the initial jolt of emotion that Perry's brain brings when R eats a part of it, R decides to bring the rest of the brain with him back to the airport (along with Julie). Instead of instantly devouring every morsel of it, embracing his zombie instincts, R instead decides to ration Perry's brain and savor each bite he takes. As he slowly consumes it, he is continuously flooded with Perry's memories, including moments from his childhood, the moment he first met Julie, the deepening of their romantic feelings for one another, his father's death, and the moment that R killed him (Marion 2011). With each influx of new memories, R longs for more, but it is not more brains that he is longing for. Instead, he longs for the familiarity of Perry; his memories seem so familiar in that it is detailing a life that R once had himself. Through the consumption of Perry's brain, Perry's memories become R's memories; Perry's feelings and emotions begin to become R's feelings and emotions. It is almost a complete envelopment of one into the other.

Perhaps the most interesting aspect of Perry and R's relationship is when Perry begins interacting directly with R, breaking away from the mere memories (Marion 63). These moments can be understood in multiple ways: perhaps Perry's ghost/spirit is trying to communicate specific messages to R (after all, why would we assume that R is the only supernatural presence in this story?), or, maybe the consumption of Perry's brain has created a drug-like hallucinatory effect. Perhaps the most likely possibility is instead that the consumption of Perry's brain has triggered dreamlike states in R (he was previously unable to dream), and Perry's memories are melding with R's own dreams and thought processes. In this possibility, Perry's presence is both literal (his brain is in R's body) and imagined, an avenue that lets R work through his own existence.

Through both Perry's memories and his communications with R, we begin to see that Perry had slowly become disillusioned with his surroundings—the perpetual quest to maintain a sense of normalcy through clinging to the way things were before zombies and always needing to define one's self in reaction to the other (here, all humans are proper and rational in the face of the zombie-other). The failure of neoliberal rationality seems most apparent when R apologizes to Perry for killing him:

> "'I'm sorry I killed you, Perry. It's not that I wanted to, it's just—"
> "Forget it, corpse, I understand. Seems by that point I wanted out anyway"
> [Marion 63].

Perry wanted out, and the only way to remove himself from a project that prized "rationality" at all costs, was to place himself in a dangerous position, thereby making an "irrational" choice.

The pairing of Perry and R is queered on many levels. Aside from the most obvious point of queerness (the homosocial relationship between these two men), at all moments of their relationship with each other, Perry and R are both in various states of death; they are both the abject, mon-

strous other. When R first encounters Perry he kills him; then R consumes—eats/eats out—Perry; and finally, they communicate with each
other because one is *in* the other. "I am in you," Perry tells R (Marion 107).
The eating out/eating of Perry is the first moment that R experiences this
level of intense pleasure. Previous brains left R with only mere seconds of
enjoyment and Perry's brain allows him to reach a more potent, even
orgasmic, state of being, to the point that R does not want it to end.

This relationship is also queered because of their connection with
Julie. This will be expanded upon more below, but throughout their interactions together, Perry continuously asks R to take care of Julie (Marion
63, 107). Finally, and perhaps most importantly, this relationship is queered
because it is positioned within a neoliberal understanding of proper/
improper bodies, proper/improper choices. While R as a zombie is perhaps
most easily read as anti-neoliberal subject (through his decay, irrational
consumption, and undead-state), it actually becomes Perry-through/in-R
that is begging for a complete undoing of social norms. R still clings to the
neoliberal possibility of success, where success is represented by
humanity/life. However, Perry not only recognizes the impossibility of
these social ideals, but also posits neoliberalism as the main culprit. His
continuous presence in R's mind, blending with his thoughts, is an attempt
to break down R's quest for normalcy/his quest to attain a yesterday.

> PERRY: Come on, R, don't you get this yet?
> He seems upset by my question. He locks eyes on me and there's a
> feverish intensity in them.
> PERRY: You and I are victims of the same disease. We're fighting the same
> war, just different battles in different theaters, and it's way too late
> for me to hate you for anything, because we're the same damn
> thing. My soul, your conscience, whatever's left of me woven into
> whatever's left of you, all tangled up and conjoined. He gives me a
> hearty clap on the shoulder that almost hurts.
> PERRY: We're in this together, corpse [Marion 107].

Here, Perry is challenging R to recognize the systemic inequalities that
have affected them both. He is asking R to break away from normative
understandings of "life," "worth," and "rationality," and to instead embrace
a queered existence that actively challenges the very notions R is working
so hard to obtain.[9] Unfortunately, whether due to the last piece of Perry's
brain having been eaten or the love between Julie and R, Perry then disappears from both R's mind and the pages of *Warm Bodies*. It is also
here where a queer, revolutionary possibility dissipates into hetero/
queered-normativity, as R loses the queered, radical possibilities that

Perry was championing for. Without Perry's queer presence in R, R is able to move closer to his neoliberal longings, slowly shaking off another layer of his monstrosity, and bringing him another inch closer to a hetero/queerly-normative-like[10] possibility.

R, Julie and Perry

Before entering the culminating sections of this essay, as well as the more climactic zombie-romance moments, it is important to briefly examine the queered relationship between R, Julie, and Perry. This relationship is unique in that at no point throughout the book are the three characters physically together at once.[11] Yet, the entire romantic relationship between R and Julie exists because R consumed Perry's brain and his memories. R has romantic feelings for Julie mainly because Perry had romantic feelings for Julie. All of the relationships—Perry and R, R and Julie—would not function without the presence of the missing other. Although this threesome is not the focus, nor is it even directly referenced within the story, by reading *Warm Bodies* through a queer lens, it becomes apparent that this relationship is the literal catalyst for the other relationships.

Love triangles are not unfamiliar in gothic or supernatural romances, especially in young adult fiction where one commonly finds competition and contempt between the two male leads over the female lead. In *Warm Bodies*, however, there is never competition for Julie between R and Perry. Yes, that could be simply reasoned to the fact that Perry is dead, but so is R, and that does not stop a relationship from forming between him and Julie. Nor is there contempt; in fact, on multiple occasions, Perry tells R to look out for Julie, to take care of her, and to care for her in ways that Perry was not able to. If Perry had continued to exist within R, to be a part of his dreams, thought processes, and emotions while R romanced Julie, a unique, almost polyamorous relationship could have flourished, a relationship that would have undoubtedly challenged both hetero- and homonormative boundaries. Unsurprisingly, though, this threesome is split up, and a more dominant, normative, acceptable couple emerges—even if one half of that pairing is the undead.

R and Julie

At its core, *Warm Bodies* is a zombie-romance story, where two unlikely lovers find themselves having to battle against forces that deem their love and choices unacceptable and incompatible. While there are many amusing similarities between the story of R and Julie with Shakespeare's *Romeo and Juliet* (balcony scene included [Marion 85]), this tale is not so much about incompatible love as it is about shaping one's love to fit a compatible mold, to change one's self enough that they are an acceptable love match. The ability to change and evolve into a higher state of being are *the* defining features of this story. Throughout *Warm Bodies*, many of the characters undergo various changes/processes of evolution, including Julie (who recognizes R's growth) and Julie's father (who finally believes Julie's pleas). However, amidst all these changes, it is in fact R who changes and must evolve the most in order to be loved, accepted, and seen as a rational, contributing citizen.

While the pairings of R and Perry and even R, Perry, and Julie invoke multiple queered readings, the queerness that manifests through R and Julie's relationship is primarily relegated to R being a zombie and Julie being human. At its most basic level, the relationship between R and Julie is tinged with necrophilic possibility without ever actually being necrophilic; they do not even share a kiss.[12] This is not unfamiliar territory, though, especially in young adult fiction. Intense yearning and longing for the monster is common, but many of these supernatural romance stories promote abstinence, and maybe this is in part to quell the necrophilic taboo (Platt). While *Warm Bodies* never explicitly highlights necrophilia, something like it is undoubtedly scattered throughout the book by mere virtue of the fact that R is dead and Julie is not. Here, the reader is encouraged to ignore the necrophilic readings since R is changing, and to instead focus on his progress as he becomes more and more un-undead/less and less monstrous through his subscription to normative values and ideals.

The power dynamic of necrophilia, as Scott Dudley states, turns on the ways that the necrophilic act attempts to "convert a subject that has become an object back into a subject again" (Dudley 288). With respect to *Warm Bodies*, since R and Julie are never actually physically intimate, it is the prospect of sex and romance that seems to encourage R to evolve into a less-dead subject. There is a familiarity in Julie's body that he longs for, and as he spends more time with her, in addition to gaining Perry's memories of her, he increasingly thinks about what it would be like to be romantically intimate with her. "I find myself imagining her dolled up for a concert, her neck-length hair swept and styled, her small body radiant in a red party dress, and me kissing her, the lipstick smearing onto my mouth, spreading bright rouge onto my grey lips" (Marion

30). Here, these necrophilic possibilities hint at a nostalgic past for R, and later Julie, as they both begin to piece together their aspirations for a time that once was but can never be again (Dudley 291).

At the same time, there is fear in both Julie and R over what may happen if they give in to their desires for one another. If they engage in necrophilic acts, they will be taking extreme risks, ones that could detrimentally effect their potential to find normalcy. On multiple occasions, Julie asks R if his undead disease will be transferred to her if she decides to kiss him (Marion 86, 122–123). On both occasions R is struck by her forwardness and desire to engage sexually and romantically with him, but the uncertainty of his monstrous contagion is too much of a risk for him to take. If they kiss, they risk the possibility of Julie becoming undead as well, thereby removing the possibility of them achieving a normative, rational, neoliberal life together, as Julie's current state of humanity is the main thing slowly pulling R up from his lowly existence. This questioning of R's contagion in relation to sexuality and romance is also deeply imbricated in a history of sexual otherness and disease, specifically the cultural fears surrounding gay sex and the transmission of STIs and HIV. Since R's queerness is watered down due to his neoliberal aspirations, any submission to his desires—his true monstrosity— via sexuality would leave him forever without hope of fully changing. Through this, R becomes neutered out of fear, and an abstinence-only approach is the only way to fulfill his (and Julie's) aspirations. Longing, however, is a necessary part of his evolution. He must long for Julie and the life she promotes in order to achieve the normativity he desires (even if queered by his undead state).

These longings, where R wishes to be human enough to meet Julie's needs, and where Julie anticipates and encourages his evolution, are scattered all throughout their abstinent relationship. In two discussions in particular, R's desire for change becomes evident, as well as the belief that his change is dependent on how badly he wants it. The first occurs just after the meeting of Julie and R, when R takes Julie back to the airport to save her from the other zombies. While having a (very slow) conversation with his zombie friend, M, R begins to explain that he is feeling something he has never felt before. M asks:

M: "Brought back ... Living girl?"
R: "Yes."
M: "You ... crazy?"
R: "Maybe."
M: "What's ... feel like?"

R: "What?"
M: "Living ... sex."
　I give him a warning look.
M: "She's ... hot. I would—"
R: "Shut up."
　He chuckles.
M: "Fucking ... with you."
R: "It's not ... that. Not ... like that."
M: "Then ... what?"
　I hesitate, not sure how to answer.
R: "More."
　His face gets eerily serious.
M: "What? Love?"
　I think about this, and I find no response beyond a simple shrug. So I
　shrug, trying not to smile.
M: "You ... okay?"
R: "Changing" [Marion 50–51].

And later, while reflecting on the same conversation with M, R recalls:

M: "How can you change? If we all start from the same blank slate, what
　makes you diverge?"
R: "Maybe we're not blank. Maybe the debris of our old lives still shapes
　us."
M: "But we don't remember those lives. We can't read our diaries."
R: "It doesn't matter. We are where we are, however we got here. What
　matters is where we go next."
M: "But can we choose that?"
R: "I don't know."
M: "We're Dead. Can we really choose anything?"
R: "Maybe. If we want to bad enough" [Marion 58].

In these conversations, R expresses how he is changing due to his relationship with and feelings for Julie (as well as Perry's memories). He also
notes that his change could, at least in part, be due to his deep desire to
change. This is key to a neoliberal politic, where one must see the ability
to obtain social and economic privileges as resting solely on one's ability
to change and adapt, to incorporate neoliberal ideals into one's life, as
opposed to seeing inequality as a precondition for the state and cultural
ideals and realities. In the neoliberal view, if one does not achieve (success, rationality, access to the free market, etc.), it is simply because one
has not tried hard enough.

　As both the story and R and Julie's relationship progress, R increasingly becomes less-undead. He remembers every moment he has had
with Julie (where previously he could not remember anything), his ability

to speak begins to improve, and most importantly, R's instincts to eat humans has subsided (he eats one person after meeting Julie and then subsequently vomits the remains) (Marion). The end of the book culminates in a showdown between R, Julie, a group of other changing zombies (R's progress ignites change in his fellow zombies) and Julie's father (who is the leader of a human army) (Marion 138). While we aren't aware of the exact events that transpire, we know that previously Julie had tried to explain to her father that R was different and that zombies retain some of their humanity, and, most importantly, they have the ability to change. The final scene fast-forwards to a future moment where the changing zombies are being welcomed into the stadium where the humans live, while Julie and R are taking a moment to enjoy the sun outside. Here R contemplates the journey he has been on, including his ability to become a more rational, and normative subject, even in his queered state. R's final thoughts close *Warm Bodies* and summarize the power of a neoliberal agenda during apocalyptic times. "The sky is blue. The grass is green. The sun is warm on our skin. We smile, because this is how we save the world. We will not let Earth become a tomb, a mass grave spinning through space. We will exhume ourselves. We will fight the curse and break it. We will cry and bleed and lust and love, and we will cure death. We will be the cure. Because we want it" (Marion 142). Just as neoliberalism advocates for individuality and success-via-hard work only, R similarly sees the possibility of a new world existing because he wants it bad enough. If they cannot change the world it is simply because they must not be working hard enough to rid themselves of roadblocks—namely, their perversity, queerness, monstrosity, and state of undeath. If R can evolve into a higher being, then there is no excuse for the other undead.

Conclusion

In *Warm Bodies*, R embodies the monstrous queer because he is read as castrated and asexual. He is a zombie on the one hand, and on the other, he risks infecting Julie if he engages in sexual relations with her. R also embodies the monstrous queer because of his consumption of Perry. Throughout the story, R is made asexual, castrated, effeminate, and monstrous because of his inability to subscribe to heteronormative values—he can never-not be a queered being because of his undead nature. However, as the story unfolds, we see that through Julie's encouragement and R's own desire, he slowly begins to unlearn some of his most deviant behaviors. And as he becomes indoctrinated into "normal" life Julie sees him as more sexually desirable. But he is still not-human. His state of being can never allow him to fully transgress his monstrosity into normalcy. Because R is always-already queered he is never able to enter into the space of the neoliberal subject par excellence. R is, however, very willing to comply with social scripts and ideals; he wants nothing more than to regain some semblance of his previous life as a rational subject. Through his allegiance to state ideals and social norms, R is increasingly given more access and privilege, including romantic and sexual access. He becomes a queerly-normative subject in a sexually perverse relationship, who, through a belief in the neoliberal myth of personal freedom, embraces a homonational-like positionality by assisting in the rebuilding of humanity and the state (Marion 142). By queering an otherwise fairly heteronormative zombie romance, it becomes evident that not even death can undo or discourage a neoliberalist project of rationality and sexual normativity.

NOTES

1. Throughout this essay I use "queer" to imply a non-normative sexuality/gender identity. This is specifically positioned in reference to hetero- and homonormativity which actively work to reflect social and political normalizing ideologies. Here, "queer seeks to go beyond these and all such categories based on the concepts of normative heterosexuality and traditional gender roles to encompass a more inclusive, amorphous, and ambiguous" positionality (Benshoff 5).

2. The perpetuation of liberal and neo-liberal ideologies under the disguise of sexual openness and tolerance has been highlighted by many theorist in addition to Duggan and Puar, including Robert McRuer, Judith Butler, José Esteban Muñoz, Lee Edelman, and Lauren Berlant, to name but a few. The links that Duggan and Puar draw out between terrorism and the "monstrous-other," in conversation with queerness and neoliberalism, are best suited for this discussion of a queered zombie romance.

3. Discussions of the "monstrous other" has been detailed by many theorists, most notable being Russo; Grosz; Creed; Benshoff.

4. See Auerbach; Gordon and Hollinger; Dennison; Overstreet; Clarke and Osborn; Click, Aubrey, and Behm-Morawitz for more recent examples of the vampire as metaphor for social fears and anxieties.

5. While there have been other romantic-comedy stories that feature zombies (*Shaun of the Dead*, for example), there are a small number that actually involve romantic and/or sexual relationships with the zombies—one notable example: Perkins' *Hungry for Your Love*. With the widespread popularity of both the book and film versions of *Warm Bodies*, it would not be a surprise if "zom-rom" became a popular genre in and of itself.

6. The films *Fido* and *ParaNorman* are two notable exceptions where zombies coexist with other humans (although not always without difficulty).

7. Here, R's attachment to and understanding of neoliberalism as being "the norm" is deeply tied to his disenchantment with the unlife of the undead. The acts of the undead are rooted in animalistic instinct, not rationality. As R catches glimpses of the living-life (through Perry and Julie), R longs to self-improve through subscription to the rational values of the living.

8. Although specific to this article and discussions of sexuality and LGBTQ identities, it is important to note that other "queered" identities are also given limited entrance into sites of access under the guise of neoliberal "multiculturalism" and "tolerance," most often when it best serves neoliberal agendas.

9. This type of failure has been brilliantly theorized by Halberstam in *The Queer Art of Failure*, which details the ways in which the notion of "success" within a neoliberal capitalism is inherently unachievable to marginalized peoples (by virtue of their existence), and specifically highlights queerness as failure and queers as failing the neoliberal project. In turn, Halberstam works to reframe "failure" as a fruitful moment of possibility and achievement.

10. "Homonormative" has primarily been used with reference to mainstreaming gay and lesbian individuals. Here, R can never attain heteronormativity (even if in a hetero relationship) because of his inherent monstrosity/queerness (even if less queer than the Boneys and after Perry's absence), nor can he attain homonormativity due to his opposite-gender desire for Julie. He remains sexually othered, and monstrously queered, even while clinging to normative ideals and understandings—queer normativity.

11. The three characters are never together at the same time in *Warm Bodies* except for near the beginning when R kills and eats Perry during Perry and Julie's scavenge for food. Interestingly, even in this moment, Julie is unaware/unable to see what is happening between R and Perry (Marion 21).

12. Interestingly, in the motion picture adaptation of *Warm Bodies*, R and Julie do kiss, and it is this kiss that is seen as the final catalyst needed to complete R's change. After they kiss, R's heart begins to pump, his blood flows—for all intents and purposes, he is more alive than he is dead. In the book, R remains undead, although considers himself to be on the road towards life/a less-dead-like state (Marion 142).

For a Good Time Just Scream

Sex Work and Plastic Sexuality in "Dystopicmodern Literature"

DENISE N. COOK

"The transformation of intimacy might be a subversive
influence upon modern institutions as a whole.... The
changes now affecting sexuality are indeed revolutionary,
and in a very profound way."

—Giddens 3

In recent years, various short stories have focused on a hitherto
untapped aspect of zombie infested society: undead sex work. This literature provides a unique lens via which to consider the implications of
plastic sexuality, Giddens' paradigm for the future evolution of human
sexuality. Although Giddens did not discuss the possibility of zombie
sexuality in *The Transformation of Intimacy: Sexuality, Love and Eroticism in Modern Societies*, elements of plastic sexuality are pertinently
reflected in recent zombie culture, not least since zombie fiction illustrates contemporary anxieties about the future. In zombie fiction, such
futures are typically indicative of what I term dystopicmodernity: a fic-
tionalized post-apocalyptic society. The term dystopicmodernity refers
to portrayals of modern societies rather than as-yet-inconceivably
advanced techno-societies. In the examples I will address here, the most
significant component of such societies is the presence of zombies. In
recent fiction, many post-apocalyptic portrayals depict the undead as a
key component of dystopian society.

Indeed, zombies are integral to what makes society dystopian in

73

these texts because, for example, the undead are so ubiquitous in those societies. In some zombie fiction, zombies are a new subspecies of humans that exist on the fringe of society; they are to be feared and killed. In other zombie fiction, such as the narratives considered in this essay, the undead are integrated into the core of society. In such societies, the service sector is comprised of zombies and humans alike. Zombies are primarily used to complete dangerous tasks, or are employed as a cheaper alternative to the human employee base. The undead may serve as domestic servants or indentured slaves, for example. Such inclusion amplifies the sense that zombies are a commonplace feature of dystopic-modern society. The omnipresence of zombies in dystopicmodern society normalizes their presence.

Despite their prevalence, zombies are nevertheless treated as different to and therefore separate from humans. Zombies are treated as sub-human by the living. Accordingly, in these dystopicmodern stories, zombie leasing companies offer clients a full range of services, including sex work. In continuity with sex-workers in reality, zombie sex-workers in popular culture are hired out or forced to perform sexual services, typically by living managers, pimps or human-owned companies. There are some exceptions to these patterns, and I will exemplify some of these concessions in the analysis of zombie fiction below. Regardless, sex work demonstrates the extent to which the presence of zombies is normalized in dystopicmodern society. The undead are integrated into all spheres of life, including sex work.

Portrayals of zombie sex work under dystopicmodernity provide an interesting vehicle via which to analyze plastic sexuality. Zombie sex work both evolves and deviates from Giddens' notion of plastic sexuality. Plastic sexuality is what Giddens describes as an outcome of post-traditional sexual attitudes (Gross and Simmons 531). In practice, sexual plasticity may potentially yield both positive and negative outcomes. Self-fulfillment is the driving factor of plastic sexuality and it is the standard by which behaviors are judged: if sex is not fulfilling, it is not moral (Rubin 15). However, plastic sexuality is also underpinned by an egalitarian ethos. Sexuality should be fulfilling for everyone equally, or one's self-fulfillment should not come at the expense of someone else's. This balance between self-fulfillment and egalitarianism is hard to maintain. That difficulty is explored in various ways in the examples of zombie-fiction I analyze below. The main source of tension here is the difference between human sexuality and zombie sexuality: the former is routinely privileged over the latter. The living typically perceive zombies as sub-human and negate the desires of the undead. That bias—which centers on zombie sexuality—is distinctly non-egalitarian. Although zombie sex work appears to offer a plastic, expanded range of sexual expressions in these dystopicmodern texts, they do so for humans only. Thus, by centralizing various forms of zombie sex work, these stories evoke plastic sexuality and expose its flaws. During the course of this essay then, I will explore what zombie sex work is, and how zombie sex work relates to plastic sexuality. To do so, I will examine several literary short stories in which zombies and sex work collude. Before engaging with those examples, I will begin by briefly explaining what is meant by plastic sexuality.

Plastic Sexuality

As Giddens defines it, plastic sexuality is dissimilar to passionate love because of its detachment from romance (2). Plastic sexuality is a form of sexual expression that is performed for pleasure as opposed to procreation (27). Furthermore, plastic sexuality varies in expression from one person to the next (2). Accordingly, plastic sexuality is connected to the identity of the individual, and so helps to mold one's identity (144). Since sexual expression varies from individual to individual, normalcy is also hard to pin-point: almost anything goes in the realm of plastic sexuality (179). Two key ideas follow. First, plastic sexuality is fluid and malleable. Second, so long as participants derive pleasure from the sexual exchange, any sexual pursuit is acceptable. These conditions can certainly lead to positive outcomes, including a greater sense of egalitarianism. Yet, the lack of explicit sexual boundaries in plastic sexuality may also lead to negative outcomes such as addiction (although Gross and Simmons 549) contend that Giddens overemphasizes how common such outcomes are.

Giddens (27) coined the term plastic sexuality to describe how our sexual attitudes have and might continue to evolve over time. Subsequent thinkers have utilized his paradigm to examine a myriad of related topics. Langdridge and Butt (65) explore erotic power exchange utilizing plastic sexuality as means to describe the emergence and normalization of sadomasochistic power play. Ross (342) argues that the Internet may help to facilitate plastic sexuality. Guy uses Giddens' *Transformation of Intimacy* as a template when recounting the evolution of sexuality, situating plastic sexuality in what he calls an "autonomous social system" (Guy 6). Gid-

dens' sexual evolution was previously expanded on in Warr's (251) elu-
cidation of how plastic sexuality affects safe sex practice. Warr explains
that as the practice of monogamy becomes less common, the importance
of safer sex becomes paramount in limiting the spread of sexually transmitted diseases. What is important here is the emphasis placed on non-
traditional forms of sexuality; that is, on how sex manifests a non-
monogamous, post-traditional world. Paul Johnson (191) is among the
thinkers who have explored related issues, coming to rather more cautious conclusions about how far sexuality has evolved. Johnson uses Giddens' model to explore ways in which plastic sexuality might affect
homo/hetero sexual binaries. In spite of Giddens' broad scale assertion
that sexual norms have become less stringent over time, sexual identity
and orientation remains fairly intact according to Johnson. In other
words, Johnson finds that the people he studies are not comfortable with
exceeding the bounds of normative intimate practices. While Giddens
conceptualizes plastic sexuality as an advance towards post-traditional
forms of sexuality, the cultural imagination shares some of Johnson's
caution when it comes to sexual "plasticity." As I will demonstrate via
my analysis of zombie fiction, zombie sexuality appears to embody many
of the traits that characterize Giddens' plastic sexuality. However,
dystopicmodern fiction is ultimately underpinned by a regressive vision
of sexuality, for men and women alike.

Zombie Sex Work

    To clarify these points, I will turn to zombie sex work itself. Zombie
sex work is depicted in short stories such as "What Maisie Knew," by
David Liss. In this and other zombie narratives, zombie sex-workers
come in various forms, ranging from prostitutes and mistresses to strippers and sex objects. Before we can apprehend *who* zombie sex-workers
are, it is important to grasp *what* zombie sex work is. In the examples I
employ below, zombies and sex work collude in four ways. The first is
the most prevalent: humans seek the services of zombie sex-workers.
The other three incarnations of zombie sex work include zombies seeking the services of zombie sex-workers, zombies seeking the services of
human sex-workers, and finally zombies seeking voyeuristic entertainment by viewing humans engaging in sex with other humans.
    The incarnations of sex work found in zombie fiction do not simply
manifest plastic sexuality as Giddens describes it, although Giddens'

paradigm provides a way into understanding what sex work means in the context of dystopicmodern zombie fiction. One of the core tenets of plastic sexuality is that sexual expressions are contingent on participants' mutual enjoyment. Pleasure and attraction are the facilitators of plastic sexuality, not romance (Langdridge et al., 68; see also Giddens 27; Gross and Simmons 536). This is because romance is not egalitarian; as Warr (245) posits, romance reinforces traditional sexual hegemony. Thus, plastic sexuality potentially provides a liberating alternative to romance's subordinating structure (Giddens 57; Rubin 9). Portrayals of zombie sex work typically follow this pattern, eschewing romance. In "The Dead" and "First Love Never Dies," zombie sex work is a financially driven exchange driven by sexual release rather than romance.

Among my examples, the only exception to this trend is the short story "Third Dead Body," but even here the romance is short-lived. In "Third Dead Body," Shelia's grandmother cursed her to "love the thing that hurts her and kills [her], even after it kills [her]" (Hoffman 84). When Shelia arises from her grave, she is compelled to love Ritchie, the client who hurt and killed her. Zombie-Shelia at first seeks to enter into a romantic relationship with Ritchie, pursuing what Giddens would call a quest-romance; a love-based relationship that starts with sexual expression (50). However, the relationship is one in which Sheila is victimized by Ritchie. In time, and spurred on by the women who gave her a ride into town, Shelia realizes that she must no longer submit to Ritchie's power. Her quest-romance is not destined to end with a happily-ever-after coupling. Eventually, Sheila turns against Ritchie, having him arrested for her murder. Indeed, since it was founded on murder and a curse, Sheila's quest for romance was doomed from the outset.

In this tale, romance is rejected in favor of mutable and fluid sexuality between human and zombie. Sheila and Ritchie's relationship is not characteristic of plastic sexuality in Giddens' sense, however. Sheila is eventually compelled to reject Ritchie because their relationship is not mutually fulfilling. During her relationship with Ritchie, zombie–Sheila is subordinate to his desires, seeking to appease him. In Sheila's case, plastic sexuality eventually manifests not as an equal partnership between Sheila and Ritchie, but via Sheila's self-fulfillment. The tale nears a close not with an idealized, conventional romantic coupling, but with Sheila's rebirth as a full sexual subject (albeit an undead one). In the conclusion, Shelia makes her way back to her grave to finally rest in peace.

Plastic sexuality is not limited by conventional modes of expression such as romance. In fact, varied expression is a key component of plastic sexuality (Ross 346; Huei-Hsia Wu 128; Guy 4), one which is representative of how discourses about sex are changing in the 21st century (Attwood 80). The zombie texts under analysis contribute to those shifting discourses. They also exemplify sexual diversity, thereby contributing to an expanded sexual imagination. For example, "What Maisie Knew" represents forms of sexuality that may appear to be illicit or forbidden by contemporary standards. In the dystopicmodern context, however, the protagonists are free to indulge in all manner of sexual expressions. In "What Maisie Knew," Walter, a promising salesman, purchases a reanimate from a zombie sex and strip club. In the club, zombie sex-worker enthusiasts ("reanimate fetishists"), enjoy the titillation that zombie sex-workers provide and also contract the direct sexual services of zombie prostitutes. Walter's visit to the club is initiated by a coworker's bachelor party: it is a public, acceptable form of sexual entertainment enjoyed at a time of celebration, rather than a seedy, private liaison. This example illustrates the kind of market-led freedom to express and explore one's sexual appetites that is characteristic of plastic sexuality. In dystopicmodern zombie fiction, these varied opportunities for sexual expression increase for two reasons. First there are new potential partners to copulate with (namely zombies). Second, from the perspective of the living clients, zombies are the ultimate plastic sexual partners. Zombie sexworkers are like the "real thing" (human sex-workers), only better. Those who consume sexual services from zombies certainly are not concerned by the risks of pregnancy, for instance, as they might be when engaging with other living humans. These zombie sex-workers are servile to the purchaser's unfettered whims. No limitations or penalties are imposed on the customer, so the living have no direct impetus to stop and reflect on their acts. In these texts, zombies represent a source of free, adaptable sexuality that is not hindered by traditional sexual morality. In short, they epitomize the goal of plastic sexuality.

These forms of plastic zombie sexuality therefore also stretch the bounds of normalcy. In dystopicmodern society, zombie sex work is both a viable and an acceptable option for sexual fulfillment. In our current social context, many find the commodification of sex distasteful. However, zombie sex work takes commodification a step further. Sexual intimacy is bound by social context (Giddens 19; Wagner 290). The context of dystopicmodernity provides a unique opportunity to redefine notions of normalcy (sexual or otherwise) because in a post-apocalyptic society, rules change. That is, the zombie apocalypse reshapes the social structure. As part of the same process, social norms are altered, because one is inextricable from the other. Sexual pleasure bridges between our most intimate personal attitudes and the social fabric that impacts on such desires. Zombies, who are usually considered monstrous, become sexually desirable. As is illustrated by fiction in which living protagonists freely and openly engage with zombie sex-workers, radical changes in the social fabric impact on one's most personal attitudes.

Similarly, plastic sexuality shapes the identity of those who participate in it (Hancock et al., 4; Hawkes 3411; Wagner 292). Thus, although plastic sexuality stretches the boundaries of normalcy and despite freedom being the *goal* of plastic sexuality, it is hard to see how plastic sexuality can facilitate such an escape. According to Gross and Simmons, "the individual is continually obliged to negotiate life-style options," and this can lead to positive and negative outcomes (540). The positive outcomes are that the individual is not stuck in any one mode of behavior and if one's sexual activity is not pleasurable there are ample opportunities to change one's sexual practices. But the negative outcomes are rather dire: constant change and a lack of self-security can lead to anomie.

"Meathouse Man" by George R. R. Martin exemplifies the perilous line between these outcomes, depicting a blue collar corpse handler (Trager) who forms his identity around plastic sexuality and zombie sex work. With savings earned from his job controlling zombie miners, Trager regularly frequents "meathouses," brothels which offer the sexual services of zombies. These brothels are havens of sexual freedom for the clients, who pay to indulge in any sexual acts they wish. In the narrative, Trager is personally invested in his amorous encounters with a zombie prostitute. Since they climax simultaneously, he is under the impression that she too enjoys their encounters. However, Trager discovers that the zombie sex-worker does not reciprocate his feelings. Rather, the zombies are implanted with microchips that make the zombie respond automatically to the client's brainwaves. The revelation leads Trager into depression and isolation. The benefit that Trager gains from the interaction is that in spite of heartache and self-doubt, he grows and develops into a passionate person who is capable of feeling what he believes to be an intimate connection with the zombie, something Trager failed to achieve in his relations with human women. Trager's case illustrates both the positive and negative outcomes Gross and Simmons refer to. Plastic sexuality can be a vehicle for personal growth, but a stable foundation is paramount to the success of shaping those sexually-defined identities. Simultaneously, because plastic sexuality is fluid, one's sexual identity must also be malleable. The liminal world of zombie-apocalypse is shaky terrain, and so does not lend itself to stable growth. Accordingly, sexual identities are typically fragile in these texts.

Egalitarianism

In its superlative form—abstracted from social circumstance—plastic sexuality should empower women and men alike. Various scholars gesture towards this ideal telos. Giddens refers to sexual freedom as a means by which power is expressed (144), for instance. In addition, Rubin (9) perceives plastic sexuality as a means for women to gain control over their sexuality and thereby yield greater power within society. *Pace* these views, portrayals of zombie sex work in fiction illustrate the flaws that arise from putting such notions into practice. Zombie sex work is rarely sexually empowering for women in these narratives. In fact, zombie sex work is typically more phallocentric in nature. In stories such as "Meathouse Man" and "What Maisie Knew," most clients are human and male, while most zombie sex-workers are female. "Zombie Gigolo" by S.G. Browne and "The Dead" by Michael Swanwick are rare exceptions to this rule, featuring male zombie sex-workers.

"Zombie Gigolo" is narrated from the perspective of the male zombie sex-worker whose clients are female zombies. He speaks rather candidly about his sexual arousal and the sexual pleasure he provides for his clients. Since his role is to sexually satisfy female clients, the clients might appear to hold the powered position in their exchange. However, should the female client fail to arouse the gigolo, the session is quickly terminated. Thus, this narrative illustrates that males have sexual privilege, even in undeath and even in the apparently plastic world of dystopicmodern sexuality. In this example, zombie sex work is closer to traditional romantic love-based sexual culture than to the egalitarian ideals of plastic sexuality. The male gigolo has sexual agency and his female clients are subject to his decisions. The females have only the power to request his services, but ultimately he decides whether he wants to see that client and for how long. This male-biased arrangement echoes Giddens' description of romantic love as "an active ... engagement with the 'maleness' of modern society" (2). In other words, romantic love is anathema to plastic sexual egalitarianism because it reinforces male hegemonic power. The romance model typically assumes that females need men in order to find sexual fulfillment.

Even though "The Dead" is based around a more equal gender balance—clients and zombie sex-workers can be either male or female—the narrative's sexual climate is far from egalitarian. First, in this story, zombie sex work is just another component of the zombie service sector. Zombie sex-workers are given to clients as corporate gifts and are mainly consumed by those who can afford to indulge in undead sex (namely the wealthy). The zombies are explicitly treated as lesser beings in this equation. In these ways, the zombie sex exchange is founded on inequality. Second, the story features a male zombie sex-worker, whose client (Courtney) is an influential female executive. Courtney has power in the exchange, and the zombie is hired simply to enact her sexual fantasies. The male zombie is given orders and performs. His opinion, if he has one, goes unacknowledged. Although this story more closely fits Giddens' definitions of female empowerment than other zombie sex-worker narratives do, it is nevertheless notable that female empowerment comes at the cost of the zombie's freedom. Although it is plastic insofar as sexuality is openly pursued and takes on a variety of uninhibited forms, sex is not based on freedom for all in "The Dead."

The same issues haunt other examples of zombie fiction in which the zombie sex-workers are female, including "Seminar Z" by J.L. Comeau, "Meathouse Man" by George R. R. Martin, "First Love Never Dies" by Jan Kozlowski, "Third Dead Body" by Nina Kiriki Hoffman, and "What Maisie Knew" by David Liss. In "Seminar Z," a living male teenager receives a female zombie sex-worker as a gift from his father. The teenager and his friends use the zombie as a source of recreational sex. In this case, it initially appears as if the zombie sex-worker's feelings are accounted for in this schema. She wears a mask, which appears to be a way of providing the zombie with modesty. However, the mask is designed for the customer's benefit. Principally, the mask is a safety device. So, when an EcoCorp InfiniZ client attempts to pry off the mask, the customer service agent implores the client to leave it in place; "InfiniZ does not recommend that you—" (Comeau 182). However, the client ignores the advice and demands that the customer service agent watches the havoc that ensues. The mask is designed to restrain the zombie, thereby privileging the customer's sexual desires over the zombie's will. Moreover, on "wrench[ing] the mask aside" the client is exposed to the zombie's true visage: the sex-worker has "the ravaged, decomposing face of an elderly woman" (Comeau 182). Thus, the mask is also designed to obscure the reality of the zombie's body and former identity: it hides the fact that the zombie was elderly and is now an animated rotting cadaver. In "Seminar Z" then, the zombie sex exchange is not a portrayal of sex work as an acceptable practice engaged in by willing participants who retain their dignity. Rather, the story is underpinned by traditionalist sexual views (albeit in an amplified form). The zombie-human sex exchange is conditional on male sexual pleasure only; the male decides when the female zombie is sexually useful and when they are not. If the male no longer derives sexual pleasure from the zombie, then the zombie sex-worker is discarded and disposed of. Indeed, the masks feature a deactivation button that allows the client to permanently terminate the undead sex-worker's services when they are no longer useful. In "Seminar Z," the zombie is not simply a lesser creature. She is reduced to a sex object. The mask implies that the zombie sex-workers have feelings (which need to be muzzled), but it also allows men to treat them as objects.

"Meathouse Man" and "First Love Never Dies" offer similar narratives. As outlined above, the sex-workers in "Meathouse Man" are undead prostitutes implanted with microchips that cause them to respond automatically to their clients' desires. Although they appear to actively enjoy the sexual exchanges they participate in, the zombies provide no input in the sexual encounters. The clients (such as lead protagonist Trager) thus assume that they are engaging in a form of plastic sexuality. The clients are free to indulge in whatever fantasy they wish to, and the zombie prostitute appears to mutually benefit from their congress. Indeed, the zombie prostitutes are programmed to achieve orgasm concurrently with the clients, fostering a sense of sexual egalitarianism. Yet the implanted microchips undercut that impression, demonstrating that egalitarianism is not possible when the sexual exchange is based solely on one party's desires. While one party is under the influence of behavior-altering neural implants, sex cannot be equal or mutually fulfilling, however free it appears to be. This underlying inequality is highlighted when Trager discovers the truth. Despite knowing that the prostitute is mirroring and performing rather than *sharing* his pleasure, Trager continues to visit the Meathouse. In the end, his sexual fulfillment is privileged over the zombie's well-being. His decision to continue frequenting the brothel supports inequality to the detriment of the fully formed plastic sexuality he originally thought he was engaging in.

In these dystopicmodern texts, it is not only zombies who are sexually exploited. "Skull Faced City" offers a different vision of inequality in which humans are sexually exploited by zombies. In this short story, zombies force imprisoned humans to have sex with each other for purpose of entertaining the zombies. The captives are not paid for their sexual performance; rather they are threatened with death if they do not have sex with one another. This form of sexual expression might be considered plastic inasmuch as it frees humans from the pressures of normative social structures and romantic love, for instance. It also creates an egalitarian state of sorts. First, the zombies are equals to one another. The male zombie in charge respects the wishes of his wife, for example. Second, the captured humans are equal to one another: they are all equally sex slaves. However, that limited form of egalitarianism comes at the expense of their sexual freedom. In "Skull Faced City," sex is ultimately non-egalitarian, since sexual power belongs to the zombies alone, and the living are divested of sexual choice. Moreover, this version of sex is not plastic, since although they are equal to one another, the humans do not share or demonstrate satisfaction. Sex is performed on demand, and is an expression of coercive harm, not pleasure. Ironically, the humans' sexual performances are distinctly mechanical and zombie-like.

None of these stories capture the sexual egalitarianism at the heart of Giddens' plastic sexuality, then. In these stories, the structures that govern sexual codes of conduct are imprisoning, and are severely biased towards the pleasure of one party over another. Indeed, in these stories, one party's sexual pleasure is typically contingent on the other party's sexual subjugation. Most notably, despite some fanciful exceptions such as the zombie-run system depicted in "Skull Faced City," or the fantastic vision of zombies who can mirror the client's passion in "Meathouse Man," these examples of zombie sex work usually privilege normative traditionalist views of sex, such as the centralization of male desire. In cases where the sex-workers are zombies, the clients are typically male. Male sexual pleasure is paramount and male sexual control is underlined in these texts. Rarely do the male clients consider the sexual pleasure of the female undead sex-worker. Even where they do—as in the cases of Maisie and Walter ("What Maisie Knew") or Trager and the sex-worker ("Meathouse Man")—the zombie's opinion is ultimately disregarded in favor of male sexual pleasure.

Thus, "Seminar Z's" gagged zombie sex-objects offer an archetypal image of the zombie sex-worker. Outside of occasional guttural growls or moans, zombies are rarely even able to express any desires they might have. This is exemplified in the case of the zombie sex-worker in "First Love Never Dies." In this tale of zombie sexual servitude, a criminal pimps his zombified daughter out to the highest paying customers. After a whistleblower informs the authorities of the situation, the police rescue the zombie daughter. However, the police discover that they cannot communicate with the bound, voiceless, undead victim, who can only moan. As such, it is impossible to tell whether she consents, suffers, or even whether she has sexual sentience. Since zombies often cannot communicate, they are effectively silenced by their limiting physiology. That is, they are muzzled at the most fundamental level.

The Dangers of Plasticity

Thus, although these texts embody elements of plastic sexuality, they lack the egalitarianism that Giddens valorizes. That lack is anchored in two core elements: (a) social structures that are oriented towards providing one individual with sexual pleasure at the expense of another individual, and (b) zombie physiology, which is not adapted to permit expression of desires. At these fundamental levels, the version of plastic sexuality offered in zombie fiction is limited. Here, plastic sexuality is stripped of its key trope—egalitarian sexual freedom—and reassembled as a kind of Franken-sexuality: a bastardized and flawed assemblage. Subsequently, it is little wonder that this version of plastic sexuality typically veers towards the ill effects Giddens outlines as potential negative consequences of plastic sexuality. These include addiction, anxiety, compulsiveness, male violence toward women, and obsession (121).

For example, Trager's frequent visits to the brothel in "Meathouse Man" are illustrative of addiction. Unable to sustain a relationship with another living human, Trager compulsively returns to the zombie brothel, where modified zombie prostitutes are programmed to reflect his own desires. Trager's compulsion is born out of anxiety; fear of being rejected by his own kind. Interacting with other humans damages his self-esteem, while the zombie prostitutes bolster his self-love. Since they mirror and reinforce his desires, the zombie prostitutes are conduits for Trager's immature narcissism. They not only conform to his desires, but also validate his desirability. Therefore, his engagements with the prostitutes are addictive because they are rooted in his self-esteem. Each visitation confirms that he is worthy of sexual attention. At the same time, it is an unfulfilling form of self-validation because it is only simulated attention. In order to satisfy Trager, that attention must be continually reinforced by repeated visits to the Meathouse. Trager's visits to the brothel are fraught with the kind of deep-seated anxiety and self-jeopardy that Giddens (71) and Gross and Simmons (539) refer to when discussing the potential pitfalls of plastic sexuality.

In Giddens' view, sexual compulsion typically manifests via two key behaviors—"womanizing" and "episodic sexuality"—which are linked by compulsiveness (81). Although Giddens' phrasing implies bias towards male sexual attitudes ("womanizing"), such forms of compulsion are not exclusive to men, and the zombie texts under discussion do not limit compulsive sexuality to men alone. Both "The Dead" and "Third Dead Body" depict women enacting sexually compulsive behaviors. In "The Dead," Courtney lusts after a nameless zombie sex-worker. Indeed, her compulsion for sex with the dead leads her to forego sex with a human male when it is offered to her. As with Trager in "Meathouse Man," the zombie's conformity to the living client's desire is more appealing than complex human relationships. Like Trager, Courtney finds sanctuary in the fantasy-world of zombie sex. "The Dead" describes zombie sex as an acceptable pursuit rather than an abnormal form of expression, so Courtney's choice is not condemned as such. However, her rejection of humanity in favor of a non-reciprocal relationship with a mindless sex-slave captures the key danger that Giddens notes when theorizing plastic sexuality: freedom may lead to power-biased, obsessive forms of sexual self-fulfillment that undercut the sexual egalitarianism we ought to strive for.

"Third Dead Body" is explicit about the damage that might arise out of compulsion. Under the sway of her grandmother's curse, undead protagonist Shelia is compelled to lust after her murderer (Ritchie). Her obsession leads her to reckless abandon as she seeks to reunite with him. Shelia hitchhikes from her grave to the city in search of Ritchie and when she finds him, she allows him to take her captive so he can escape from authorities. In this case, Sheila's curse-based obsession is analogous to compulsion since both sway the individual's sexual behavior, causing them to act in unsound and potentially harmful ways. In fact, the curse and compulsion are akin to ardent sexual lust, which may also blind the individual to the potentially self-effacing consequences of fulfilling their desires. "Third Dead Body" thereby captures the dark side of plastic sexuality Giddens hypothesizes about in *The Transformation of Intimacy*.

Another of Giddens' hypothesized negative outcomes—that plastic sexuality might lead to violence against women—is manifested in "What Maisie Knew." After discovering that zombies talk about their previous human lives during sex or if they suffer pain, living human protagonist Walter purchases a zombie sex-worker, Maisie: the undead version of a women Walter previously murdered. Walter's intent is to stop Maisie from telling others about Walter's crime. Over several sex sessions, Walter discovers that Maisie remembers everything about the night he murdered her. Fearing that she will enact revenge on him, Walter has Maisie destroyed: Maisie is taken to a gathering of male reanimate fetishists who dismember her corpse with hand tools. Maisie's disturbing fate at the hands of these men manifests an extreme version of Giddens' concern regarding violence towards women. Giddens (153) hypothesizes that such violence is the result of a failure to "sustai[n] basic trust," related unresolved issues regarding "mastery and control," and "repressed emotional dependence upon women." Walter's fear that someone might discover his secret is indicative of his inability to sustain trust, since it spirals into a paranoid compulsion to destroy Maisie entirely. Violence is expressive of Walter's desire to assert "mastery and control." Such control is inextricable from his sexuality since Walter purchases, imprisons, and has sex with Maisie. He has complete control over her. His decision to have her killed is the ultimate articulation of that control. Since she belongs to him, it is not necessary to have her dismembered. Nevertheless, Walter does so out of fear over her ability to eventually take revenge. Walter's reaction underlines that he considers Maisie to be powerful: she ultimately has the power to ruin him if she exposes him. In order to repress his dependence on her (to use Giddens' terms), Walter enacts extraordinary violence on her person. What is notable here is that Walter is concerned with himself: his guilt over the murder he committed and his fear that he will lose control. Maisie is reduced to simply an embodiment of Walter's inner-conflicts. To Walter, Maisie is a cipher, not a being. In "What Maisie Knew," then, plastic sexuality is undercut by the same narcissistic projection we see elsewhere in stories about zombie sex work. Tales such as "What Maisie Knew" highlight that personal sexual freedom could easily slip into harmful self-indulgence. This, as Giddens recognizes, is one of the main dangers that encumbers plastic sexuality.

Conclusion

At its best, plastic sexuality opens a door to endless sexual possibilities (Young; Johnson; Langdridge et al.). Yet, at its worst, Giddens believes that plastic sexuality could have dire consequences for men and women alike (Giddens 65; Gross and Simmons 540). In Giddens' view, plastic sexuality may be fragmentary, and could lead to destructive behaviors (see also Sanders 401). Whilst researchers such as Gross and Simmons (549) are less convinced that plastic sexuality is problematic, the representations of plastic sexuality offered in dystopicmodern zombie fiction underline the darkest potentials of sexual plasticity.

Although the dystopicmodern context differs from our own everyday environments, these depictions analogize social and sexual concerns that are relevant to our lives. Giddens uses real-world examples to conceptualize the directions in which sexuality might be heading. Zombie fiction provides an alternative way of hypothesizing about the same issues Giddens raises. As Glassner (xi) observes, popular culture commonly reflects our societal fears and assumptions about the future.

As such, portrayals of zombie sexuality paint a mixed picture of sexual freedoms and sexual dangers. Zombie sex-workers may seem farfetched and fantastic compared with the everyday realities of sexual expression that we engage in. Consequently, we might fail to see the connections between sexuality under dystopicmodernity and under our present social circumstances. However, it is worth noting that, as I have demonstrated throughout this essay, the potential pitfalls of plastic sexuality—narcissism, distrust, violence against women—are all-too familiar and are readily applicable to our daily sex lives. In contrast, the ideals that plastic sexuality could represent—egalitarianism, mutual pleasure, sexual expression free from moral judgment—seem, troublingly, all-too distant.

Laid to Rest

Romance, End of the World Sexuality and Apocalyptic Anticipation in Robert Kirkman's The Walking Dead

Emma Vossen

"I can't believe I'm saying this but the dead, they're a manageable threat. I can see the mistake I made wanting to run not being willing to stand and fight ... I've seen how we can organize, plan, how if we do things right if everyone does their part we can survive anything ... we can rebuild the walls, stronger, taller make our community better than it ever was ... I think about the road ahead of us, and for the first time it seems long and bright. After everything we've been though, all the people we've lost I suddenly find myself overcome with something I thought we'd lost ... hope. I want to show you this new world I want to make it a reality for you"
—Rick Grimes to his son Carl after the destruction of their home and community [Kirkman ch 14].

Apocalyptic Anticipation

In 2007 film scholar Kirsten Moana Thompson established and traced the phenomenon that she refers to as "apocalyptic dread" throughout late 90s and post–9/11 American cinema. Thompson's analysis builds on Soren Kierkegaard's concept of "dread," which includes "theorizations about the paradoxical and ambivalent dimensions of anxiety (dread)" that "suggest that the implications of knowledge and freedom of choice are not just liberating, but also deeply terrifying" (Thompson 18). Thompson observes that horror narratives built on anxieties about both the future and the present became increasingly popular around the turn of the millennium. Narratives of global catastrophe often represent these apocalyptic fears in the form of monsters, including the zombie.

These apocalyptic narratives, Thompson argues, are a "new manifestation of a long-standing American apocalyptic tradition" that was built out of puritanism and has since reemerged many times in cinema, from the science fiction films of the cold war, to the demonic horror films of the 1970s (18). Thompson contends that this American apocalyptic tradition "reach[es] a hysterical peak in the nineties in a cycle of horror, disaster, and science fiction films explicitly focused on the approaching millennium" (18). The last phase of this trend includes the post–9/11 horror films, in which "the dread took new forms with anxieties about the rise of Islamic fundamentalism and terrorism from within" (Thompson 18). This same tradition of apocalyptic dread can be traced not only within cinema, but within the medium of comics as well. The same apocalyptic fear that Thompson tracks was reflected in the early Cold War pulp comics,[1] and the genre subsequently underwent an extreme dystopian turn in the late 70s and early 80s alongside film (Thompson 2). This turn can be seen in the extreme popularity of Reagan-era dystopian comics, including Frank Miller's *The Dark Knight Returns* (1986), as well as Alan Moore's *Watchmen* (1986–1987) and *V for Vendetta* (1982–1989).

The idea of apocalyptic dread can be traced throughout the lineage of science fiction and horror in both film and graphic fiction: both art forms attempt to confront our ambiguous future. Fredrick Jameson's esteemed observation that science fiction is oftentimes dystopian because it embodies our inability to imagine a collective future, has since been taken up by Constance Penley who instead insists that we can imagine a future, and dystopia instead illustrates that we "cannot conceive the kind of collective political strategies necessary to change or ensure that future" (qtd. in Thompson 2). Both theorists illustrate that dystopia represents our desire for global change, even if we would not want to live in the apocalyptic worlds of our dystopian fiction. Almost twelve years after 9/11, dystopian narratives remain popular, but contemporary dystopian science fiction comics and films demonstrate that we have

moved beyond our inability to conceive of the collective political strategies to escape capitalism, and accepted that there is no political strategy
that will take us into a post-capitalist, utopian future.

Many of us have conceded our utopian dreams, admitting that capitalism, and the social and ideological constraints that accompany it, are
too pervasive to overcome. Indeed, it is becoming harder to distinguish
between our current pre-apocalyptic existence and our dystopian imagination. The period of apocalyptic dread that Thompson chronicles is
over. We are now living in a time in which our films and comics stand
not for our fear of apocalypse, but instead reflect what I will refer to as
"apocalyptic anticipation."[2] Because we have no political strategy that
will lead us to a more advantageous post-capitalist world, we are instead
searching for a larger, greater end that is above political distinction, an
end that is all consuming. Recently, the zombie apocalypse has become
the most popular of dystopian end-points. These dystopian zombie narratives no longer represent our dread that the world might end, and
instead offer a fantasy in which we anticipate and invite the apocalypse,
hoping that it will liberate or relieve us not only from our debt and more
quotidian economic constraints, but also from our increasingly bleak
looking future. Rather than offering portentous warnings, many new
apocalyptic narratives are optimistic and romantic versions of the end
of the world. They offer escapism from the present, allowing readers to
imagine what day-to-day life would be like in a near future post-
apocalypse. The post-apocalyptic world is one in which it is hard to take
anything for granted. Having lost their quotidian luxuries and possessions, survivors are forced to acknowledge and appreciate the simple
pleasures of companionship.

To illustrate this phenomenon, this essay is focused on a prominent
example of anticipatory apocalyptic fiction: Robert Kirkman and Charlie
Adlard's wildly popular zombie epic *The Walking Dead* (2003-present)
(Gaudiosi). *The Walking Dead* comic sets a new standard for the zombie
narrative by focusing not on the monsters, but rather on the humans
living amongst them. The protagonists are visibly concerned about finding food, shelter, and weapons, as is characteristic of post-apocalyptic
narratives. However, these details are mechanical rather than pivotal to
The Walking Dead's thematic interests. The primary concern, instead,
is attaining and sustaining human contact. These survivors are not simply concerned with killing or avoiding zombies; the impetus for their
very continued existence is to find a suitable home in which to settle
down, begin anew, and very importantly, to fornicate. What makes this

series such a distinct artifact in the saturated zombie subgenre is the prominent roles that sex and relationships play in sustaining the story-line. Narrative conflicts revolve less around a zombie threat than they do the narrative tropes of romantic melodrama, focusing particularly on emotional and physical relationships. The story is ripe with lies, love, murder, sex, cheating, pregnancy, jealousy, mental illness, friendship, family, sickness, and mourning. Moreover, Kirkman's characters disappear, switch partners, die off, and reappear much like one would expect from any daytime television drama.

These interpersonal and physical connections are pivotal. Kirkman's text is an exemplar of apocalyptic anticipation, and its optimism about the end of the world is represented through the characters' relationships. Apocalyptic anticipation is also demonstrated by the characters themselves who are living full, satisfying lives, as opposed to characters in other zombie narratives who are impelled by the most basic fight for survival. Instead of simply attempting to survive for the sake of living, Kirkman's characters only live—only desire to survive—if they have someone for whom to live. Kirkman's characters are forced to prioritize what is important to them as humans when almost all of their pre-apocalyptic responsibilities and belongings are lost.

Fans of Kirkman's narratives have devoured his zombie tales because they offer soap-opera style indulgence and escapism that, in our current economic struggles, only seems plausible after the end of the world. For many young people today, it is hard to fantasize about the possibility of getting married, owning a home, having job security, having children, or living without debt. Subsequently, all of these typical milestones no longer seem achievable, economically plausible, or, more importantly, worthwhile. Furthermore, environmental disaster and political catastrophe have led many to question the "point" of participating in the classic, conventional adult rites of passage. Developing a lasting partnership seems fruitless in a world where day-to-day existence is so difficult for the individual. There is no clear impetus to have children when one is unable to provide for them and their future looks bleak. Apocalyptic destruction of the current world, offers a clean break and a fresh start where these milestones and possessions (as well as economic constraints on them) no longer exist. This fresh start inspires new life-aims and causes characters to re-prioritize which relationships are worth pursuing. Thus, in contrast to the difficulties we face in the real world, the apocalyptic world presents romantic fantasies of falling in love and building a family that seem worth pursuing. The apocalypse essentially offers utopian escapism. Yet, we cannot imagine a new world, a better world, without first imagining the end of the one in which we currently live. Kirkman's narrative embodies this apocalyptic anticipation, providing hope that a new future may be both possible and appealing.

In recent years, many other popular texts have represented the apocalypse in this anticipatory fashion. Noteworthy examples include Max Brooks' *New York Times* bestsellers *World War Z* (2006) and the *Zombie Survival Guide* (2003), the latter of which sold a million copies in its first year (Staskiewicz). Contemporary zombie narratives such as those by Kirkman and Brooks are well received not because they depict apocalyptic terror, but because they anticipate and desire the dead rising and unhinging societal order. *The Zombie Survival Guide* is an imaginative tool that provides escapism while positioning itself as a piece of very real "non-fiction." The deadpan text is written as a survival manual that helps its reader prepare for and live through the impending zombie threat. The manual chronicles what is treated as a very real history of zombie attacks in the past, and includes a blank "outbreak journal" in which the reader can record their observations of current zombie activity (Brooks). These texts by authors like Kirkman and Brooks are just a few artifacts in a burgeoning line of narratives that reflect apocalyptic anticipation, a vein of art that not only envisages life beyond contemporary socio-economic shackles, but that also depicts post-apocalyptic life in a hopeful and appealing light.

The preoccupation with the zombie-induced apocalypse is founded on not only on the fantasy of capitalism's finale, but a return to—or reopening of—the American frontier. In the introduction to *The Unfinished Nation*, Alan Brinkley explains that "to many Americans in the late nineteenth century, the West seemed an untamed "frontier" in which hardy pioneers were creating a new society" (Brinkley). It was from this perception that America's romantic frontier mythos was born. Americans believed in a destiny that promised them both the physical terrain and a social space in which they could reinvent themselves, a new land unfettered by the constraints of the old. The post-apocalyptic landscape of these zombie narratives functions as a reopening of the conceptual, romantic frontier well known in American history. In this zombie frontier, characters reinvent themselves and live a life that holds concrete tangible purpose: that of simple survival. The pan-zombie genre is no longer about the fear of one's world crashing down, but the pleasure of escaping the drudgery of capitalism and the trepidation its currently fragile economy causes. The implausibility of the dead coming back to life represents how unlikely it is that capitalism can be overcome, that revolutionary utopia can feasibly be achieved. The utopian impulse can instead be seen in the desire for apocalypse in Generation Y and Z's zombie narratives.[3] The generation born after the year 2000 has been called "generation Z" (Anatole): a label that captures the sense that this grouping represents the end of the proverbial line (since Z lies figuratively at the end of alphabet). Generation X's fear of the end of the world was represented through the films and comics of the time (as was demonstrated by Thompson); generation Y and Z's anticipation of the end of the world is represented through their dystopian apocalyptic texts. At some point in recent years, the end of the world stopped representing horror, and began representing hope. The current youth would still like to imagine a better place, a better time, a better way of life, but can only imagine these feats and indulge their utopian impulse if it takes place after the end, the complete destruction, of this world. Instead of representing utopia as an unrealistically perfect place, these texts instead represent a future that can only be achieved through destruction of current society.

The Walking Dead: Twilight *for Zombie Fans*

The Walking Dead comic, written by Kirkman and illustrated by Adlard, has been serialized over the past ten years, totaling over 100 issues and well over 2000 pages, and has continual success in its adaptations as both an extremely popular television show (McMillan) and an award-winning videogame (2012). What sets Kirkman apart from his predecessors in this genre is his commingling of romantic, family drama with horror; the aesthetics of the latter serve to reinforce the sentimentality of the former. Indeed, horror serves mainly as the backdrop to a complex and fundamentally social and romantic drama. This unique combination of traditionally unexpected elements has proven immensely popular. Indeed, these zombie narratives are incredibly popular with this generation, and there are discernible shifts towards a more positive sentimentality in what was once the modus operandi of horror. Examples of this optimistic and romantic shift in tone and theme can be seen not only in *The Walking Dead* but also in movies like *Shaun of the Dead* (2004) and *Zombieland* (2009), and more recently in Isaac Marion's popular book and its film adaptation *Warm Bodies* (2013). *Warm Bodies* is the story of a beautiful young girl and a surprisingly attractive zombie who is brought back to life by their love (Marion). *Warm Bodies* shatters the living/dead binary and establishes instead a continuity, a spectrum of life in which the recuperation of a zombie's humanity can only be fully established through love. Love is thus framed as the fullest extent of an interpersonal existence.

Kirkman's ongoing comic series *The Walking Dead* epitomizes this same trend, being as much about sex and romance as it is horror and apocalypse; Kirkman's characters learn how to fully "live" and love after the end of the world. Indeed, Kirkman has claimed the success of his series can be directly linked to its focus on human relationships. He explains, "*Twilight* is to *Dracula* as *The Walking Dead* is to [George A.] Romero movies. I'm the Stephenie Meyer of Zombies. I watched Romero movies and I was like, yeah, but what if they had more kissing?" (*The Nerdist*). Kirkman argues that it is not zombies that makes *The Walking Dead* so popular, but rather traditional soap opera elements such as romance, betrayal, and sex. Soap operas and similar dramas have long functioned as a type of escapist wish fulfillment in their indulgence in fictional American luxury. Whereas soap operas and dramas of the late 80s and 90s focused on the exciting sex and love lives of the rich and beautiful, Kirkman's zombie-filled dystopia has become a choice form of utopian escapism for those who see economic success as unattainable, and who would rather imagine a social order unhinged and a world that required a return to the primal apocalyptic pastoral.

Kirkman's departure from Romero hinges on optimism: the notion that the end of the world provides opportunity to build a new and better world, not just the chance to watch the old world crumble. Kirkman's zombie narrative bears all the thematic dressings of horror, with its macabre scenarios and constant threats from the innumerable hordes of the undead but, more often than not, its plot is indulgent and driven by palpably erotic fantasy fulfillment. Kirkman explains that his approach to the series is to "take what is really cool about zombie movies and then just add soap opera stuff. So it's like action heroes crying, people falling in love, people being sad … I think that's what makes it popular" (*The Nerdist*). *The Walking Dead*'s protagonists are concerned less with slaying zombies than they are with being better people. Frequently, this equates to being a more sexually and romantically fulfilled person. Sex is emphasized in *The Walking Dead* as that which separates "the living" from "the dead." The survivors' primal sexual urges and desire for personal companionship separate the living from the monstrous "other." Sex, and the momentary escape that accompanies it, is the force the characters use to fight against the temptation to give up, to become inhuman.

However, that is not to suggest that sex creates a dichotomy between the living and their undead counterparts. The zombies provide a backdrop, the fictional conditions which facilitate the living characters' interactions. Being constantly confronted with death means that the survivors must prioritize what really matters to them during what are potentially their last days on earth. Protagonists are frequently impelled to participate in the acts that accentuate their humanity. After being exposed to death so frequently, the living characters must come to terms with the possibility that they could be next. The survivors therefore live in a state of perpetual acceptance of death. The survivors' lives are defined by their proximity to death. When not ensuring that they are staving off death by fulfilling the basic needs of sustenance and safety, the protagonists live every spare moment as if it were their last. This mode of living sets them apart from the dead. The zombies' omnipresence underscores how pivotal life and death are to existence.

The zombie highlights how inadequate it is to think of life and death as entirely separate states. *The Walking Dead*'s characters instead adopt a more postmodern view of death in which "alive" is measured by relative quality of life. As Jeffrey Jerome Cohen explains in his study *Monster Theory*, postmodernism itself is akin to Frankenstein's monster. It is a history, a theory, and a culture that is "composed of a multitude of fragments, rather than of smooth epistemological wholes ... bound together to form a loosely integrated net—or, better, an assimilated hybrid, a monstrous body" (3). Monsters enable postmodern theoretical examination because they inhabit liminal spaces, policing what Cohen calls "the borders of the possible," and calling into question binaries such as 'us' and 'them'" (12). Zombies epitomize this view of postmodern monstrosity, since the undead inhabit the liminal space between human and inhuman, between living and dead.

If one simply survives rather than lives, the line between living and dead begins to blur. Rick Grimes, the series' protagonist and leader of the survivors, lectures his group on this topic:

> The second we put a bullet in the head of one of those undead monsters—the moment one of us drove a hammer into one of their faces—or cut a head off. We became what we are! ... You people don't know what we are! We're surrounded by the DEAD. We're among them—and when we finally give up we become them! We're living on borrowed time here. Every minute of our life is a minute we steal from them! You see them out there.

You KNOW that when we die we become them. You think we hide behind walls to protect us from The Walking Dead? Don't you get it? We ARE The Walking Dead! WE are The Walking Dead [Kirkman ch 4].

Unlike the invading governments and aliens of many other dystopian texts, zombies are not outsiders looking to conquer America. They are not "evil incarnate." Rather, zombies are us. They come from within and they embody the multitude of fragmented identities that constitutes America itself. Rick's speech encapsulates Kirkman's thesis. Rick's realization underscores why the comic is so full of sex and romance. The decision to kill (or otherwise) is a complicated matter. What is much more complicated in Kirkman's new world is the choice whether to live or die: if one chooses the former, is one truly living or just surviving on borrowed time? In these narratives, a beating heart is not enough to evince life. Just like the zombie who slowly comes back to life in *Warm Bodies*, a survivor's life is placed on a continuum of "living" in which survivors attempt to move as far away from the undead as possible. In these narratives one is never fully alive, or fully dead; they are instead a human existing somewhere in between these two extremes. If one does not sufficiently "live" as a sexual or romantic being, then one may as well be one of the zombies from whom the group is trying to protect themselves. Simply put, a zombie's "life" is quite over; they cannot sleep, love, make decisions, make memories, or have sex. Those in the community taking control of their life and actively having lots of sex are those that remain furthest from the dead, in a psychological, existential sense. In postmodern zombie narratives such as Kirkman's, living protagonists frequently seek to maintain the fantasy that humanity and zombidom are contrasting modes of existence. In *The Walking Dead*, however, that desired separation is critiqued; contemporary society's constraints and rules are directly compared with the lack thereof in the post-apocalyptic state.

Yearning in (and for) the New World

The Walking Dead follows lead protagonist Rick Grimes, who wakes up from a coma in his local hospital to discover that he is the only living person in a small town overrun with the titular ghoulish horde. By the second issue, Rick escapes from the hospital and serendipitously finds his wife (Lori), his young son (Carl), and his best friend (Shane) at a camp outside of Atlanta. From this point on, the narrative follows Rick's struggles to protect not only Carl and Lori (who is pregnant), but also the community of survivors with whom they travel (Kirkman ch 1). As the story progresses, almost every character partakes in coupling at some point, giving the group a reason to keep moving, to continue looking for other survivors, and to find a secure place to settle down. Because making money and sustaining wealth are no longer goals in this world, the characters focus on the happiness that human interaction offers instead. In this zombie-infested apocalyptic environment, when an eligible, desirable individual becomes sexually available, there is no time for the timidity, rituals, or shame that characterize contemporary sexual standards and courting rituals. Here, bachelors and bachelorettes make themselves readily available to each other almost entirely without any hesitation or heed to heteronormative socio-sexual customs. Characters establish very quickly what they have to offer and their willingness to have sex in a timely and efficient manner in order to not be passed over by potential partners. As one survivor, Maggie, explains, "we've gotta be proactive or we're going to end up alone" (Kirkman ch 2). Coupling is more than just a choice, it is a survival technique. Pairings like Rick and Lori, or Maggie and fellow survivor Glen, search for places where they can properly raise not just existing children but children they want to bring into the world. Sexual desire and romantic partnership stimulate the characters' will to keep living despite the fact that almost everyone they knew before the apocalypse is likely dead.

This sexual desire mirrors apocalyptic anticipation and the collective desire amongst generation Y and Z for the end. Kirkman's characters demonstrate collective desire for a new and better world through their romantic satisfaction, utopian hope, and general contentment in spite of the hardships they face. The characters find and form life-changing relationships that they did not previously have. Their world is constrained, but also offers new opportunities. Sometimes the characters' sexual satisfaction is fleeting but, this type of momentary escape makes life worth living, since they provide hope for the future in otherwise bleak circumstances.

For some of Kirkman's protagonists, sex is the primary reason to keep going in the face of seemingly hopeless circumstances. One of the more endearing characters in the series is relatively young Glen, who humbly admits being sexually interested in a slightly older fellow survivor, Carol. When Carol couples up with Rick's second-in-command, the strong and reliable Tyreese, Glen realizes he has lost his chance, and quietly reassesses his position in the group. Kirkman and Adlard demonstrate Glenn's episodic loss of desire to live through many silent panels of Glen looking longingly at Carol. The otherwise proactive Glen vacillates between survival and aimlessness throughout the first three "camps" that the characters inhabit (Kirkman ch 2). Glen's attitude towards his own life is unclear during this period: it is implied that Glen may take his own life, or that he may recklessly gamble with his well-being by volunteering for dangerous missions to forage for supplies. Just when it seems like Glen is about to see an early grave, the survivors are taken in by a veterinarian, Hershel, and his young adult family. One of Hershel's daughters, Maggie, inquires after Glen's gloomy temperament, to which he replies, "Everyone around me is pairing off ... I don't want to end up alone too" (Kirkman ch 2). Maggie's succinct and pragmatic response—"if that's what you're after, I'll fuck you"—might seem terse, but it spurs possibly the most authentic and earnest romance of the entire series (Kirkman ch 2). The two become arguably the most psychologically stable couple in the book, killing zombies en tandem throughout the day, and enjoying each other's company at night. They become self-sufficient as a pair, and provide for the greater group. As the couple's relationship becomes more serious, they begin to consider their new world version of marriage as well as the possibility of having children, although they readily admit that they first require a permanent, stable home and community. Their ideal designs are rooted in sexual chemistry, motivating their desire to instigate a new society. Because they have nothing to lose and everything to gain as a young couple, Glen and Maggie are able to very quickly get on with their life together. Their pragmatic outlook, and the lack of financial barriers allow them to very quickly become serious about their relationship and live happily together, getting married and having children. The normative pleasures of marriage and family seem increasingly unattainable and futile in today's world of widespread unemployment, educational debts, ever-increasing cost of living, and prohibitive housing costs. For Glen and Maggie, the apocalypse simplifies this romantic process immensely.

Social constraints that currently inhibit sex and relationships are typically tossed off by *The Walking Dead* characters. There is no time for traditional courting in the wake of the apocalypse. The characters' sexual liberation represents their liberation in all facets of life including, most importantly, the freedom to be themselves and to follow their desires. For example, because they are not separated by institutions such as school systems, employment, and retirement, large differences in age cease to be a factor for many of the characters when selecting romantic partners. Age has little relevance as a societal qualifier within *The Walking Dead* because it has very little to do with how soon one may die in a landscape populated with the shambling horrors. All characters are effectively at the same "stage of life" as they all share a goal: to survive. Driven by the desire to spend their limited days with someone else, the characters feel free to couple up with who they want regardless of age or other socially constructed obstacles. For instance, near-geriatric survivor Dale questions why his twenty-something spouse Andrea would want to be with someone so old, askingn "How many good years can I have left?" Andrea quickly replies, "Nobody has any good years left" (Kirkman ch 3). Andrea and Dale's relationship is life changing for both of them. Andrea is with Dale for the rest of his life and her life is better and more satisfying because of their partnership. Shortly after Dale's death, Andrea explains to Rick: "Over the course of a year I inherited a family—I grew up—I loved the woman I became and the life I had. And now it's all gone. I'm all alone and all I can think about is how I'm that girl again, the girl I was ... the one I didn't like" (Kirkman ch 12). During her sexual attachment with Dale, Andrea implicitly displays her refusal to recede into some existential infancy; her ability to find in Dale a reason to keep living marks her and those like her as alive, and thus distinct from the undead.

Despite being surrounded by death and decay, having no luxuries and being constantly uprooted, Andrea valorizes her post-apocalypse life, characterizing it as more satisfying and honest than her previous existence. She attains all the achievements and satisfactions she could not find in normal society, including falling deeply in love with a much older man and adopting children. After Dale's death, and a series of other unfortunate events Andrea is left with nothing, not even herself (as she had come to be). At this point in the narrative the survivor-community is at its most utopian in terms of supplies, security, and stability; yet, without a partner, Andrea spirals into self-loathing. This depression does not last long as Andrea again finds a new world happiness when she finally gives in to her long-suppressed feelings for Rick (who is also recently widowed) and consummates that relationship. Both Rick and Andrea reached near zombie status in terms of emotional "living" after losing their respective partners (Lori and Dale), but their partnership reignites their will to live. Right before this coupling takes place, Rick claims that although he is physically alive, he emotionally "died a long time ago," to which Andrea replies, "Have you forgotten? Death doesn't affect people quite like it used to. Don't you think it's about time you came back to life?" Andrea then kisses Rick for the first time (Kirkman ch 15). Although they have both experienced substantial losses, together they gain hope for their future, they know that they must live everyday as if it is their last in order to be proud of the people they have become.

Andrea is not the only person who feels that their new life is an improvement over their old world life. Glen and Maggie are depicted as exceedingly happy throughout the series, and Carol displays a similar favoring of her new, post-apocalypse life. She explains to Lori, "I've almost got things better now—Tyreese is better than my husband ever was ... I mean look around you. Look at this place. We could have it all here. We could rebuild—make a new life" (Kirkman ch 3). The focus here is on creating a *new* life, not re-creating the ultra-structured life they had previously. In fact, at one point Rick settles his survivors down in a gated community that Carl considers to be *too much* like their old life. Carl, having grown-up in the wake of disaster refuses to buy into the fantasy the community offers. He claims the members of the community are "all stupid. The roamers didn't go away because you can't *see* them. I hate this place, Dad. It doesn't feel *real*. It feels like everyone is playing pretend" (Kirkman ch 12). Despite Rick's initial reluctance to Carl's point of view, he eventually realizes that there is no benefit to living in a simulation and alters the community's practices, adopting a more pragmatic approach to the zombie threat.

Kirkman's zombie narrative offers readers a fantasy that is as liberating as it is unimaginable. *The Walking Dead* depicts a world without capitalism, without traditional social structures and the designations that go along with them. When these structures are uprooted, life decisions are no longer limited by economics or socially circumscribed mores. This post-apocalyptic world invokes a new kind of American dream, one of self re-creation. Kirkman's characters can completely reinvent themselves. As such, they are conduits for fantasizing Generation Y and Z readers, whose prospects seem bleak, but who hope for post-apocalyptic escape. For many characters in *The Walking Dead*, post-apocalyptic existence is an improvement over their previous lives. They have the opportunity to transcend their imposed roles within the social order: a gym teacher becomes a soldier; a policeman becomes a leader; a lawyer becomes the lone warrior; a young girl becomes a mother; a prisoner becomes a farmer; a thief becomes a husband. Social upheaval allows them to overcome self-hatred or self-doubt and truly live as the people they always wanted to be.

Sex, Desire and Hope

Rick and his fellow survivors have the power to change their world, their living situation, and their day to day lives in a way that often feels impossible for *The Walking Dead*'s readers. This better life may be filled with "kill or be killed" encounters, but it is new, empowering, and relatively unaffected by the weight of history. This hope for a better life is represented primarily through the characters' romantic and sexual satisfaction. In this new world, sex is readily attainable regardless of differences in gender, age, race, sexual orientation, or ability, as long as the protagonist is willing to be a stable and loving partner. Even if characters have not found permanent partners, they can typically find someone else willing to participate in a type of "last hurrah," since neither participant can be sure whether they will ever have another chance to indulge in the act. For example, upon discovering that the world is over and realizing that he is free after years of incarceration, one prisoner (Axel) chooses to stay within the safety of the prison. Faced with the possibility that he will die when the group's prison camp is invaded, Axel engages in consensual sex with Patricia, another survivor. This experience is a source of satisfaction for them both and would have never happened in the old world. The post-apocalyptic climate may be fraught with danger, but as Axel and Patricia's liaison illustrates sexual interactions are frequent, accessible, and necessary: sex is a source of life-affirming sociality in this environment.

Characters also find comfort in observing sex. Such a sight inspires hope and optimism for the observing character's own future and for their own visceral escape. Sex signifies that the characters are physically safe, and that their immediate needs are met. For example, Donna walks in on Dale and Andrea having sex soon after the group has arrived at their first settlement, Willshire Estates (Kirkman ch 2). Although Donna initially recoils from this display of physicality between the elderly Dale and twenty-something Andrea, Donna leaves with a sense of genuine optimism. As she says to her husband Alan directly afterwards, "you know, I still don't approve of those two, but Andrea is a grown woman and she can make her own decisions. It's just nice to see people happy with all that's going on. I'm happy for them ... seeing [Dale and Andrea] together ... knowing that they can put their lives back together, it gives me hope" (Kirkman ch 2). Donna's reaction at this moment reflects her practical optimism: she interprets sex as the sight of people truly living, and it inspires her to change her attitude. Donna acts as voyeur in this scene much like the reader does throughout the rest of the text. Like Donna, we are voyeurs on the characters' progress, satisfaction, and freedom—both sexual and otherwise—which stand in contradistinction to the constraints that we face in our day-to-day lives.

Unfortunately, Donna's voyeuristically inspired enthusiasm is short-lived. The next morning the newly hopeful Donna is careless in her inspection of homes that the characters seek to inhabit. She joyfully explores the house, exclaiming, "This is going to be so fun. It's going to be like one of those home shows but better!" (Kirkman ch 2). Almost immediately after making this proclamation, the left side of her face is torn off by a stealthy zombie. Killing off Donna is not a means of cynically undercutting optimism per se. Rather, the incident debunks her over-compensatory enthusiasm. In this scenario, Dale and Andrea use sex to cope with their changing lives. In contrast, Donna is inspired into blind idealism. Such naivety frequently leads to a gruesome demise in Kirkman's narratives. Unrealistic expectations about the future—such as Donna's statement regarding their potential abode—are kept in check by the realities of the zombie plague. In *The Walking Dead*, the characters who survive are pragmatic about life and death; they are satisfied with what happiness they find and do not attempt to recreate their previous lives. Dale and Andrea's relationship reflects the type of new world optimism that Kirkman proffers. They enjoy their freedom but remain cautious and aware that they could die at any moment. Donna and Alan on the other hand are unfit for this new world, as are most characters who seem to value the old world and its ideals. They are incapable of appreciating their new world for what it is. They seek to simulate their old lives instead of finding happiness that is more attuned to their surroundings (as Andrea and Dale do).

Soon after Donna's death, her bereaved husband Alan expresses his despair, saying to Rick that "[e]verything is just hard." Rick's reply—"I know, nothing's easy anymore. Nothing" (Kirkman ch 2)—corroborates Alan's reversal of the idealism Donna previously espoused. Yet that is not to say that the narrative perspective concurs with Alan's pessimism. Their conversation is contrasted by parallel panels depicting Glen and Maggie walking hand-in-hand. The text box containing Alan's despair overlaps two panels portraying Maggie and Glen sneaking off to have sex. They have found an escape that is in fact "easy." This contrast between the couple's depiction and Alan's dialogue implies that, even at the end of the world, sex is a fundamental aspect of existence. Finding, protecting, and maintaining a sexual partner and attaining this new world happiness becomes, for many, their raison d'etre.

Conclusion: A Postmodern Zombie Narrative for Gen Y and Gen Z

Post-apocalyptic zombie texts are not the only narratives in which these millennial anxieties of apocalyptic anticipation are depicted. For example, the directionless angst of the current generation—commonly labeled as "generation jobless"[4]—can be seen in the everyday setting of Lena Dunham's award-winning HBO series *Girls* (2012). Dunham, who has been both congratulated and criticized as the "voice of her generation" (Walker), plays the show's central character Hannah: a privileged and lost twenty-something living in Manhattan. One poignant example of 21st century anxiety can be seen in the first season when Hannah is getting an STD test and explains to the gynecologist that she has a fear of AIDS, only then to immediately retract her statement:

> these days if you are diagnosed with AIDS it's actually not a death sentence. There's so many good drugs and people live a long time, so. Also, um, if you do have AIDS there is a lot of stuff people aren't going to bother you about. Like for example no one is going to call you on the phone and say "did you get a job" or "did you pay your rent" or "are you taking an HTML course" because all they are going to say is "congratulations on not being dead!" [*Girls*].

Eventually, Hannah concludes with the epiphany "Maybe I actually am not scared of AIDS. Maybe I thought I was scared of AIDS and what I really am is ... wanting ... AIDS" (*Girls*). Under the crushing pressure of contemporary adulthood, Hannah naively fantasizes that even the cruel death of AIDS could be a possible relief from the expectations of societal participation. Hannah at this point acts as a representative member of Generation Y. She feels hopeless and craves a life she feels is worth living, an escape from her current zombie-like existence. She wishes upon herself a type of personal apocalypse that will free her from the directionless banality of unpaid internships. In line with Thompson and Kierkegaard's assertions, the chronically overeducated and under-employed individuals who comprise Generation Y are more aware than any previous generation of the "contradictions presented by a secular, modern, knowledge-based society," in which "millennial and apocalyptic beliefs ... have proliferated" (Thompson 18). Generation Y's and Z's collective existential yearning for the end represents a desire to return to a "simpler" time: a time in which surviving is life's principal challenge; a time in which individuals might congratulate one another for "not being dead!" The post-apocalyptic landscape of *The Walking Dead* functions in the same manner. Such narratives are particularly resonant with those individuals who identify with the sense of collective disempowerment Thompson and Kierkegaard evoke.

Zombie narratives are especially pertinent in flagging these themes. The zombie apocalypse causes social upheaval and necessitates starting anew. It illuminates how zombie-like existence within capitalism can feel. Sarah Lauro, author of "The Zombie Manifesto," argues that unconsciously "we are more interested in the zombie at times when as a culture we feel disempowered." She goes on to explain that zombie narratives provide "a great variety of outlets for people" during periods of dissolution, such as the global economic crisis (Kinnard). In contrast to the unconceivable scale of capitalism or international financial ruin, the zombie offers a singular threat to survival that signifies all of our problems and anxieties. As such, the zombie summates the threats of debt, unemployment, global warming, war, homelessness, disease, and so forth.

Yet zombies are not the primary focus in *The Walking Dead*. Rather, they catalyze social reorganization, and this is the principal source of both trepidation and anticipation for Kirkman's characters and readers. Those of us fortunate enough to live in relative affluence have so much control over what we want to do with our individual lives, but so little control over how we function in the larger web of society. Kirkman is particularly attuned to these notions. Indeed, the publishing blurb on the back of the comics highlights how pivotal these anxieties are in shaping *The Walking Dead*'s ongoing story of apocalyptic anticipation:

> When is the last time any of us REALLY worked to get something that we wanted? How long has it been since any of us really NEEDED something that we WANTED? The world we know is gone. The world of commerce and frivolous necessity has been replaced by a world of survival and responsibility.... In a matter of months society has crumbled—no government, no grocery stores, no mail delivery, no cable TV. In a world ruled by the dead, we are forced to finally start living.

This summation centralizes and universalizes a desire to stop going through the motions and "start living" again. The blurb suggests that *The Walking Dead* performs a particular function for individuals struggling with their position in a capitalist world, whose identities are delimited by class, race, gender, nationality, among other socially constructed impositions. Readers are encouraged to fantasize about an all-encompassing end of days, and indulge in their personal desire to hit the road and return to the frontier, a situation where things really "matter" in a tangible, immediate sense. This monstrous world overrun with the dead may initially seem daunting, but it may also be an improvement compared with the world as it currently exists. For all its dangers and challenges, the version of post-apocalyptic sociality represented in *The Walking Dead* simplifies what parts of being human are valuable. Fear that they may soon be dead (or worse, undead) motivates the characters to focus on what makes them feel alive: attaining sex and love. Throughout *The Walking Dead*, these traits—living, loving, and fucking—are characterized as the essences of life itself. Although the series' combinations of utopian, dystopian, optimistic, and hopeless sentiments may seem paradoxical (much like the dead-alive nature of zombies does), the world depicted is one in flux. Resultantly, it is a world pregnant with possibility.

NOTES

1. As has been chronicled in the anthology *Comic Books and the Cold War* (2012).

2. A term that was also used in Matthew Barrett Gross's *The Last Myth*, although he uses it to describe a phenomenon of fear of the apocalypse, much like Thompson's "apocalyptic dread" and unlike the ideas that I am attempting to advance here.

3. Typically generation Y is considered those born roughly between 1980 and the year 2000. Generation Z is comprised of individuals born any time after the year 2000, although often times those born in the late 90s are also considered part of generation Z.

4. Sharon Bartlett and Maria LeRose's 2013 documentary enshrines this phrase in its title.

Queering and Cripping
the End of the World

Disability, Sexuality and
Race in The Walking Dead

CATHY HANNABACH

Since its 2010 debut on AMC, the television show *The Walking Dead*[1] has garnered vast popular and critical attention. Embedded within the contemporary obsession with a zombie apocalypse, the show is part of a broader cultural project seeking collective ways to navigate a post–2008 imploded capitalist system that many economically vulnerable and privileged populations are still experiencing as "the end of the world." In doing so, the show raises questions about post-apocalyptic racialization, kinship ties in the absence of social institutions to finance them, and intimacies that include cannibalism, disembowelment, and homosocial/homoerotic zombie orgies. Bringing queer disability studies to bear on the show, in this essay I ask how disability, race, and sexuality intertwine in *The Walking Dead* to reflect histories of zombie representation as well as anxieties over early 21st century neoliberal capitalism.

While many scholars have examined the racial and colonial politics of zombie constructions,[2] little work has examined how popular representations of zombies reflect norms of ability and disability. This is a problematic omission in existing literature as the links between zombification and diverse forms of embodiment are encoded into the visual representation of the walking dead. In popular culture, zombies and people with disabilities are constructed in problematically similar ways: communication practices, gait, and cognitive reasoning skills attached to zombie representations mirror those attached to depictions of people with autism, cerebral palsy, and other various disabilities. Simultaneously mapping disability onto the living dead, and mapping death-in-life onto people with disabilities, zombie culture contains some deeply troubling ableism. Yet here I ask how a more radical queer crip reading is possible, one that values the ways compulsory able-bodiness, compulsory whiteness, and compulsory heterosexuality are questioned, troubled, and ultimately challenged within one particular zombie cultural production. Doing so requires drawing on the burgeoning field of queer disability studies, an interdisciplinary and radical social justice-oriented field of inquiry. Queer disability studies does not just look for the queer, disabled characters in a given text or history, seeking to bring them out from invisibility and into the light. Rather, queer disability studies critically interrogates the social construction and intertwining of heterosexuality, able-bodiness, white supremacy, and patriarchy, revealing the ways power and hegemony are at work in the ways they currently animate social and political life.[3]

I demonstrate here that in *The Walking Dead*, "queer" has little to do with who (or what) characters have sex with and much more to do with anti-normativity. Indeed, the queer elements of *The Walking Dead* are found in the practices, embodiments, and desires that resist white, bourgeois heteronormativity and its attendant demands, while simultaneously revealing their centrality in both viral zombie narratives and contemporary neoliberalism. In this sense, queerness in the show is always an intersectional constellation, as race, gender, sexuality, and disability intertwine.

Viral Politics in Zombie Capitalism

A number of cultural studies scholars have sought to make sense of the current zombie obsession in U.S. popular media by attributing it to the 2008 economic collapse and consequent recession. Henry Giroux, for example, writes eloquently about "zombie capitalism," a form of global neoliberalism that has created a new world order that "views competition as a form of social combat, celebrates war as an extension of politics, and legitimates a ruthless Social Darwinism in which particular individuals and groups are considered simply redundant, disposable ... easy prey for the zombies" (Giroux 2). For Giroux, it is the 1 percent and their institutions (to use the language of the Occupy Movement) that are the zombies, as their ideologies spread through contemporary culture and politics like a virus, infecting the rest of us 99 percent in the process. David McNally also mobilizes the viral zombie metaphor to explain global neoliberal capitalism, but for him it is the exploited who are the walking dead: "those disfigured creatures, frequently depicted as zombies, who have been turned into *mere bodies*, unthinking and exploitable collections of flesh, blood, muscle and tissue" through the processes of alienated labor and commodity fetishism (McNally 4, emphasis in original). While these economic explanations for the zombie revival are convincing in many ways, their primary focus on political economy often fails to engage with the explicit ways that race, sexuality, and disability shape both how global capitalism operates and how the viral zombie functions to knit together political, cultural, and economic anxieties.

The Walking Dead demonstrates the ways these cultural, political, and economic concerns feed each other. The show takes place in a post-apocalyptic Atlanta, Georgia, overrun by zombies called "walkers." A mutated virus has been introduced to the human population that causes them to turn into zombies upon their death, after which they attack and consume humans for food. The show follows a core group of human survivors as they struggle to stay alive, avoid the walkers, and figure out how to maintain social bonds in a world largely absent of the political and economic institutions that are designed to support them. The few human survivors, led by the straight, white patriarchal sheriff Rick, must navigate a state-less, service-less world that even capital seems to have abandoned, drawing only on their own strengths and bootstrap-agencies for assistance. In many ways, The Walking Dead's setting, while hyperbolic, embodies a logic that is central to neoliberal capitalism: privatization of social services and basic human needs is enabled through the withdrawal of public state support, and individuals are left to fend for themselves in a hostile world with only their ambitions and families on which to draw. In this way, Giroux and McNally are correct in their assessment of neoliberal global capitalism's zombie production. The Walking Dead offers us a world in which there are no working banks, grocery stores, apartment buildings, or schools even though the buildings that housed these public institutions litter the landscape, haunting and taunting the human survivors in their lack of safety. In post-apocalyptic Atlanta, only independent, able-bodied, virile folks are imagined to be able to survive while those whose embodiments or identities are interdependent with others and with a social safety net face death or abandonment. As Robert McRuer and Abby Wilkerson argue, neoliberalism disproportionately harms populations that have historically been positioned to rely more heavily upon public services—such as people with disabilities, poor people, queers, trans* people,[4] immigrants, and women—while it simultaneously enshrines the heterosexual nuclear family as the "proper" private location of support (McRuer and Wilkerson 3).[5] In neoliberalism, unpaid labor in the heterosexual family by spouses, parents, and children is understood to substitute for public support, and marginalized populations are expected to invest in the heterosexual nuclear form as a safeguard against poverty and death. In *The Walking Dead*, these populations similarly face potential annihilation as those who are elderly, have physical or cognitive disabilities, are pregnant, or cannot or will not attack zombies with weapons are quickly killed or abandoned. The tenuous kinship ties still remaining are expected to provide for basic human needs. All of the groups represented as "families" in the show are either heterosexual couples or children and parents related through heterosexual unions. While the entire group of survivors shares some of the affects and practices associated with "family" in its heteronormative sense (economic interdependence, primary affective bonds, and shared domestic space, for example), heterosexual couples and child/parent units are granted primacy over the group as a whole, leaving the heteronuclear family intact even in a post-apocalyptic world that in many ways might seem to require a more expansive and heterogeneous network of kinship and community. The ultimate neoliberal world, *The Walking Dead* reveals the centrality of disability and sexuality to global capitalism, even when that political economy has been annihilated.

Zombies as Others, Others as Zombies

If disability and sexuality shape the ways humans navigate the show's landscape, they also dovetail with race to construct the ubiquitous antagonist of the show: the viral zombie. Kristin Ostherr and Priscilla Wald have demonstrated that zombie narratives since the Cold War have heavily drawn on virology, as virology offers a ripe metaphor for cultural paranoia over potentially "infectious" people and ideas that could move undetected through supposedly "normal" populations. In these viral zombie narratives, anxiety over the loss of humanity has been represented as a theft of the body—which can be seen, for example, in novels and films such as *Last Man on Earth* (1964), *The Omega Man* (1971), and the recent *I Am Legend* remake (2007) starring Will Smith fighting viral zombies, all adapted from Richard Matheson's Cold War novel *I Am Legend* (1954).

The viral zombie also has a specifically racial, sexual, and disability history even as disability seems to be largely absent from most critical analysis. The zombie has roots in Afro-Haitian spiritual traditions and the zombie's blackness has historically been central to the horror it produces in the white United States imaginary. Drawing on racialized histories, zombies are often represented as mindless bodies, staggering around and often maimed, unable to fully communicate or participate in the social contract. In this way they join the list of marginalized populations who have similarly been constructed as the "others" against which the (neo)liberal social contract has been defined—most notably women, people of color, queers, trans* people, and people with disabilities.[6] Significantly these groups have been excluded precisely through their imagined lack of rationality and interdependence (rather than independence), as well as their embodiments that exceed white, cisgendered,[7] able-bodied norms. These historical constructions are deeply imbricated in popular constructions of viral zombies, particularly within *The Walking Dead*.

The specifically Afro-Haitian history of the zombie, which lurks in the shadows of all zombie representations including those on *The Walking Dead*, render even more clear the intertwining of sexuality, disability, and race. For example, the show explains the zombies as infected with a virus that brings death and life-in-death. Viral narratives in popular culture often mobilize sexual and racial panics that locate disease, disability, and death in sexually and racially "othered" bodies. In *The Walking Dead*, the zombie's historical racialization as Afro-Haitian and alignment with "improper" desire that can spread a virus to unsuspecting and undeserving humans raises the specter of HIV/AIDS and draws on even while it disavows this connection.

For example, in the first season the survivors head to the Centers for Disease Control, assuming that answers about the virus and zombies would be available there if anywhere. After meeting with the head researcher in charge of eradicating the zombie virus, Edwin Jenner, the group learns that no cure has been found, even though French scientists had come close. In choosing to highlight the CDC and American-French viral research relationships, the writers of the show invoke the specific history of the AIDS pandemic, as both played key roles in publicizing

HIV/AIDS in its early years (often with highly discriminatory effects) and constructing viral origin and transmission narratives that became the dominant ones circulating today. French and U.S. scientists share credit for discovering that HIV is the virus that leads to AIDS (Wald 244–45), and it was the CDC played a key role in associating certain scapegoated populations with HIV/AIDS and encouraging bans on specific populations donating blood (Treichler 47–60; Bayer and Feldman 20–27).

In the early years of the AIDS pandemic, Haitians (and later, African Americans) were targeted by the CDC and other health agencies as especially dangerous vectors of HIV, and in public health policy, immigration law, and popular cultural representation they were depicted as the "walking dead"—technically alive but soon-to-be-dead infected bodies capable of contaminating and killing "good unsuspecting Americans" who were white and middle class. This framework also shaped how Haitian immigrant women were positioned, as their reproductive and sexual practices were understood by the U.S. state to be capable of infecting the body politic with the HIV virus (Hannabach 32–35). Intertwining Haitian, gay male, and female subjects through their presumed shared "bad blood" that could spread viral disability in the form of AIDS, such histories reveal the ways the zombie has long been constructed through race, sexuality, and disability.

This historical construction heavily shapes how *The Walking Dead* represents both zombies and humans. What separates the zombies from the humans then is that the zombies are ruled by a need for human flesh that in the logic of the show is coded as anti-social. While the heterosexual desire valued on the show is also a desire for human flesh and a type of communion through that fleshly encounter, the zombies are constructed as different in the effects their desire has on their object: death. If heteronormativity and its attendant gender, racial, and class ideologies require a fleshly desire that reproduces heteronormativity in the form of children (presumed to grow up to be straight and start the process again), the zombies enact a rather queer form of desire and reproduction. The compulsory heterosexuality and compulsory able-bodiness that bind the show's humans together are entirely irrelevant to the zombies, whose desire for fleshy consumption defies gender, sexual, and familial boundaries. Zombified wives attack their human husbands, zombified adults rip apart their own children (and vice versa), and zombies of all genders descend in bloody orgies to satiate their cravings for consumption, sexual mores be damned. Essentially, the compulsory sexual norms structuring

U.S. society no longer bind the zombies nor shape their desires, even as the human survivors cling to them. Indeed, the zombies quite explicitly refuse marriage ties, coupledom, childrearing, and gender norms, desiring instead some rather queer corporeal communion and reproducing not through heterosexual intercourse but rather through promiscuous orgies of flesh and blood with bodies of all genders. The HIV/AIDS metaphor codes the zombie virus as a challenge to heteronormativity in ways similar to AIDS narratives that blamed the virus on sexually deviant bodies, including gay men (Wald), Haitian mothers (Hannabach), and sex workers (Treichler).

Heteronormativity is not the only social norm that the zombies of *The Walking Dead* violate, however. Robert McRuer writes that "compulsory heterosexuality is intertwined with compulsory able-bodiness; both systems work to (re)produce the able body and heterosexuality. But precisely because these systems depend on a queer/disabled existence that can never quite be contained, able-bodied heterosexuality's hegemony is always in danger of collapse" (McRuer 31). Quite literally, the zombies are the constitutive outside of the human, they are what the humans are defined against, and the zombies' sexual and reproductive practices are a key component of what renders them inhuman in this world.

Not only do the zombies perform a version of queer disability, they trouble the boundaries separating queer from straight, disabled from able-bodied, and human from inhuman. Further, they reveal the ways that disability functions differently for different kinds of subjects. For example, *The Walking Dead's* white men are continually rendered disabled through traumatic injury, yet this form of disability is "overcome" to avoid threatening white patriarchal heterosexuality. The show opens with the straight white male protagonist Rick in the hospital, waking from the coma he fell into after being shot. Staggering out of the hospital, still weak and injured, Rick realizes that his wife Lori and son Carl are missing, the city is seemingly empty of humans, and blood-thirsty zombies are running amok. It turns out that Lori and Carl have escaped with Shane, another sheriff who is Rick's partner, and are camped out in the woods with several other survivors. Thinking Rick dead, Lori and Shane begin a sexual relationship that is depicted as partly out of desire for each other and partly out of a desire to have Shane fill the open role of Carl's father, thus preserving the heterosexual nuclear family in the midst of chaos. The show essentially begins in a place of straight white male disability, which is overcome through Rick's reclamation of his physical strength, leadership abilities, and heterosexual family. Later on, Rick and his newly reclaimed wife and son join up with a few other human survivors to form the core group of protagonists. Eventually confronting Shane about his affair with Lori, Rick further solidifies his right of sexual access to Lori as well as his control over the reproduction of white masculinity exemplified by his relationship with his son Carl.

Unlike Rick's law-and-order form of straight white masculinity, another of the core group members, Merle, embodies a specifically racist, misogynist, and homophobic "white-trash" form of masculinity. After repeatedly harassing the women and people of color in the group, threatening the group's survival, Merle is handcuffed to a rooftop by Rick and left to die by the women and T-Dog, an African American man who Merle had a history of attacking. To avoid being eaten by zombies, Merle is forced to cut off his hand, rendering him an amputee who eventually finds and joins the suburban enclave of Woodbury, which is introduced in Season 3 and which I address below. Merle's amputation, while represented as traumatic, does not threaten his masculinity or white supremacist claims to bodily and cognitive superiority. In fact, while in the town of Woodbury Merle devises a weaponized prosthetic that he uses to attack zombies and threaten human characters—the prosthetic consists of a metal tube with a bayonet attached to the end, essentially turning his amputated arm into a stabbing phallus. In Woodbury, Merle uses this prosthetic to attack Glenn, an Asian American man who belongs to the core group of protagonists, as well as help the Governor of Woodbury sexually assault Maggie,[8] another member of the core group and Glenn's girlfriend. Essentially, the amputation that might have challenged Merle's claim to violent white heterosexual masculinity is "overcome" through technology that in fact bolsters and expands the violent ways such an institution can manifest.

There are a number of other instances of white male disability throughout the show, and all are presented as sudden and unexpected. For all of these characters, disability and bodily disruption are experienced as a break in their normal life course, a sudden interruption to the physical abilities, sexual access, and economic future to which straight white masculinity has historically been granted entitlement. The trauma each of these characters experiences is predicated upon not expecting disability to play a role in their life, at least until old age. In some ways, the zombie apocalypse might even be seen to allay fears of disability in old age, as the human characters don't even know if they will live that long. Further, rather than challenge the sexual, racial, and corporeal norms governing the world of *The Walking Dead,* these experiences of disability all shore up such norms. As David Serlin argues in *Replaceable You,* people with disabilities or with bodies considered "different" can often be reincorporated into the body politic through prosthetic and other medical technologies that have historically been made available to white men (Serlin 2). However, what about disabled bodies that do not have access to these technologies of social incorporation? Those irredeemably queer bodies, those bodies that are rendered the constitutive outside to the social, and whose disabilities are rendered not through sudden, unexpected traumatic injury but rather through historical processes of racialization, sexualization, and gendering enjoy no such reincorporation.

In contrast to the white men who experience disability as sudden and surmountable, the women and people of color in the show are disabled in more structural and sustained ways. Lori, who is entirely defined in relation to the men in her life (Rick's wife, Carl's mother, Shane's lover), becomes pregnant during the second season and is unsure of the fetus's father. Her pregnancy is presented as "disabling" both her and the rest of the group, as it is the reason why characters are forced to risk their lives obtaining pregnancy tests and baby formula, the reason why the group cannot move as quickly or as strategically as the male leaders desire, and the reason why Rick and Shane fight with each other. Eventually, Lori's pregnancy is presented as the reason why Lori's son Carl is forced to kill his mother, to save the baby and prevent its zombification. Lori's dependency upon the group is attributed to her pregnancy, and sets her apart from the other women characters. While almost all of the women on the show are dependent upon men for survival, support, and basic human existence, pregnancy in particular is pathologized. Feminist scholars have been right to critique the pathologizing ways pregnancy has historically been constructed as a disabling condition in legal and cultural frameworks that take white masculinity as their norm (Samuels 55–56). However, feminist disability studies scholars have also pointed out that this critique also often leaves intact the ableist assumption "that disability is inherently contaminating and that certain bodily conditions themselves are disabling" (Hall 6). In the framework of the show, women in general and pregnant women in particular are rendered disabled not in the sudden, surmountable ways the white men are, but rather in their very constitution by the social order that defines them as dependent.

Relatedly, the African American characters on the show are disabled in ways quite different from the white characters. In *Social Death:*

Racialized Rightlessness and the Criminalization of the Unprotected, Lisa Marie Cacho argues that "disease and disability figure centrally whenever there is the need to represent state-sanctioned violence as necessary for national survival [because] disability is the language of devaluation, contagion, and control" (69). In the history of U.S. law and culture, queerness, non-binary gender, and non-whiteness have been construed as disabilities that justified state and extra-state intervention.[9] Unlike the white characters on the show who suddenly become disabled yet have their sexual and gender propriety remain intact, the African American characters are positioned as constitutive "others" who must be eliminated or managed in much the same way diseases are. In all three seasons of the show broadcast so far, African American men have been killed, harmed, and incarcerated disproportionately to the white characters (men and women both). For the most part the show itself is entirely uninterested in interrogating the racism at work in this representation. However, a brief scene in Season 2 opens the possibility for critique even as it shuts it down. In "Bloodletting," the second episode of the season, T-Dog and the other characters realize that a wound T-Dog had suffered when cutting his arm on a rusted car frame has become infected. The blood infection has been getting worse, and T-Dog begins to fear for his survival. Significantly, his fear focuses not only on the zombies but white humans and their historical propensity for racist violence. Speaking with Dale, the older white grandfather-type of the group, T-Dog notes the precarity of both blackness and disability in the neoliberal zombie world:

> T-DOG: "They think we're the weakest. What are you? 70?"
> DALE: "64."
> T-DOG: "And I'm the one black guy. You realize how precarious that makes my situation?"
> Dale: "What the hell are you talking about?"
> T-DOG: "I'm talking about two good-ol'-boys cowboy sheriffs [Rick and Shane] and a redneck [Dale] whose brother [Merle] cut off his own hand.... Who in that scenario do you think is going to be the first to get lynched?"

This scene is exceptional in its direct address of structural racism and white supremacy, as well as the ways it links both to ableism. T-Dog correctly notes that black bodies have always had more to fear from the white state than the other way around, given the histories of racialized slavery, mass lynchings, and criminalization/incarceration—all of which have been justified as protecting white, heteronuclear families from black male threats. Similarly, he links race to disability, noting the ways disability in the form of Dale's old age and his own blood poisoning make them likely targets of violence from the other white characters, as well as the neoliberal world itself. Dale here speaks as the "good white liberal" who cannot believe that race and disability would matter in the biopolitical context of the apocalypse (partly because he cannot understand racism and ableism as structural, as something other than individual prejudice), but T-Dog points out that racism and disability have always grounded U.S. state practices and heteronormative community formations, as well as histories of visual representation. Zombies or no zombies, black life has always been rendered precarious in the U.S. state and visual culture even as that black precarity has grounded the construction of the white, bourgeois heteronuclear family. Black people have historically been enslaved, tortured, lynched, murdered, raped, and incarcerated so that white heterosexual family life can be enshrined. Similarly, compulsory able-bodiness lives at the heart of U.S. politics and culture. In a rare moment of explicit critique, T-Dog and the show itself forces viewers to confront the ways race, sexuality, and disability dovetail not merely in the fictional and futural world of the zombie apocalypse, or even in the present day world of the viewers, but across the entire history of the United States. Just when we think the show might be opening up space to critique the ideologies that thus far the show seems deeply invested in maintaining, the moment is closed down. Dale reduces T-Dog's structural critique to hallucinations caused by a fever, and the show cuts over to the white characters' escapades in the woods. At the end of this remarkable scene, ultimately structural racism and ableism are reduced to the delusional fantasies of a black disabled man in need of cure. Despite this attempt at foreclosure though, the show can't manage to entirely erase the lingering effects of T-Dog's radical and structural critique of compulsory white heteronormativity and its attendant compulsory able-bodiness. T-Dog is eventually killed off, as are all of the black male characters, save one—Tyreese—as of the time of this writing (the end of Season 3). Yet his critique seems to haunt the show's subsequent episodes, demonstrating how possibilities for resistance to the show's ideologies lurk within the very fabric of visual culture itself.

Sexual Politics and Queer Crip Possibilities[10]

If T-Dog's scene opens up a critique that even the apparatus of the show can't entirely close down, the representation of another African

American character—Michonne—further explores the queer crip possibilities at work in *The Walking Dead*. It is true that *The Walking Dead* is deeply invested in heteronormativity and seems unable to deal substantially with explicitly gay, lesbian, or bisexual identities. Indeed, there are neither self-identified LGBTQ characters nor same-gender sexual encounters in three seasons of the show, leaving viewers with the impression that the show's producers think that all the queers in the prominent gay tourism location of "Hot-lanta" have either been eaten by zombies or become zombies themselves. No self-identified queer characters in Atlanta seems about as plausible as the extremely low number of African American characters in a city that is known for its very large and vibrant LGBTQ and African American populations.[11] However, just because there are no self-identified LGBTQ characters does not mean there are no queers, any more than the fact that nobody saying the word "disabled" on the show means that disability is absent. Indeed, if a queer crip reading of the show looks for and values moments when heteronormativity, white supremacy, and compulsory able-bodiness are troubled and exceeded, the character of Michonne offers some incredibly rich queer crip pleasures. From her introduction to the series all the way through her every scene, Michonne remains the most resistant and "othered" body on the show. Simultaneously marked as African American, queer, butch, and disabled, Michonne represents all that the show seems to be working against. Yet because of this she provides one of the clearest examples of the tenuousness of compulsory heterosexuality, compulsory able-bodiness, and compulsory whiteness in post-apocalyptic Atlanta.

Michonne is introduced in the last scene of Season 2. In it, the camera follows Andrea, a young white woman and one of the core group of survivors, fleeing zombies in the woods while trying to find the rest of the group that has abandoned her, thinking her already dead. Pinned down by a zombie and about to be killed, Andrea is saved by a hooded, sword-wielding figure who swiftly decapitates Andrea's attacker. This savior turns out to be Michonne, who drags behind her two black, shackled zombies that have had their arms and mouths brutally cut off. Michonne's physical prowess is established in her first action and repeated throughout subsequent scenes as she easily slices through attacking zombies, outruns and out fights most of the men in the show, and wields her katana sword with a master's skill. Comfortable with weapons and physical violence, Michonne waits for no savior and rejects dependency on men, distinguishing her from all of the other women on the show. She is coded as butch in relation to the other women characters, queering her gender presentation. Her hair is in braids, she wears no apparent makeup, and perhaps most tellingly, she walks with her head held high, physical prowess, and even a bit of a swagger—all visual signifiers that in the world of the show are only attributed to men, never women. Considering that all of the white women on the show are coded as feminine, we might be wary of the racism at work in constructing femininity itself as white and thus excluding Michonne, particularly given the U.S. history of excluding black women from femininity[12] and queer black women from queer femme communities (Bryan 147). Indeed, there are very few African American women on the show including Jacqui, a mother and wife who kills herself at the CDC; and Sasha, a member of another survivor group who eventually joins the Governor at Woodbury. However, these other black women are also quite feminine in relation to Michonne, which renders her butchness not as synonymous with black womanhood per se but rather as something that explicitly queers her in contrast to the other black and white women.

In addition to her gender presentation, Michonne is queered through her emotional and erotic attachments. After saving Andrea, the two women become close, with Michonne tending to and often risking her life to save Andrea from various illnesses and attacks as they live and travel together for several months.[13] Throughout the first half of Season 3, while there is no sex depicted between them, their relationship is visualized through tropes associated with romantic and sexual coupledom: they are framed by the camera as physically close to one another, they touch often (particularly significant considering how rare it is for other characters to touch or be touched by Michonne), their emotional commitment is clearly to each other, they embody a vaguely butch-femme dynamic, and, perhaps most telling, Michonne becomes very jealous when Andrea's emotional and bodily attention shifts to another sexual partner. When Andrea begins a sexual relationship with the Governor of Woodbury, a terrifyingly brutal and abusive character whose violence is immediately obvious to Michonne, the women essentially experience a break-up. Citing the long-standing and offensive stereotype in lesbian cinema, literature, and cultural productions of the supposed "straight girl" who leaves the supposed "real lesbian" for a man, *The Walking Dead* renders their break up legible to audiences who have already learned to read the codes signifying their erotic and emotional entanglement. Richard Dyer explains that visual culture often relies upon iconography to signify homosexuality without having to (or being able to) explicitly depict it, using "a certain set of visual and aural signs which immediately bespeak homosexuality and connot[ing] the qualities associated, stereotypically, with it" (Dyer 300). By employing camera angles, framing, costumes, blocking, and eye line matches that we have been trained to read as signifying sexual coupledom, indeed the same ones used in the show to represent heterosexual couples such as Lori/Rick and Maggie/Glenn, *The Walking Dead* can plausibly render Andrea and Michonne a lesbian couple and make their relationship central to the narrative without ever having to explicitly declare it. Given the obvious coding of this relationship, we might wonder after the show's coyness. However, doing so forgets the historic relationship between onscreen homosexuality and connotation,[14] as well as what Danae Clark[15] and Katherine Sender[16] call "gay window dressing": the strategic usefulness of deploying ambiguous signifiers that can be read as gay or straight, depending upon the audience. In this way, Michonne can be queered through her removal from normative constructions of gender (femininity) and race (whiteness), thus offering a momentary critique of those ideologies, even while the show as a whole can maintain its overarching ideological investment, much in the same way T-Dog's critique functions.

Michonne's queerness is additionally marked through disability in ways that reveal the intertwining of racial, sexual, and gender norms. After being ambushed by Merle and the Governor's men, Michonne and Andrea are kidnapped and taken to Woodbury where they encounter the Governor for the first time. Michonne is immediately suspicious of the man and refuses to engage with him in any way, plotting their escape. The Governor is also immediately suspicious of Michonne, and troubled by her gender presentation, ease with weapons, and protection of Andrea. Most particularly, Michonne's refuses to answer the Governor's questions or engage with the social systems he represents, instead remaining silent and glowering. The white patriarchal town of Woodbury demands that this black, queer, butch body explain herself in its terms, and she continually refuses to engage or acknowledge these norms as valid. The show constructs Michonne as disabled in this context in much the same way people with non-normative communication strategies are assumed to be developmentally disabled, stupid, or mad. For example, stereotypes of the "mad woman," the "retard," the "stupid person of color," and the "stoic butch" who "just won't communicate" reflect this configuration, aligning all of these figures with the zombies in the show who similarly employ nonnormative communication strategies that the humans cannot or will not comprehend.[17] While it may seem surprising to read Michonne as disabled (after all, she is one of the most physically capable characters and doesn't sustain any long-term serious injuries through Season 3), disability studies reminds us that disability is constructed by culture, as it is cultural institutions that "disable" particular bodies through constructing them as "other." In this way, Michonne's blackness, queerness, communication practices, affects, and butchness are all rendered "disabilities" in the world of the show, disabilities that exceed and ultimately critique the ideologies of compulsory able-bodiness, compulsory heterosexuality, and compulsory whiteness.

Part of what frustrates the Governor about Michonne is her refusal of the gender norms, sexual practices, and racial hierarchies that the Governor and Woodbury represent, as well as her revealing of the brutal violence that undergird them. From their first introduction, Michonne reads the Governor as violent and dangerous. In contrast to the zombies, whose violence and threat to the core group of survivors is obvious to all of the characters, the Governor's threat remains hidden to all but Michonne. Unlike Andrea, she never buys into the façade of a social contract and a community based around (coerced) consent. She recognizes from the beginning the brutal and constitutive violence that undergirds Woodbury's social order, which includes torturing zombies in the name of scientific experimentation, and refuses to play along. For this, the Governor absolutely hates her. The show tries to suggest that his brutal and terrifying rage stems from specific actions of hers (such as killing his daughter, who is a zombie), but this is ultimately unconvincing as his hatred of this black, queer, butch body is more clearly tied to her very being rather than any specific actions she takes. As the show pits Michonne and the Governor against each other for the affections of Andrea, it subtly invokes sexual histories of race and disability whereby white heteronormativity is defined against and through racialized queer disability. While the show itself does not seem interested in critiquing these histories, indeed its conservative politics cause it to uphold and naturalize them, Michonne persists, fiercely attacking those who attack her and her loved ones, and refusing to allow such a system to define her desires, embodiment, or relationships.

As is clear, AMC's *The Walking Dead* offers a rich site to analyze the ways that sexuality, disability, gender, and race intertwine in contemporary zombie media. Further, it elucidates the histories of violence that stitch together global capitalism, compulsory able-bodiness, and white heterosexual patriarchy. The show raises complicated questions about these histories and offers moments of disruption that are never entirely smoothed over by the narrative attempts at closure. A queer disability studies reading elucidates queer and resistant possibilities throughout the show, particularly regarding the intertwining of race, sexuality, and disability in zombie representations. Placing the show alongside the other zombie media examined in this book, we can also further trace the ways political, cultural, and economic systems rise again long after their supposed death. Ultimately, *The Walking Dead* demands that we reckon with the radical possibilities of non-normative bodies in all of their queer, disabled, and racialized forms. If zombie representations carry with them long histories of violence and exploitation, then critical reading practices can intervene in these histories and construct other, more heterogeneous socialities.

NOTES

1. The television show is adapted from Robert Kirkman, Tony Moore, and Charlie Adlard's comic book series of the same name. Due to space constraints, this essay focuses on the television show only. The comics contain significant differences in narrative and character development, which renders some of the details of my argument only applicable to the television show. For example, in the television show, Michonne (who I analyze extensively later in this essay) is a much queerer character than she is in the comics, and in the show the narrative information about viral transmission and the zombie virus is discovered in a different manner (and through a different character) than in the comics. Many *Walking Dead* television audiences are also fans of the comics, and analyzing how those transmedia audiences render intertextuality might make for an interesting larger project.

2. See for example Christie and Lauro; Moreman and Rushton; McAlister.

3. For more on queer disability studies, see Kaefer; McRuer; McRuer and Mollow; McRuer and Wilkerson.

4. Trans* refers to all non-cisgendered people, including transgender people, transsexuals, transvestites, genderqueers, gender non-conforming people, and others.

5. It is important to keep in mind that these marginalized groups have been historically written out of the social contract; indeed they are the bodies against which liberalism (and neoliberalism) has been defined. Through unequal suffrage laws, slavery, discrimination in housing and employment, mass criminalization and incarceration, ableist constructions of public space, colonial genocide, heterosexist and privatized health care systems, and racist immigration laws, these populations have disproportionately been denied the basic means of survival to begin with, and then are blamed in neoliberal discourse for being "drains" on the state coffer and used as justification for cutting public services. For more on these histories, see Spade.

6. In making this claim, I do not mean to equate the historical ways these populations have been and are defined, nor do I mean to reproduce the violent analogies proclaiming these populations mutually exclusive. Rather, following interdisciplinary social justice scholars I want to emphasize how these populations have been historically produced against the white, male, heterosexual, able-bodied citizen through shared discourses of medicine, law, political policy, economics, and popular culture (Cacho; Chen; Smith; Spade; Mogul, Ritchie, and Whitlock).

7. Cisgendered refers to people whose assigned gender and gender identity align; in other words, people who are not transgendered.

8. Merle incarcerates Maggie and plans to interrogate her about the rest of the group's whereabouts. The Governor tells Merle that he will take over, at which points the Governor proceeds to sexually assault her and threaten her with rape. While Merle does not directly assault Maggie in this scene, he sets up the situation, enables the Governor's actions, and defends the behavior afterwards.

9. The history of the eugenics movement is but one evocative example of this. Throughout the 19th and 20th centuries, the term of "feeblemindedness" functioned as a catch-all category that physicians and lawmakers attributed to lesbians, gay men, transgender people, bisexual people, sex workers, African Americans, Native Americans, people with physical and mental disabilities, unwed mothers, poor and homeless people, and immigrants to justify forcibly sterilizing them (Cacho; Wilkerson; Hall; Garland-Thomson; Ordover; Briggs; Schweik).

10. I draw here on the work of Carrie Sandahl and other disability studies scholars who argue for "crip" as both a radical adjective and verb analogous to and intertwined with "queer." For Sandahl, "cripping spins mainstream representations or practices to reveal able-bodied assumptions and exclusionary effects. Both queering and cripping expose the arbitrary delineation between normal and defective and the negative social ramifications of attempts to homogenize humanity" (37).

11. See E. Patrick Johnson; Howard.

12. See Somerville.

13. The relationship between Michonne and Andrea is significantly different between the television show and the comic series. In the show, it is the central relationship for both characters in Season 3. In the comics, the two women barely know each other and do not have any kind of intimate relationship.

14. See D. A. Miller.

15. Clark discusses gay window dressing in "Commodity Lesbianism."

16. Sender discusses gay window dressing in *Business Not Politics.*

17. For more on how communication norms have been used to construct these figures in popular culture, medicine, law, and even queer communities, see Gilbert and Gubar; Hall; Garland-Thomson; Gates; Halberstam *Female Masculinity.*

Re-Animating the Social Order

Zombies and Queer Failure

TREVOR GRIZZELL

Zombies are failures. Whether it is in the realm of reproduction, control, or life itself, zombies fail to fit into the social order in ways that make sense, and instead have a knack for bringing about the failure of society at-large. In contemporary popular culture, works like *The Walking Dead* prominently feature zombies as plot devices, with zombies infecting characters with unknown pathogens, making spaces unlivable, and creating a generalized sense of panic that serves to push the narrative forward. I do not think it is a coincidence that queer people have frequently been accused of these same actions and similarly seen as less-than-human and societal failures, with accusations of contagion and difference similarly upholding normative standards of intimacy and life. It is this articulation of queerness and the zombie that I analyze, asking how the figure of the zombie might offer new visions of queer politics. As Judith Butler questions in an analysis of violence and mourning post–9/11, "if the humanities has a future as cultural criticism, and cultural criticism has a task at the present moment, it is no doubt to return us to the human where we do not expect to find it, in its frailty and at the limits of its capacity to make sense" (*Precarious Life* 151). Along these lines, I call on a variety of contemporary and historical works in cultural theory and criticism to suggest we might find in the zombie new perspectives on failure and the human (and non-human, for that matter) that may give us a certain queer view of culture, a reconceptualization (or what one might call a re-animation) of the social order that gestures towards a politics of the zombie that might be, in its seeming elision of life and meaning, more livable and meaningful for queers and other non-normative persons. Through this queer re-thinking of the zombie, I want to continue critical work begun by other scholars that questions what meanings we might gather from the supposedly meaningless and anti-social zombie, and reveal the ways in which the zombie can encourage us to rethink how we understand life, intimacy, and interactions between the human and non-human.

To talk about the politics of the undead is in many ways to take part in a type of theorizing that might seem unnecessary, wasteful, or unconnected to real-world concerns; zombies aren't exactly knocking down the doors of the average citizen on an everyday basis, after all. As numerous scholars have shown, however, the *ideological* issues present in depictions of the zombie are extremely pertinent; definitions of life and death (and the meaning attached to these definitions), notions of proper kinship and reproduction, and rhetorics of control and excess serve to buttress innumerable inequalities in contemporary society. Even if the subject matter may seem silly or illogical, that shouldn't stop us as critics from engaging with it; if anything, this underlying assumption of uselessness should be immediately suspect and indicative of a critical gap worth examining. In *The Queer Art of Failure*, Judith Halberstam encourages us to engage these seemingly "childish and immature notions of possibility" in order to divine new ways of encountering and understanding the world and its underlying components and structures (23). In many ways I am engaging with her notion of low theory, a type of theorizing that "makes its peace with the possibility that alternatives dwell in the murky waters of a counterintuitive, often impossibly dark and negative realm of critique and refusal" (2). It is in the pursuit of low theory that I find myself knee-deep in the charnel house, digging through discarded parts to find meaning in seemingly meaningless corpses, a vibrancy in death that might let us live, if not better, at least differently.

The core lens through which I am examining the figure of the zombie is that of queer failure, exemplified in recent theoretical work by Halberstam's *The Queer Art of Failure*. As Halberstam asks, "what rewards might failure offer us?" (3). Rather than being simply an inability to succeed and an impetus to "do better," instead failure might be reimagined as an opening for critical intervention or even an intervention in and of the social itself. From a queer theoretical perspective, the failure to complete a task or live up to a normative standard is a crucial moment in which ideology and behavior are incongruent. I argue that in examining these incongruities, and even purposefully situating ourselves alongside them, we can discover deeper effects of failure and how it calls attention to alternate ways of doing or being, or at least provides respite from the never-ending call to be interpellated in the social order, to "make sense."

I will examine three main classes of failures in which the zombie takes part. First, I look at the ways in which definitions of kinship and reproduction are remade in the wake of the zombie, looking specifically at the symbolic death of the Child and queer forms of intimacy and reproduction. Second, I suggest that the concepts of animacy and necropolitics illustrate the failures of life and vitality to accurately define and represent the world post-zombie, opening spaces to form new ways of understanding agency and meaning-making. Finally, I analyze the zombie's engagement with rhetorics of control, excess, and purity through its inability to contain itself bodily and behaviorally, its inherent impurity, and the ways in which the excess of ideology plays out in zombie literature. In these three classes of failure (family/life/control) exist a wealth of contradictions, paradoxes, and elisions that call attention to new or alternative forms of existence and intimacy that we might call queer or critical because of their (sometimes violent) questioning of implicit norms that disenfranchise those whose identities or actions lie outside of the bounds of the social order.

Failure I: Babies Making Babies

In a memorable sequence from director Zack Snyder's 2004 remake of germinal zombie film *Dawn of the Dead*, an at-term pregnant woman is bitten by a zombie inside of the mall that survivors are using as a refuge. Fearful that she will "turn" into a zombie and infect others with whatever contagion causes zombification, her male partner ties her to a bed but does not kill her. Soon after, she begins labor and seemingly dies; she quickly re-animates as a zombie and gives birth to her child. When another survivor comes to check on the couple and finds that the mother has turned, she shoots the zombified woman, causing a firefight in the room that leaves everyone dead. When the other survivors elsewhere in the mall hear the gunshots and come to investigate, they come across the dying shooter and quickly determine that a gunfight had taken place. Examining the other bodies in the room, they find a small bundle of cloth in the father's arms. After opening it up, the audience is presented with a close-up of what looks to be a dead child, its pale blue skin and sunken-in eye sockets seemingly lifeless. The baby then flings its arms wide and screams, revealing grey eyes that mark it as undead. The audio of the baby screaming continues while the image cuts away to the hallway outside of the room, and a gunshot is heard silencing the zombified child while the film leaves the viewer with slow-cutting images of empty locations in the mall.

This striking scene, and the seconds-long existence of this zombified baby, provides a wealth of imagery and incitements to thought that epitomize, in many ways, how the zombie brings about and evinces the failure of the standard family structure, reproduction, and intimate human interactions. Following Mel Chen's statement that "queering is ... violating proper intimacies," I argue that in the restructuring of human intimacies, the zombie can be seen as engaging in a process of queering the social order (11). For my definition of intimacy, I refer to Staci Newmahr's discussion in her work *Playing on the Edge*, in which she states that intimacy "depends on the cultivation of a belief in the privacy of a particular experience. What is intimate is that which is normally not apparent, accessible, or available" (171). I argue, through looking specifically at this sequence from *Dawn of the Dead*, as well as more general conceptualizations of zombies in other fictional works as they relate to reproduction, the body, and toxicity, that zombies undermine simplistic understandings of bodies through their violent, unthinkable acts that radically restructure normative models of the family, (a)sexual reproduction, and pleasure.

If the proper intimate relationship between mother and child is one in which the mother gives the gift of life to a child, this scene from *Dawn of the Dead* begins to queer (re)production by instead presenting a mother giving *undeath* to her baby. The womb itself becomes a queer mechanism here, as it inverts the general understanding of birth practices (giving undeath rather than life). Thinking through Sara Ahmed's conceptualization of orientations, from its queer birth this undead child is already oriented away from the social order and towards alternative forms of development and reproduction. As Ahmed argues, "the orientations we have toward others shape the contours of space by affecting relations of proximity and distance between bodies" (3). As a zombie, the child will seemingly never grow up, in the sense of puberty and body development, and as such will never be able to reproduce in the normative method; in this respect, the process of infection has oriented the child away from normative models of intimacy and love.[1] Instead, however, the child would be able to (re)produce as a zombie does: through the act of biting or sharing blood or other bodily fluids. This queer act of (re)production is not limited due to qualities of sex, gender, or even species as standard sexual reproduction is; zombification as a process knows few limits other than necessitating a subject for infection. The incest taboo, as well, ceases to be meaningful in a system in which children may (re)produce with parents or siblings may infect siblings with no extraneous consequences of consanguinity. One might think back to the *Night of the Living Dead* and the scene in which the young girl Karen is found feeding on her father who soon reanimates as a zombie, for example, to see how a child can become the giver of undeath to her parents.

Definitions of bodily pleasure and intimacy are also complicated by the zombie, as the mouth for the zombie becomes the privileged site of bodily intimacy rather than the genitals and the point through which the zombie makes its bodily connections. This intimacy, however, is not explicitly sexual; on the contrary, it tends to be violent and frequently traumatic for victims of zombie bites or infection. As the definition of intimacy I presented earlier shows, intimacy does not have to be pleasant for either or both parties. After all, "to violate, and be violated, are intimate experiences" if we conceive of intimacy as gaining access to something thought to be inaccessible (Newmahr 176). In this way, the bite of a zombie could be seen as an intimate act for both parties; the bite victim experiences something thought to generally be off-limits or taboo (the bite of another person) as well as the foreknowledge (and accompanying anxiety, dread, and fear) that they will likely become a zombie and experience a heretofore unknown way of existing, while the zombie experiences the specific taste of the victim and transmits the otherwise-contained contagion to the victim. The violation of human skin by zombified human jaws creates a vision of intimacy that is at once horrifying and wondrous, life-ending and existence-creating; thanatos and eros combine in this almost inconceivable act that disrupts the meaning-making structures of the social order.

As these examples have hinted, intimacy is not a solely private concept. As Lauren Berlant states, "the inwardness of the intimate is met by a corresponding publicness" (1). Intimacy, as a private experience, is always understood relationally to other forms of action, and it is this liminal space between public and private that the figure of the zombie illuminates, bringing the intimate explicitly to the public. As many depictions of zombies in media show us, the act of a human being bitten or eaten by a zombie seems to be most horrifying when it is seen by others. The public display of an intimacy like violent infection or murder amplifies its cultural disruption, and we can see this even beyond zombie media and in current news. As recent events have shown us with Rudy Eugene, the man referred to in some media reports as the Miami Zombie who was recorded on video eating the face of another man while supposedly high on bath salts (with this video quickly making its way around the Internet, accompanied with images of the victim's devoured face [see Koplowitz]), all intimacy is not treated equally. To know someone on the level of taste, or to feel how one's teeth might sink into another person's flesh and the force needed to remove skin, is to cross the line of propriety and know *too much* of another person, and for this act to be seen or recorded is even more anathema (while at the same time being a curiosity for a public discouraged from seeing such intimate acts).

These taboo forms of intimacy are not limited solely to material bodily interactions; even the meaning of time and age affect what forms of intimacy are seen as acceptable, and the zombie similarly disassembles these understandings. The child is not the only age-defined figure that is given new meaning in the zombified social order. The temporal shift brought about by the zombie also changes the meaning of what it means to be elderly. Bodies that may have been considered past their prime, waning and quickly losing usefulness, once zombified become equalized with bodies that may have once been youthful and far from the processes of decay that are thought to characterize old age. While the zombie still decays, it equalizes the process. The zombified child of *Dawn of the Dead* is the same as the elderly woman from the same film. In a similar way, the (re)productive capability of the elderly becomes awakened in the zombified form, with contagion taking the place of gametes. The elderly person, seemingly incapable of contributing to the continuation of society through their own reproductive processes, is now able to (re)produce a new social order, one in which the state of decay of one's body seems not to matter as long as one's brain is intact. Through its reworking and redefinition of time and the life cycle, the zombie calls attention to the ways that temporality affects our understandings of what sorts of intimacy are allowed for certain individuals (in this case, those of certain ages).

The figure of the Child as evinced by Lee Edelman in his work *No Future* provides a fantastic model for examining in greater detail the complex meanings of this zombie child. Edelman states that in the social order, the figure of "[the] Child remains the perpetual horizon of every acknowledged politics, the fantasmatic beneficiary of every political intervention" (3). Rather than representing a real child, Edelman discusses how the *idea* of the Child serves to prop up the social order in an unchanging state whose purpose is to "save the children," creating a future that is *re*productive (producing itself over and over again) rather than productive to protect the eponymous and imaginary Child.

If the Child in Edelman's formulation embodies innocence, propriety, and the continuation of society as-is, the zombie child embodies desire, chaos, and the beginning of a radically new form of being. At every point that the social order's Child is deployed to cover up realities of society or individual behaviors, the zombie child shows its instabilities. While Edelman's Child lacks desire or passion, the zombie child is id uncompromised. Where Edelman's Child is meant to remain a symbol for all that is pure, the zombie child destabilizes notions of children as pure and innocent, becoming a fully (re)productive subject at birth that is only held back from eating as it pleases by its physical being. When Edelman's Child gets trotted out whenever the social order is being threatened in order to buttress a flailing social order, the zombie child serves as a marker of a radically different (and productive rather than *re*productive) future.

In response to the Child of the social order, Edelman bases a model of queerness around the death drive, what he describes as "the inarticulate surplus that dismantles the subject from within," an excess within that serves to destabilize the subject (9). Through heterosexual reproduction (and the desire for gays and lesbians to take part in similar activities through creating families after the heterosexual model), the state is able to reproduce itself and finds its greatest use out of sexuality. Edelman, however, sees queerness as finding its place with an identification with the death drive and a denial of reason and the logics of life; queerness "attains its ethical value precisely insofar as it accedes to that place [of the death drive], accepting its figural status as resistance to the viability of the social" (9). Only through a denial of the social order and politics itself can queerness truly be queer, and with this definition, the zombie (and specifically the zombie child) embodies a form of queerness that is so radical it must be destroyed. The zombie child is not simply dangerous on a physical level; its *very existence* is a threat to the social order, as it represents radical possibilities that are inconceivable under social norms as they are. As such, the zombie child is never innocent, never a life worth saving (as so much political rhetoric surrounding abortion may tell us), only an unknowable Other in the path of the unrelentingly reproductive social order.

If we take Edelman's argument in a slightly different direction, we can see the ways in which women's bodies have been instrumentalized by the social order in order to stabilize and continue the existence of the state *vis-à-vis* the Child, such as through state incentives for having and rearing children, the outlawing of abortion, or the presentation of motherhood as a patriotic or moral act. While the social order of Edelman's Child holds mothering and heterosexual reproduction as stabilizing and necessary for the continuation and reproduction of life and the social order, in zombie culture the female capacity for reproduction takes on a *destabilizing* effect; the womb is no longer a safe haven for children but a possible incubator of the undead, its membranes and flows nurturing children with whatever contagions may be present in the environment. Female bodies as sites of reproduction become dangers rather than blessings, sites of disorientation rather than orientation, even if the child does not become infected by a zombifying contagion.

In the second season of AMC's television adaptation of *The Walking Dead*, Lori (the wife of Rick, the main character) becomes pregnant and wonders whether it is worth bringing a child into the newly chaotic and undead-filled world. Her acquisition of morning-after pills (which in the logic of the show would seem to cause an abortion) is greeted with anger from Rick, who strongly encourages her to keep the child. A season later, Lori's pregnancy leads to her death as she begins labor with the baby in breach position and another survivor must cut open her abdomen (with no anesthetic) to pull the baby out while Lori's son sits nearby. After its birth, the child (now named Judith) brings new needs to the group, in terms of cleaning supplies and formula that cause rifts and complications within the group. Rather than a symbol of society's continuation and naturally unending reproduction of itself, then, the Child (figured here as Judith) in this world becomes a marker of society's inability to reproduce itself without intense cultural, physical, and emotional work. While in the show Judith is presented as a symbol of hope, Edelman's reading of the Child brings an anxiety to this specific text that counteracts the normative progress narrative, instead creating space for us to question how we might re-figure or sidestep the social order as-is. She marks an unstable space in which hope is revealed to be not just a desire for a better future, but a desire for a *specific type* of future that relies on the recapitulation and reinforcement of normative structures (that may be outdated or no longer viable) to come into existence.

Failure II: Beyond Life and Death

In a scene from the first season of *The Walking Dead*, the character Andrea sits with her dying sister Amy, who has been bitten by a zombie, and waits for her to turn into a zombie. The sequence, shot from a variety of angles that imply Amy could awaken at any moment and attack Andrea, similarly infecting her with the zombie contagion, continues for an extended period of time, showing Andrea caressing Amy and talking to her. Even as Amy dies and lays motionless, Andrea still continues to talk to and hold her sister, getting even closer to her physically to the point that the audience feels increasing anxiety about an impending attack. Extreme close-ups of the sisters' faces and a swelling melancholy soundtrack add to this anxiety over the inevitable reanimation and its possible consequences for Andrea. When Amy finally turns into a zombie and begins groaning and grasping for any nearby flesh, Andrea pulls her sister in close to her own neck and strokes her hair a final time before pulling back and shooting her in the head, ensuring that she will no longer be re-animated.

The key paradox underlying the re-animatedness of the zombie is that in actuality, the body is never *not* animate. Processes of growth and decay continue in the human body after it dies, with bacteria, viruses, and microorganisms continuing to thrive in the body as an ecosystem. While the self (in the Cartesian sense of the mind) may have died off, the body does not cease to be meaningful; it literally lives on in both old and new forms, as habitat and nutrient for organisms of all types and as material. The zombie in one way, then, calls attention to an anxiety (whether founded or not) of human beings as creatures without "souls," as lacking an essential humanness, as being able to function without what we may think defines humans as sentient, whole beings. The horror of the zombie as a returned family member who may not remember the family or friends they may now be eating or attacking is not solely a fear of the fragility of the social order and unconventional forms of intimacy as referenced earlier, but also an attack on the very definitions held by culture at large on what counts as alive and/or animate.

These cultural anxieties surrounding life and animacy are explicated clearly in the work of theorist Mel Chen. Wondering "how [we might] think differently if nonhuman animals ... and even inanimate objects were to inch into the biopolitical fold," Chen wants to displace life as the center of biopolitics and introduce concepts that may offer new ways to ponder "how matter that is considered insensate, immobile, deathly, or otherwise 'wrong' animates cultural life in important ways" (6, 2). For these purposes she deploys the concept of animacy, which she defines as "a quality of agency, awareness, mobility, and liveness" (2). She argues that animacy gets deployed culturally in hierarchies, wherein the excess or lack of animacy makes subjects more or less meaningful or worthwhile. From an animal rights perspective, then, Chen's argument suggests that animals are perceived as less animate in the sense that they seemingly lack agency or awareness, and therefore their needs are not generally seen as worth much. When an animal is seen to be more animate or inspires animacy in people, however, these priorities can shift; we might think of how a seeing eye dog supports the animacy of a blind person (through mobility and awareness) or how pets (that inspire lively affective responses in people) easily gain more sympathy and legal protection than most livestock. At the bottom of the hierarchy we find organisms or objects that seem to have no vibrancy or animacy to them (such as dirt or mountains), and therefore warrant little protection that does not come from a place of economic or emotional concern.

People, as well, fit into these animacy hierarchies, as one must be properly animated to be considered human. Many racial stereotypes are rooted in these hierarchies; one might consider media portrayals of Latinos as hyperemotional, as being too animate, or portrayals of Asian-Americans as cold and unfeeling, lacking a proper level of animacy. Similarly, these hierarchies of animacy intersect with disability in a number of ways. Major funding has historically gone to find cures for disabilities such as para/quadriplegia that limit normative mobility, and recently research into curing autism (which has as some of its "symptoms" alternative forms of emotionality and nonnormative affective responses) has become a major fundraising cause.[2] Raced and disabled corporealities and psychologies that lie outside of the normative constraints of animacy must be condemned, curbed, or fixed, rather than understood or taken on their own terms.

Chen's ideas surrounding animacy continue the theoretical work attending to the concept of biopolitics, or an examination of the ways in which the state and individuals make sense of the world through the control, dissemination, or interaction with conceptions of life and their intersection with human bodies. Her complication of biopolitics, moving from Foucault's classic emphasis on life to one on animacy, leads us towards a more nuanced way of examining the zombie and its place in the social order. Where Chen sees the solution to biopolitics' emphasis on life as the intervention of animacy, however, Achille Mbembe's work instead presents the idea of necropolitics as a complication to biopolitics. While biopolitics in its standard form holds the distribution and control of life as the defining feature of sovereignty, Mbembe suggests that it is not only the distribution of life, but death as well that defines sovereignty. While biopolitics makes sense of government policies to allow life or take it away, it does not properly represent the state of terror, or "being in pain" as Mbembe puts it, deployed in the name of sovereignty in contemporary societies (39). In these situations, an economy of death comes about where control over death becomes an integral political issue. As Mbembe states, "Under conditions of necropower, the lines between resistance and suicide, sacrifice and redemption, martyrdom and freedom are blurred" (40). Looking at slavery as an example of how necropolitics has operated in the past, Mbembe points out how suicides committed by slaves once they were caught by slave catchers were instances of agency, "for death is precisely that from and over which I have power. But it is also that space where freedom and negation operate" (39).

In this way, Mbembe presents death as something that is not simply the negation of life, but a *productive* act or event in and of itself. This theme continues in his discussion of the work of Georges Bataille:

> Death is therefore the point at which destruction, suppression, and sacrifice constitute so irreversible and radical an expenditure—an expenditure without reserve—that they can no longer be determined as negativity. Death is therefore the very principle of excess—an *anti-economy*. Hence the metaphor of luxury and of *the luxurious character of death* [15].

Mbembe's remarks on necropolitics here provide us with a new lens for understanding the zombie as not simply the removal of reason, the destruction of order, the end of meaning, but instead as an *overabundance* of meaning, as a wealth of knowledge that cannot easily be interpellated into the social order. The physicality of the zombie reflects this, as well; the zombie is never singular, but always operates *en masse*. The hungry, desire-driven hordes of the undead overwhelm the social order as-such, and social structures must be re-ordered to deal with (if not accommodate) the non-normative behaviors and bodies of zombies.

To not be interpellated is not, however, an inherently pleasant place to be—on the contrary, the visibility of difference frequently leads to violence and attempts to force a subject to make sense (which we can see in the response of humans to zombies in most zombie literature), and Mbembe recognizes this in his model of necropolitics. Underlying Mbembe's reading of necropolitics, both contemporary and historical, is an inherent distrust of the Other:

> The perception of the existence of the Other as an attempt on my life, as a mortal threat or absolute danger whose biophysical elimination would strengthen my potential to life and security—this, I suggest, is one of the many imaginaries of sovereignty characteristic of both early and late modernity itself [18].

This model of necropolitics can be seen in the majority of zombie literature, directed towards both human and nonhuman Others. This perspective, fueled by paranoia, suggests an economy of life that is incapable of being sustained for extended periods without crashing. Mbembe himself purports as much when he asks, "What is the relationship between politics and death in those systems that can function only in a state of emergency?" (16). Along the borders of Mbembe's model, then, we can see traces of a utopian vision of politics that can account for radically nonsensical knowledge, a politics that may find in excess new methods for being rather than Others who become objects of paranoid suspicion and eventual destruction or assimilation.

Chen and Mbembe's models when read alongside one another give an even more complex view of life, death, animacy, and the place of the zombie in all of this. Read through Chen's analysis of animacy, Mbembe's necropolitics lets us see animacy as not only something that living things engage in, but as practices tied to things that may (soon) be dead or non-living, as well. When models of life and death begin to bleed into one another and when the choice to live and the choice to die are each considered part of a spectrum of animacy, it becomes an even more useful model for examining the zombie, a figure that is neither dead nor alive and acts with an unknown amount of agency. Through the zombie, this failure of life and death to be stable or accurately define what it might mean to be animate or lively becomes even more apparent, requiring us to think more deeply on how we define the subjectivity, usefulness, and agency of people, things, and creatures around us. Rather than objects devoid of meaning, Mbembe and Chen's models allow us to see zombies as critical figures in and of the social order in their excessive meanings that defy social control and bring us to question the meanings of life, death, and Otherness.

Failure III: Volatile Bodies

Going back as far as George A. Romero's infestation of a mall with zombies in *Dawn of the Dead* and its politicization of the zombie as an anti-capitalist figure (the consumer as mindless drone), the zombie has served for multiple artists as an allegory for human excess in a variety of forms, whether that be material, sexual, gastronomical, or emotional. Even for the living in zombified landscapes, excess is commonly presented as wholly negative with no redeeming qualities. To be excessive in the world of the zombie is in many ways to ask for death; overeating leads to sluggishness and a lack of supplies, rampant sex brings about complications in the form of children or difficult-to-treat disease, and wanton tears and crying call attention to one's vulnerability and location for dangerous Others, living and dead alike. To be a proper subject in the world of the zombie, then, is to be always in control of one's body, desires, and instabilities; to be human is to be in control, and to be zombie is to be embodied in excessive ways. Using theoretical work from Stacy Alaimo, María Lugones, and Mel Chen, and sequences from *The Walking Dead* as key texts, in this section I will discuss how the projection of excess onto the zombie both distracts from and accentuates the excess of human existence in contemporary American culture at the same time that it calls attention to ways of being that look beyond normative models of purity and control.

One of the key ways in which the zombie is excessive is in its toxicity and inability to contain its (pro)creative potential. As presented earlier, the zombie's non-normative methods of (re)production, coupled with its near-constant desire to feed, make it a model of toxicity that is defined in many ways by excess. While the genitals are frequently privileged as points of toxicity, leakage, or a general openness to other organisms, the queer (re)productive potential of the zombie extends our understanding of the body as a point of contact and intimacy with other bodies, creating what seems to be an excessive openness. The zombie puts forth an image of radical accessibility and openness, a body that permeates its surroundings as it is permeated by them. With its internal organs and fluids open to the world, entrails dragging along behind it as it shuffles along to (re)produce more zombies through its vaguely-defined contagions transmitted by the simplest of bodily contact, the zombie is intimate with the world and others in ways that living humans seem not to be.

While this bodily excess seems to be easily consolidated into the figure of the zombie, contemporary ecocriticism and science studies inform us otherwise. Ecocritic Stacy Alaimo argues for a conception of trans-corporeality, a "theoretical site ... where corporeal theories, environmental theories, and science studies meet and mingle in productive ways" which she sees centered around the idea that "the human is always intermeshed with the more-than-human world" (3). While mainstream cultural understandings of intimacy, interpersonal connection, and boundaries tend to assume that the body is a discrete object, Alaimo argues instead, calling on contemporary biology and cultural theory, that we must understand and examine how the human body is always connected with environment and other human and non-human beings and how these connections are articulated with systems of oppression. New definitions and conceptions of intimacy can become visible as models that privilege touch as the main method for intimate interfacing cease to be as meaningful, given that microscopic bits of others and the environment constantly enter our bodies through simple acts of living (eating, drinking, breathing, touching).

Through Alaimo's model, the zombie becomes visible as an explicitly toxic literalization of the transcorporeality of the human body, a being that suggests anxieties concerning purity and toxicity in its excessive contagious intimacy. In reading bodies not as discrete objects but instead as permeable objects that have a reflexive relationship with our environment, Alaimo's model encourages us to critically assess the ways in which we influence environments and how they might influence us in both material and ideological ways. In her model, the discrete categories of Subject and Object become blurred as we notice how intimately connected humans are with each other, as well as the objects and spaces around them, zombies included.

The viewer may find it difficult to believe Rick (a white man) as he tells Glenn (a Korean-American man) that race doesn't exist anymore in an attempt to halt a conflict between Glenn and a white supremacist early in the first season of *The Walking Dead*, as the show itself enacts standard racist and sexist tropes that put white men in charge and others in subordinate positions to either be protected (in the case of most female characters) or utilized when necessary as bodies for work or sacrifices for the plot (most characters of color). Beyond even the show's inability to escape from racist logics in its depiction of a dystopia where race no longer exists, is the fact that race *does* still matter to the survivors, in more ways than one. On a basic level, the survivors in *The Walking Dead*, and most zombie literature, take on a perspective that zombies are not like them in a process of counteridentification that labels zombies as a class separate from humans. This very process reflects a certain form of racism (for lack of a better word), one that displaces the Other of contemporary "real" society (racialized persons) for a new Other (the undead). While not the same, both of these situations rely on models of self/other that privilege one group over the other as rational, stable, controlled, and intelligent, leaving the dis-privileged half of the binary with qualities generally seen as negative: bestial, associated with the body, irrational, out of control.

Underlying each of these situations is a need for purity, a necessity to categorize and hierarchalize, privileging the purity of whatever side of a binary may be acceptable (whiteness, straightness) and denouncing the ability of the other side to ruin this sense of purity and rightness with as little as a single non-normative sex act or a perceived racial marker. This yearning for purity, for philosopher María Lugones, denies the complexities of existence, identity, and community. Lugones presents two models of attempting to understand identity differences, "curdling, or an exercise in impurity" and "splitting, or an exercise in purity" (123). While splitting (an atomistic view) attempts to create distinctions between the various parts that create a whole (whether that be a community or a person), something curdled (an organistic view) recognizes the interweaving, interrelated nature of the whole. In her model "something in the middle of either/or, something impure, something or someone mestizo, [is] both separated, curdled, and resisting in its curdled state"; in this impure subject's curdled state, it refuses to be ordered in a recognizable way (123).

The zombie, I would argue, encourages this model as well. As discussed above, the zombie fails to be defined by the social order. Rather, it exists in a space between life and death, human and non-human, sentient and bestial, calling attention to the inadequacy of these binaries to define the zombie, and in the process encouraging us to look more closely at the ways these binaries affect social subjects or communities. While we can read the zombie as encouraging this level of complexity in critical analysis, most zombie texts tend to engage in the same sorts of simplistic calls to unity and purity that we find in culture at large. To read the zombie as not separate from the human, then, is to take a more radical approach, one that might even go so far as to say that not only are zombies like us, but we are like zombies.

Rick's statement also reveals how the desire for a pure, unified humanity denies the cultural histories and effects of racism that go beyond epithets and even human-on-human violence. Even if race were to no longer consciously matter to the survivors, this does not change the fact that racism has already irradiated the soil, *literally*, through the material effects of racist ideology.[3] A "post-racial" society is always marked by its history of race, as is a "post-class" or "post-gender" system. The end of homophobia will not bring back the wooded cruising areas clearcut to try to keep communities free of perceived sexual perversion. Even the destruction of the human race will not remove dioxin and other toxic materials from the area once populated by workers at a PVC factory (or from their buried bodies, for that matter) that were considered "safe enough" to live in. To see the world from a trans-corporeal perspective, as the zombie might encourage us to do, is to see the lasting material effects of our cultural and ideological histories.

Conclusion

Through these texts and examples, I've attempted to curate a heteroglossic view of the zombie as producing new ways of being at the same time that it destroys or renders murky old ways of life (and death, for that matter). In cultural tropes surrounding zombies and in these examples specifically, the failures of the zombie to live up to the social order or reproduce it point to new, queerer ways of experiencing and understanding the body, identity, environment, and society. In its seemingly nihilistic actions, the zombie manages to bring about new forms of meaning and ways of looking at everyday phenomena, and so I continue to consider what it might mean to embody the zombie's politics. I align myself with Robert McRuer as he "argue[s] for the desirability of a loss of composure, since it is only in such a state that heteronormativity might be questioned or resisted and that new (queer/disabled) identities and communities might be imagined" (149). I think we may already have some models of this decomposing in zombie literature, instances where characters may, for one reason or another, start to connect with the undead in ways that refuse the dictates of the social order, in the process destabilizing norms. I think of the ending scenes of *Shaun of the Dead*, for example, in which we see humans coming to live with zombies as citizens in their own right. While we don't get a sense of the complete destruction of the social order here, as Edelman might desire, we see the gentle pulling apart of society and questioning of norms as romances and friendships form between the living and the undead, illuminating the failures described in this piece and how society might try to make sense of them. While zombies may not be an immediate threat to our livelihood, maybe in considering their effect on our culture and politics we might find more understanding, complex, and livable or enjoyable possibilities for those who operate outside of the norm and cannot, or choose not to, assimilate.

NOTES

1. A possible complication in this scenario is the father's protecting and caring for the child. At this point in the film, I think his actions actually act as more of a queering of the norm than a supporting of it, however, as we've previously seen that he is so indebted to a normative family structure that he would watch his wife become zombified and give birth to a zombified child rather than end her life and her "unnatural" birth. In this situation, the presence of the zombie queers the nuclear family, as it turns supposedly rational decisions (encouraging birth of child, protecting family) into irrational ones (proliferating the undead, protecting zombies).

2. For more on some of the issues surrounding autism and medical treatment, see Rosin.

3. Here I'm specifically thinking of the history of uranium mines built on Native land in the United States, and the subsequent worker exploitation and environmental degradation taking place that continues to this day in the name of "clean" nuclear energy.

Gay Zombies

Consuming Masculinity and Community in Bruce LaBruce's Otto; or, Up with Dead People *and* L.A. Zombie

Darren Elliott-Smith

Traditionally the vampire remains a clear "top" to the zombie's "bottom": within the undead cohort, the zombie is a marginalized upstart and notably sits outside the literary tradition. Often depicted as an uncharismatic and often comic creature, the zombie is often satirically deployed as a representation of "mindless" conformity or consumption. For James Twitchell the zombie is "an utter cretin, a vampire with a lobotomy" (Twitchell 15), and Kyle Bishop underscores the figure's "limited emotional depth, [its] inability to express or act on human desires." Being bound to physical action he suggests that the zombie "must be watched" (Bishop "Raising the Dead" 196). This suggests both a compulsion to look at the figure of the zombie and a *wariness* of a monster that must be kept at a remove, for fear of being "turned" or being infected.

Such anxieties also bear comparison with the guardedness inherent in homosexual panic. In recent queer-influenced horror film the zombie figure is used both as a cipher for homosexuality and for a sub-cultural critique *within* western gay male culture. This article focuses specifically on the shambling, semi-articulate, gay zombies from Bruce LaBruce's melancholic and pornographic zombie films *Otto; or, Up with Dead Peo-*

ple (2008) and *L.A. Zombie* (2010). LaBruce's appropriation of the gay zombie figure is used as a means of exploring sub-cultural anxieties within a white, bourgeois, homonormative community, but similarly the emphasis on zombie "performance" reveals Otherness as celebratory. LaBruce's *Otto; or, Up with Dead People* uses the zombie to attack both oppressive homophobia (in the film's poignant portrayal of zombie/queer bashing) and to critique the bourgeois homonormativity of its middle class Berlin clubbing milieu. His comic contemplation of the deadening gay scene reveals the isolation and disillusionment within certain gay communities. The film's depiction of the young gay zombie Otto as both "consumed" and a reluctant "consumer" (a satirical riff on gay male top/bottom sexual politics) locked within an inescapable capitalist ideology also points the finger at urban gay culture's role in the privileging of property.

The messy physicality of the zombie also connects with the zombie film's frequent utilization of pornographic tropes. The hard-core sexual elements in *Otto's* "gut-fucking" imagery magnify the gay man's oral eroticism in cannibalistic orgies that supplant anality with orality. LaBruce's follow up film *L.A. Zombie* develops *Otto's* hard-core scenes of necrophilic gay sex and, as such, forms its own critiques of gay men's erotic valorization of masculine forms as meat and the emerging zombification of a capitalist gay porn industry. Yet despite the radical potential of gay zombie sex as a method of alternative reproduction, it is often alienating rather than empowering.

Zombie Bottom Feeders

In George A. Romero's definitive series of zombie films (1978–2008), the zombie becomes identified with consumption rather than production, it becomes *counter*-productive, developing into a compulsive flesh eater. Romero's socio-political horror films are the first to conflate the figure with cannibalism in its ravenous corporeality, a new configuration that proved so effective that flesh eating was quickly established as a core trait of the cinematic zombie. Peter Dendle asserts that Romero "liberat[ed the figure] from the shackles of a master, and invested his zombies not with a function to serve, but rather a drive" (Dendle *The Zombie Movie Encyclopedia* 6). Though Romero's zombies lose their individuality *en masse*, their capitalist cannibalism reveals a contradictory desire to regain individual subjectivity via consumption, but also, conversely, a desire to "fit in" with the consumer community. Indeed, in the individual's aspiration for difference from others, a certain element of homogeneity is achieved resulting in a clonish sameness. This same homogeneity is also integral to queer appropriations of the zombie. White male homosexual culture also encourages a sameness defined by materialism, being accepted into the "scene" and an adherence to a hyper-muscular gym body image.[1] This recognizable difference-but-sameness is resonant with what Leo Bersani calls the homogeneity of homo-ness in same sex, "a desire for the same, from a perspective of a self already identified as different from itself" (Bersani "Is the Rectum a Grave?" 6). This also takes the form of a valorization of an ideal masculinity (which inevitably takes the form of macho heterosexuality) that the gay subject also dis-identifies[2] with.

So, What's So Queer About the Zombie?

The zombie manifests a somnambulistic, perpetually threatening and liminal sexuality that is bound to the corporeal and arguably has been treated with repugnance. In spite of the obvious analogies, the exposure of internal bodily spaces, bodily fluids and primal urges, it has remained largely an anti-erotic object. Gregory A. Waller concludes that zombies are not "sexual beings" at all and that they rely on an even more basic feeding instinct (flesh rather than blood) than the vampire (280). However in "Contagious Allegories: George Romero," Steven Shaviro considers Romero's postmodern zombie as a critique of the Western capitalist system perpetuated on mindless consumption that can be also read erotically. Shaviro writes that "zombies mark the rebellion of death against its capitalist appropriation ... our society endeavors to transform death into value, but the zombies enact a radical refusal and destruction of value" (84). In terms of erotic pleasure, it is via the viewers' identification with the victims on film during the zombies' attacks that they are subjected to both a threat of penetration and of being devoured. This can be paralleled with the subject's fear of his/her body being penetrated or consumed by another (sexually or otherwise) or, worse still, a fear of *actually enjoying* it. Shaviro concludes that the voyeuristic anticipation of watching and waiting for the zombies to attack their victims provides an erotic frisson of passive pleasure as a spectator which works to titillate the viewer, encouraging enjoyment in the implied orgasmic intensity of the climactic attack. This anticipation then gives rise to a jouissance[3] symbolized via the frenetic externalization of the body's insides spilling outward.

The cycle of European zombie films in the 70s and 80s foreground the figure's conflation of *sex* with *death*. The soft-core nudity present in Jesus Franco's, Lucio Fulci's, and Jean Rollin's zombie films are heavily influenced by the increasing availability and popularity of pornography and the aesthetic of what Russell calls the "fantastique [...] a sub-genre with a predilection for the erotic" (88). Yet in titles such as *Zombie Flesheaters* (1979) and *Zombie Holocaust* (1980) it is the *female* body that is eroticized. In such films it is not the zombie figure per se that is coded erotically, but rather it is the sexually charged methods in which the zombie *attacks*, tears open victims' and consumes flesh that are emphasized alongside the zombie's own body as essentially *penetrable* and *penetrating*, objectifying the corporeal in all its messy goriness. In this sense the zombie film's visualization of the vulnerable body also reconfigures it as a site of eroticized, penetrable sexual wounds. Such films often feature zombies thrusting fists and sinking teeth into the fragile bodies of their victims, who in turn, writhe in the implied orgasmic intensity of being turned inside out and devoured. As Russell points out,

> [Such films] create a disturbing link between physical pleasure and physical pain. These films frequently link sex with bodily trauma ... [at times] it seems as if bloody wounds and sexual orifices are on the verge of becoming interchangeable [131].

Whereas the erotic pleasure of zombie attacks remain implicit in these European titles (for the most part zombies do not "have sex"), in the representation of the *gay* zombie the erotic potential of the body as a penetrable/penetrating site of jouissance is explicitly realized. *Gay* zombie porn (and zombie porn per se) is first visualized in Vidkid Timo's *Night of the Living Dead* pastiche *At Twilight Come the Flesh-Eaters* (1998), which juxtaposes a low budget black and white porn parody of Romero's socio-political horror with behind the scenes sex between the porn film's crew and cast in color. While *Flesh Eaters* does not feature the penetration of bodily wounds, the hard-core straight zombie porn film *Porn of the Dead* (2006) features explicit sex between male/female non-zombie performers and grotesquely made-up zombies, who are sexually penetrated anally, vaginally and via wounds in their deteriorating flesh.[4]

LaBruce's forays into gay zombie porn uses the zombie figure to celebrate one's difference from heteronormative standards, but it also operates to satirize Western gay male sub-cultures that are presented as homonormative, assimilative, bourgeois and "dead." Homonormativity, in Lisa Duggan's formulation of the term, refers to

> a politics that does not contest dominant heteronormative assumptions and institutions, but upholds and sustains them, while promising the possibility of a demobilized gay constituency, and a gay culture anchored in domesticity and consumption ... monogamy, devotion, maintaining privacy and propriety [*The Twilight of Equality?* 179].

Within the male homosexual community, homonormativity tends to a white, middle class, youth-oriented clonishness that aspires to a hypermasculine body ideal. Conversely gay zombie narratives often foreground differences *within* the amorphous horde, playing down the symbolism of infection (and its obvious connection with AIDS signifiers) and instead focusing on sub-cultural tensions, critiquing stereotypes and highlighting the psychic trauma of "fitting in."[5]

The infectiousness of the zombie also opens up the figure as a symbol of a quickly spreading epidemic of death, decay and *queerness*, which is passed from individual to individual in a viral fashion via a bite. The zombie's bite brings death, emaciation, decay, and a desire to feed on the flesh of others. The concept of zombie-ism as sickness, with its signifiers of bodily wasting, weeping sores and signs of rot clearly offers the figure as an AIDS allegory, alongside the vampire (the chief icon of queer infectiousness).[6] As a reanimated corpse that continues to "live," the zombie establishes an undead community via viral communication. It is via these alternative methods of unnatural reproduction (infectious bites or scratches—and now sex) that the zombie figure threatens society's infrastructure. As such, the zombie offers an alternative to heterosexual reproductive futurism. In the very same body, the image of the crumbling, decaying body of the (homosexual) zombie is both a signifier of ageing and mortality—the eventual consequences of an antireproductivity that the gay man stereotypically represents—that continues uncannily to thrive.[7]

The zombie acts upon very primal instincts, eating to "survive" even though it is already dead. Traditional zombies represent extreme lawlessness. They can be understood to be an embodiment of the id; they are ruled entirely by appetite. Their insatiable drive to cannibalize their victims can be read as a sublimation of an equivalent sexual drive. This calls to mind Leo Bersani's discussion of the homophobia displayed by the press in the 1980s, stimulated by the AIDS crisis in "Is the Rectum a Grave?" which, for him, "reinforce[d] the heterosexual association of anal sex with a self-annihilation originally and primarily identified with the fantasmatic mystery of an insatiable, unstoppable female sexuality" (Bersani "Is the Rectum a Grave?" 222). Furthermore, the gay zombie in fact represents the return of a repressed feminine appetite in the *already annihilated* gay man while, again, echoing cannibalistic terminology.

In "Oral Incorporations: *The Silence of the Lambs*" Diana Fuss discusses the slippage between homosexuality and cannibalism via Freud's *Totem and Taboo*, which can also inform a useful reading of the flesh eating gay zombie in LaBruce's films. In "Three Essays on the Theory of Sexuality," Freud suggests that the remnant of aggression in the sexual instinct "is in reality a relic of cannibalistic desires" ("Three Essays" 72). In the "cannibalistic" oral stage of sexual development the infantile subject's sexual activity is not separated from the ingestion of food which leads to a collapsing of desire and identification where the subject's "sexual aim consists in the incorporation of the object" (Freud "Three Essays" 116–17). In *Totem and Taboo* Freud analyzes an event in which the powerful father of a "primitive horde," who is surrounded by a harem of females, casts out his sons from the tribe. Jealous of the father's power and access to the tribe's females, the outcast brothers then conspire to murder and consume him, assimilating his patriarchal power (Freud *Totem and Taboo* 95). Yet Freud also infers a homosexual motivation behind the siblings' cannibal desire as an indicator of their "homosexual feelings and acts" (*Totem and Taboo* 167).

Fuss goes further to suggest that "gay sex has always been cannibal murder ... [where] identification [is akin to] oral cannibalistic incorporation" (84). The central drive of the identification process is an introjective impulse to assimilate the object, to consume and become nourished by the very qualities that draw the cannibalistic subject to it initially. The (gay) cannibalistic subject consumes the Other (the masculine ideal) whom he erotically desires and disidentifies with. By considering oral incorporation as an extension of (and perhaps parallel to) anal incorporation, Fuss reclaims the *oral eroticism of homosexuality* "alongside the scene of intercourse *per anum* between men, [the] spectacle of male homosexuality, [is] one based on oral rather than anal eroticism" (84). For Fuss, both mouth and anus have castrating potential as "each comes to symbolize the gaping, grasping hole that cannibalistically swallows the other" (84). Oral incorporation as a simultaneous desire to annihilate and homoerotically consume the other sheds light on the flesh eating zombie's symbolic potential as a potentially queer monster.

In LaBruce's films the forlorn, isolated, nihilistic gay zombie is often caught in a tension between exclusion *from* the communal (and from life itself) and a desire *for* the communal, a carnivorously motivated desire to identify with (and consume) other men. The zombie as sexualized Other represents a celebration of the corporeal erotic, rendering the entire body as an erotogenic zone that is both penetrable and penetrating. LaBruce's depiction of sympathetic gay zombie figures paradoxically represents a radical celebration of the conflation of cannibalism and homosexuality, a horrific representation of the gay shame provoked by such monstrous visualizations and, further still, a disenfranchisement with the various gay sub-cultures that the individual/zombie is expected to assimilate into.

"Death is the new pornography!"

Otto; or, Up with Dead People's eponymous zombie anti-hero represents a nihilistic, sexually indifferent and apolitical gay male subject who is desperately seeking masculine company. LaBruce re-works the zombie figure into themes of his oeuvre: the marginalized subject who is fetishized by what LaBruce calls "reactionary revolutionaries"; the eroticizing and consumption of hypermasculine iconography and the conflation of hard-core pornographic tropes with anti-capitalist proclamations. LaBruce's generically hybrid film fuses melodrama, music video, existential drama, fictional documentary, pornography, gore-saturated horror, and satire. The film dramatizes the anxieties faced by Otto (Jey Crisfar) when he fails to assimilate into the horde and, instead, re-establishes his individuality and his marginalization. In *Otto*, the mob not only represents violent zombie-phobic humans, but also the harsh exclusivity of a zombie community (albeit a fake one) that also demands conformity. The conventional formula of the zombie narrative is to pitch an Us (humans) vs. Them (zombies) opposition, before revealing the zombies as the return of the repressed, as undead versions of ourselves in our human potential for monstrous violence. *Otto* transforms the binary into an Us (the film's gay "fake" zombie actors) vs. Us (gay "authentic" zombies) opposition, pitting homosexuality against *itself* in a critique of gay subcultures. More importantly, LaBruce's self-reflexive and parodic narrative offers a critique of the banal deadness of gay male subcultures, particularly those of the very homogenous "dead" clubbing scene in Berlin. LaBruce's self-reflexive presentation of the gay zombie highlights the figure as an agent of parody and pastiche where zombie drag becomes yet another example of gender performance that offers the gay male subject hypermasculinity. Zombie drag becomes a method of gender performance that highlights the gay male subject's humorous, if anxious, negotiation with idealized masculine gender tropes. The performative,[8] self-referential, and seemingly celebratory, pleasures of zombie drag via *Otto's* faux-zombies, Otto's own "costume," and in *L.A. Zombie's* heavily made up alien drag, allows for a self-assertion that draws attention to the constructedness of mainstream generic and heteronormative gender forms; it can also operate as a form of self-divestiture. Here the jouissance implied in the loss of self is not only afforded to the subject via masochistic identification in fatalistic sex, but also via an immersion in the active pursuit of appropriation, performance, costume, and generic layering.

The eponymous central protagonist in *Otto* is unlike other horror film zombies in that he is not part of a consuming horde; instead La Bruce sees him as the "rebel," the "outsider"—a solitary, marginalized individual: "with Otto I intended to make him into more of a misfit, who didn't relate to the other zombies."[9] Otto is different even from the *other* gay zombies depicted in the film—he is a semi-articulate, mostly lucid creature whose undead confusion is portrayed as amnesia. Unlike the groaning, cannibalistic automata of the film's more stereotypically traditional zombies, he represents a newer generation that, according to the film, had become somewhat more refined: they had developed a limited ability to speak and more importantly to *reason*.

The film questions the actual existence of real zombies by ambiguously presenting Otto as (possibly) the only authentic zombie among fictional undead actors, while never offering or discounting either a supernatural or rational explanation for his undead status. LaBruce also borrows Romero's stylistic use of color and black and white from *Martin* (1977) to swap between an apparent reality and the fictional "film-within-a-film" world by literally including the conceit of not one, but two films being made within the overarching narrative—hence the film's undecided title. Throughout LaBruce's film we are unsure of which film we are watching, *Up with Dead People*, the "political-porno-zombie-movie" fictional art-film on the rising up of a horde of gay zombie insurgents (with its pretentious, art-house black and white aesthetic), or *Otto*, a documentary film on a troubled adolescent who is convinced he is a zombie (with its alternate color, digital video style). The two eventually become interchangeable in LaBruce's overarching narrative. To make matters more complex, scenes from each of the films are often juxta-posed with one another, shown out of chronological order and both are "directed" by the film's fictional radical feminist filmmaker Medea Yarn (Katarina Klewinghaus). LaBruce interweaves Medea's films in frag-mented form, presenting behind the scenes sections of the making of her films alongside scenes from the films themselves and including scenes from Otto's journey to Berlin, which exists outside of the behind the scenes conceit.

Otto is not the typical *abject* corpse zombie. He is a slight adoles-cent, with a grey complexion, dirty brown hair and milky blue eyes, a decidedly blank face with bruises and congealed blood on his face and lips. More *coolly wasted* than decomposing, his look strikes one as more of a cultivated, *deliberate style* than that of archetypal rotting cadaver. Indeed, his wasted emo-teen aesthetic[10] (displayed via his disheveled hoodie, striped sweater and shirt and tie combo) support the film's depic-tion of zombie-ism as modish and clearly conflates various youth cul-tures (such as emo and punk). As such, he stands out as different from the more masculine skinhead style of the film's faux-zombies. In an online interview with Ernest Hardy LaBruce declares that his intentions for the character of Otto were, from the outset, deliberately ambiguous:

> I wanted to make a zombie who was a misfit, a sissy and a plague-ridden faggot. I deliberately leave it open to interpretation whether Otto is sup-posed to be a "real" zombie or merely a screwed up, homeless, mentally ill kid with an eating disorder, who believes that he's dead [Hardy].

In Otto's first direct-to-camera address from Medea's documentary, he states:

> It's not easy being the undead—the living all seem like the same person to me and I don't think I like that person very much ... I was a zombie with an identity crisis and, until I figured it out, I was stuck eating whatever non-human flesh was available.

The "sameness" to which Otto refers to can be read to symbolize that of conformist homonormative culture from which both Otto and LaBruce feel alienated. Alongside his identity crisis, Otto is an amnesiac, with occasional flashbacks to what he refers to as "the time before." Throughout the narrative, he longs to rediscover his "true self" and to reconnect with other people in order to determine what has brought him to this point. In one sense, his journey as a neophyte zombie might be understood as the (re)discovery of his sexuality, yet from early in the narrative he seems drawn to other male zombies, thus his homosexuality is a given. Together with his resolute declarations of his true zombie-ism, this would suggest that Otto is sure both of his sexuality *and* of being undead. It is his sense of not belonging, and of his failure to fit in with the fake or dead subcultures offered to him in Berlin, that causes him to question his identity.

In several interviews, other characters discuss Otto's function as a *tabula rasa* (both for Medea and extra-diegetically for LaBruce). Fritz Fritze (Marcel Schlutt), who plays the revolutionary leader of skinhead gay zombies, discusses his rival zombie lead:

> He [Otto] was the "Hollow Man," the empty signifier, upon which she could project her political agenda.... Otto is a blank slate, onto which LaBruce can project anxieties about the alienating effects of both bourgeois homo-normative and gym-body oriented gay clubbing cultures. Upon first meeting Medea Yarn, Otto is cast as an actor in her zombie film (as a "fake-zombie") and, at first, he appears to fit in seamlessly into her zombie imitator-group. Medea comments on his appearance that, "there was something different about Otto, something more ... 'authentic.'"

Otto's authenticity can also be read in terms of his *difference*, not only from humans but from the other zombie-actors too. Still, there remains an ambiguity as to whether he is more proficient at acting than Medea's other "zombies," really a zombie, or merely a psychotic who believes he is a zombie. Medea and Fritz both identify his persona as a reaction against an oppressive capitalist system, from which they believe he is retreating into a narcoleptic state. The authenticity of the zombies Otto meets on his journey through Berlin is questionable. The presence of Medea's actor-zombies undermines the authenticity of all zombies within the film. The legitimacy of the homeless zombies that Otto encounters also remains dubious, not to mention the pseudo-documentary and Otto's own claims of zombie-ism.

As with Romero's films, the zombies in *Up with Dead People* represent the once-consumed masses returning to consume "the living," who LaBruce (via Medea Yarn) recasts as conformist bourgeois homo-normativity. The zombie, like the homosexual, has arguably been so thoroughly assimilated into the dominant culture that it has taken on normative traits and become conventional, even banal. Like contemporary homosexuality in some Western cultures, these gay zombies are simultaneously tolerated and intolerable. Though "commonplace," Berlin is hardly a utopia for the undead. As Medea states, the *gay* zombie is considered even more abject to their oppressors, who then take to zombie-bashing where the "gay undead [are] hunted down and murdered even more ruthlessly than previous generations." Such zombie-bashing includes Maximilian's (the film's anti-hero Fritz's zombie lover) murder at the hands of a right-wing gang of youths, Otto's "stoning" by infantile youngsters, and later his zombie-phobic beating by a group of Middle Eastern/Arabic young men in the film's final sequence.

Otto's apolitical indifference masks his longing to follow the "smell of human density" and to be accepted into a community of others *like himself*, attracted by "some overpowering smell ... the smell of flesh ... Berlin." Through his film's fake zombies and the concept of zombie drag, LaBruce references a fashionable trend within popular culture, which celebrat+*es the figure of the zombie in events, theatrical performance, installation art and literary parodies.[11] If the zombie is adopted to highlight difference and revel in the pride of marginalization, it also conversely evokes an assimilationist ethos that is essential to the figure. To wear zombie-drag *en masse* paradoxically declares both difference and conformity. Otto is considered by the film's non-zombies to be indistinguishable from other gay zombies, but *within* a gay subculture that has largely adopted the zombie skinhead look, he is considered "different." Similarly, LaBruce parallels the conformity of gay cruising culture with zombie-ism, saying, "It really is pretty much like *Night of the Living Dead*. People are in a kind of somnambulist, zombie-like state; people are in a sexual trance almost. It's not really about the individual" (Castillo).

If the homogenous gay club culture is depicted as dead, the truly dead Otto seems the *least* zombie-like of the film's characters (in his possession of speech, free will and autonomous thought). In several sequences in LaBruce's film Otto comes across a succession of the counterfeit undead. In one scene he is picked up by a gay fake zombie outside a club named *Flesh* (a reference to the gay cruising "meat-market" as cannibalistic) which is hosting a themed fancy dress "Zombie Night." He is cruised by another male "zombie" presented as a classic skinhead with close-cropped hair, a black bomber jacket, and a tight white t-shirt with red braces and Doctor Martens. He persuades Otto not to enter the club, declaring, "It's *so* dead...." Instead, he flatters Otto on his assumed "costume": "you put so much effort into your ensemble ... really, really cool!" before sniffing him and commenting, "Wow! You even smell authentic!"

The comic misreadings of authentic and inauthentic zombie style become more explicit as the two head back to make love in the skinhead's apartment. As they kiss, blood begins to trickle from their interlocked mouths and the scene fades to black. A fade up reveals the apartment as a scene of carnage with Otto having eviscerated the skinhead. The white sheets, walls, and posters are splashed in arterial spray, bloodied handprints, and gore. Slowly the corpse of Otto's "trick" then begins to move. Propping himself up on the bed, his entrails lying on his stomach he proclaims, "That was amazing ... can I see you again some time?" In this "biting" satire on the deadness of gay clubbing culture in Berlin, Otto turns the tables on the city's meat-market whereby the consumed twink becomes the consumer. Initially, Otto seems as soulless and empty as the other zombies, who symbolize the perpetually empty consumers of capital, but, instead, he eventually becomes consumed and used by the seemingly radical systems (Medea Yarn's documentary) that also seek to critique capitalism.

The original cuts of many of LaBruce's works include hardcore gay sex, later excised under various theatrical and home entertainment release stipulations. The shaky performance of actual sex adds to LaBruce's low-budget, realist, and exploitation aesthetic in opposition to sanitized, mass-produced gay pornography. For LaBruce such formulaic porn perpetuates an unrealistic representation of gay sex, whereby the body becomes an eroticized object in a capitalist mode of industrial production:

> Gay porn [is] fascist in that it has the same iconography as the Third Reich: the idea of the perfect body. It's body fascism. They're often fucking like pistons, very mechanical [...] with its slick monolithic aesthetics, its cold production-line uniformity, and its easy propagandistic appropriation of the gay agenda [qtd. in Hays 185].

In *Otto* Medea declares, "Death is the new pornography!" While it is undeniable that part of the horror genre's appeal lies in its symbolic conflation of sex and death, in which fucking and killing are both coded as masochistic, for LaBruce's zombies, fucking and killing become *literally* interchangeable. The previously symbolic coding of *le petit morts* is now realized *explicitly* linking physical pleasure with physical trauma. The director champions the sub-genre's queer expediency that "zombie porn is practical: you can create your own orifice" and has long since upheld the radical potential of zombie pornography, "zombie porn is the wave of the future ... get ready for a revolutionary zombie porn extravaganza!" (interview with LaBruce).

Peter Dendle suggests that sex between or with zombies symbolizes an "unapologetic revealing of humanity" (*The Zombie Movie Encyclopedia* 6) in the exposure of one's physical innards. The opening up of the body to externalize one's guts represents sharing one's inner feelings with others in an exchange of the self with another individual or within a community. Indeed, LaBruce's camera, like that of the European softcore zombie film, opens up the body. It sexualizes the various orifices and inner "piping" (the rectum, the anus and the intestinal tract) but simultaneously reveals the human subject as an empty shell that will, nevertheless, *do* for sex. The gay zombie opens up the entire body's potential to both *penetrate* and *be penetrated*.

In one significant scene, Fritz returns home to find his lover Maximilian (Christophe Chemin) dead, having shot himself in the head. He is later reanimated as a zombie but, rather than being repulsed, Fritz begins to passionately kiss him, and Max returns his kisses with an infecting bite upon the neck. Having turned Fritz into a zombie and then eating his intestines, Max is later shown sitting quietly awaiting his lover's return to consciousness. When Fritz is later reanimated, Max proceeds to penetrate the hole in his undead lover's stomach with his penis, effectively fucking him into (and *in his*) immortality. Setting aside the male body's dual oral and anal orifices, an entirely new erotic entry point is ripped in Fritz's stomach—direct to the site of digestion. Consumption, digestion, and assimilation seem to be the order of the day in the symbolism of this sequence which itself becomes a satire of *gastric* incorporation. If we understand the zombie's drive to orally consume living flesh as a literalizing of desire for the love object, gutfucking is an extension of this desire while satirizing the (gay) zombie's penchant for unnatural procreation. Literally planting seed into his partner's stomach, Maximilian bypasses the mouth and or anus. The frequent scenes of "reanimation" and "recruitment" in LaBruce's film represent zombies as both incredibly potent and fertile. This symbolic impregnation of Fritz, taking Max into his stomach, is a comic literalizing of an unnatural reproduction only capable of replicating a dead subculture.

L.A. Zombie: *Sex as Alienating*

LaBruce's *L.A. Zombie* (2010) develops the director's fascination with the pornography genre and the monstrous icon of the zombie. It builds on the concept of the homeless, vagabond zombie, featuring a gay alien zombie (porn star François Sagat) who, in the opening titles of the film, is seen emerging from the ocean waters after apparently crash landing off the coast of Los Angeles. The film is episodic and fragmented in style, following the unnamed zombie across the city in his various sexual encounters via disconnected set pieces that invariably end in a male character's death and a necrophilic, climactic sex scene between the zombie and corpse. In what could be fantasy sequences, Sagat's zombie proceeds to either penetrate their dead bodies (via various bodily wounds or via anal sex) with an enlarged scorpion stinger tipped penis or masturbates over them, ejaculating black alien semen, which has life-giving qualities. Before long, the dead male victims eventually reanimate and reciprocate Sagat's sexual advances. The zombie is once more presented ambiguously, deliberately leaving the viewer uncertain as to whether Sagat's character is an actual zombie, or whether the zombie incarnation of Sagat is seen as part of his own schizoid self-image. LaBruce achieves this ambiguity via juxtaposing hard-cuts between a human-looking Sagat (dressed in a ripped hooded sweater) and the zombie-Sagat (who is overly made-up in lurid green, black and blue make-up and body paint). The exaggerated artificial visualization of the alien zombie's make-up and Sagat's oversized hyper-muscularity also augments the suggestion of both zombie *and* masculinity-as-performance, while simultaneously working to feminize the monster (via the draggy make-up and his swollen "breasts"). With each episode, Sagat's zombie form becomes more excessive, symbolizing the emergence of either the zombie's "true form," or a further split of the character's more extreme fragmented personality and the emerging dominance of the alien zombie. Sagat turns a darker green and, in the metamorphosing into his alien alter-ego, his protruding vampire-like incisors grow disproportionately large to the point where they erupt from his face almost destroying all of his humanoid features. The projection of Sagat's excessively Othered zombie (now also an *alien*) via these phallic, increasingly extruding teeth represents both an escalating narcissistic desire to consume and be nourished by the hypermasculine, but also symbolizes a excessive phallic response to a masculinity in crisis: via a loss of property (homelessness), a loss of self-worth (poverty) and a loss of subjectivity, sexuality and community.

Unlike the zombies in *Otto; or, Up with Dead People* who are fucked into immortality and continue to remain shambling, rotting zombies, there is clearly a more redemptive element to the undead sex in *L.A. Zombie* in that the dying and the dead are actually brought back to life or restored in intact human form. The film's opening sequence features the nameless zombie being mistaken for a hitchhiker and being picked up one evening by a young male passing driver. Via multiple cross-cuts LaBruce establishes the ambiguity of the zombie figure, the film's spectator sees Sagat's character as the greenish, alien zombie and yet via the reverse point of view shot of the anonymous driver, he appears human. Startled, the driver crashes the car. A fade up frames the overturned car with the driver having been thrown on to the road, lying in a pool of his own blood and flesh. His chest is shown clearly ripped open and his heart eventually ceases beating. Sagat's alien zombie then crawls out of the wreckage seemingly unharmed, and stumbles over to the driver's corpse. Straddling the cadaver, the zombie pulls out his large black, erect stinger-tipped penis and proceeds to penetrate the gash in the driver's chest, thrusting in and out underneath his still heart. With each thrust the heart begins to pulse and pump once more, causing the driver to reanimate and writhe in ecstasy, his eyes fluttering open. Eventually the zombie withdraws and ejaculates oily black semen over the driver's chest and face. Later the bloodied, but restored driver is framed sitting relieved near to the car wreckage, his chest having healed itself. Soon the monster turns, looks unmoved and stumbles off into the night alone.

These sex sequences between the undead in *L.A. Zombie* underline the curative and recuperative qualities of alien zombie sex and, in particular, the healing power of his ejaculate. In the course of the film the zombie "comes across" (physically and sexually) a dead homeless man whom he has sex with in his cardboard box shelter, a stabbed gangster who has double-crossed his partner for money who is erotically resurrected in a storm drain, and several gunned down victims of a drug deal gone awry (played by muscular gay porn stars including Erik Rhodes and Francesco D'Macho). In all instances, via corporeally penetrative sex, the zombie is able to bring the dead back to life. Despite Sagat's zombie's protruding teeth, which would seem to suggest his desire for oral consumption and his castrating qualities, LaBruce's L.A. zombie does not eat flesh or cannibalize his victims, instead he is seemingly driven only to resurrect or restore others. This perhaps suggests that unlike the cannibal zombies of *Otto; or, Up with Dead People*, who long to orally assimilate and consume machismo, Sagat's already-hypermasculine zombie seems sated and engorged with it. Instead of desiring and consuming masculinity Sagat *becomes* the end product of consumption: a grotesquely unsatisfied hypermasculine "ideal" in the form of a zombie-phallus.

Conclusions: Gay Zombie Sex as Anti-Communal

Within narratives like *Otto* and *L.A. Zombie*, LaBruce underscores that sex *between* zombies is shown ultimately to alienate. While the camera eroticizes the internal in a "frenzy of the visible"[12] that provides an initial jouissance, it eventually proves to be distancing. For LaBruce, there seems to be little physical trauma or pain involved in the scenes of evisceration or death. Rather than lingering on and highlighting the sensational *un*pleasure caused by painful, seemingly traumatic sex, LaBruce's low rent aesthetic renders sex almost mundane, banal, unerotic and hollow. In essence, LaBruce's depictions of undead "empty" sexual relations seems to echo Bersani's valorizing the potential of gay men's promiscuity as "anticommunal, antiegalitarian, antinurturing, antiloving" ("Is the Rectum a Grave?" 22). Yet in *Otto; or, Up with Dead People's* denouement Otto's romantic love-making with Fritz in his crisp clean bed sheets seems to yearn for redemption, a reconnection with masculinity and the gay community. His pallor, scars and bruises seem to disappear in the healing white light of Fritz's bedroom and, for a moment, Otto appears "normal." However, the morning after reveals the promise of redemption to be false. Fritz wakes to find a note on his pillow, on which is sketched a gravestone reading "Otto: RIP."

Otto is later shown leaving Berlin to journey north seeking further connections. In the film's final shots he is shown hitchhiking on a country highway, speaking directly to the camera and in voice over on his decision:

> I really didn't know what my destination was.
> But something told me to head north...
> Maybe I'll find more of my kind up there and learn to enjoy the company.
> Maybe I would discover a whole new way of death.

LaBruce's film suggests that sex and death provide neither an end nor an answer. Instead, Otto continues in a limbo-like state, never knowing others like him, never knowing where to go, unable to separate reality from fantasy and never experiencing the "suicidal ecstasy" ("Is the Rectum a Grave?" 18) connoted in the conflation of sex with death. In his reading of *Otto*, Shaka McGlotten (182–193) rightly states that there is little evidence of Bersani's melodramatic "shattering of the self" he finds in gay sex (Bersani *The Freudian Body* 38). Instead, McGlotten sees in Otto a passive indifference to any polemics (such as Medea's radical political posturing). But this apathy seems to achieve empowerment.

McGlotten reads Otto's zombie Other as a site of queer identification with apathy; Otto is able to "enact a freedom from the responsibilities and obligations that are the ordinary stuff of life" (McGlotten 185), to ape heterosexual coupledom, to seek out one's soul mate, or to indulge in gay male promiscuity. He reads Otto as a powerful "fantasy/model of an agency that is empowered as it is automatized," seeing LaBruce's treatment of the zombie figure as a more useful approach to zombie theory that has in the past, for him, only operated as a metaphor for racial and political difference, infection, consumerism, or the savage proletariat drone.

Otto's final journey is read by McGlotten as "speculatively optimistic" (182), in its refusal of self-immolation, living on as if in limbo; his conclusion is that Otto's search for "a whole new way of death" can be seen as a radicalized acceptance of one's own indifference towards life yet being inspired to live it anyway. To me this seems somewhat flaccidly optimistic. McGlotten reads Otto's indifferent sociality as a radical uncaring form of connecting with others, albeit driven by an automated desire to do so. Yet if Otto's final search is presented as utopian fantasy, given LaBruce's cynical tone in the film's overt nihilism and via the development of the zombie figure in *L.A. Zombie*, I would argue that LaBruce's zombies demonstrate that the idealistic pursuit of a shared communality is futile. Otto's zombified status (whether the result of an actual or symbolic suicide) can be seen as an act of self-divestiture. However, the drive to devalue the self becomes meaningless in the (hypocritically capitalist) economic exchange of Otto by Medea who re-values him as her muse. We can read Otto's journey in two ways: as a symbolic suicide or a journey of discovery into the unknown, both of which will eventually prove unsatisfying. Otto ironically continues, "[a]t one point I did consider ending it all, like at the end of Medea's movie. But how do you kill yourself, if you are already dead?" In this final shot, by a rural roadside of saturated yellow fields and blue skies, a rainbow appears behind Otto's head. Framed in this way by the most venerable of queer symbols, Otto's words take on a new resonance. LaBruce's ironic rainbow, I would suggest, simply resets Otto on a seemingly indifferent drive, on "Auto" as McGlotten puns (190), to connect with others like himself, a drive to fulfill societal demands for the communal that will ultimately be doomed to fail. Like Otto, Sagat's mute alien zombie chooses to withdraw from the symbolically dead cruising communities of West Hollywood stumbling instead into a nearby cemetery. The nameless zombie is framed crying abject tears of blood as he grieves over his previous attempts to sexually reconnect with others (shown in flashback) while standing over a grave. He then proceeds to dig himself into a grave with his bare hands, seemingly wishing to return to the disconnection of the earth unsatisfied by his earlier attempts to physically and emotionally connect with others but, like Otto, even in "undeath" he is unable to escape the assimilationist, numb homonormativity that is offered as community.

NOTES

1. Niall Richardson argues that the interpretation of the gym body or the hypermasculine body should not only be understood as an "attempt to reinforce essentialist ideas of male power." Instead it is entirely dependent on the context or culture in which it is construed. "Hyperbolic muscularity" may indeed be making an "ironic comment on masculine ideals," whereas "gay scenes maintain a fetishistic interest in hyper-muscular torsos" (38–9). LaBruce's valorization of the hyperbolic muscular body of François Sagat in *L.A. Zombie* therefore "may be interpreted as adoration of muscularity, or as a camp comment, comparable to drag, which is attempting to challenge or overthrow regimes of masculinity" (39).

2. According to José Muñoz: "Disidentification is a performative mode of tactical recognition that various minoritarian subjects employ in an effort to resist the oppressive and normalizing discourse of dominant ideology" (91). In terms of gay male identification, the subject simultaneously recognizes himself in the image of an unattainable phallic masculine ideal (symbolized in the heterosexual male) but also acknowledges that it is different *from* his homosexual self.

3. Jouissance is defined as an increased enjoyment or pleasure that is connected to Lacan's concept of desire and has sexual aspects. Whereas Freud sees desire as a drive where the subject seeks a reduction of tensions to a low level, Lacan, argues that the two elements of pleasure are diametrically opposed. His jouissance can be seen as connected to an increase in tension and the compounding of desire, a sexually based concept with potentially self-immolating consequences: "It starts with a tickle and ends up bursting into flames" (83). This influences Bersani's own utilization of the term throughout his works, "sexuality would not be originally an exchange of intensities between individuals ... a condition in which others merely set off the self-shattering mechanisms of masochistic *jouissance*" (Bersani "Is the Rectum a Grave?" 41).

4. For a wider reading of *Porn of the Dead* see Steve Jones "Porn of the Dead."

5. See Darren Elliott-Smith for a wider overview of gay zombie narratives in film and television, including titles such as *Flaming Gay Zombies* (2007), *Gay Zombie* (2007), *Creatures from the Pink Lagoon* (2006), *The Nature of Nicholas* (2002), and the BBC's recent television serial *In The Flesh* (2012).

6. Ellis Hanson considers the figure of the vampire to be the utmost in monstrous metaphors for the spread of AIDS within the gay community (324–326). The metaphor of the AIDS patient as the dead or "living corpse" has been acerbically rendered in zombie films such as, *I, Zombie: The Chronicles of Pain* (1998), in which the infection and decay of zombie-ism is directly paralleled with sexually transmitted disease.

7. For example, Todd Haynes' film *Poison* (1991) features a section entitled "Horror," a black and white 1950s mad-scientist parody which configures the 1950s McCarthy-ist fear of the unseen threat of secret communism and veiled homosexuality.

8. Judith Butler's concept of the "performative" questions the supposed biology of binary gender as constructed via the repetition of acts and behaviors where social performance *creates* gender, a performance which imitates culturally prescribed and impossible ideals. In *Gender Trouble*, Butler argues: "acts, gestures and desire produce the effect of an internal core or substance, but produce this *on the surface* of the body ... such acts, gestures, enactments generally construed, are *performative*" (173).

9. From a personal interview with LaBruce and Darren Elliott-Smith, 24 April 2008.

10. The romanticized stylized zombie teen "look" can also be seen worn by R (Nicolas Hoult) in the film version of *Warm Bodies* and in the group of countercultural teen zombies in *Night of the Living Dorks*.

11. These include social website *Crawl of the Dead* which advertises zombie pub crawls, festivals and marches across the world including, Iowa's *City Zombie March*, the *Zombie Walk* in London and Canada and the World Zombie Day held in London in October 2008. In art exhibitions undead still-life and performance art is a regular feature. LaBruce himself recently exhibited his "Untitled Hardcore Zombie" at the Soho Theatre in London and at Peres Projects Los Angeles in 2009. Contemporary zombie appropriation also extends to literature in Seth Grahame-Smith's *Pride and Prejudice and Zombies* spawning a series of parodic sequels and prequels including *Sense and Sensibility and Sea Monsters*.

12. In *Hard Core: Power, Pleasure and the Frenzy of the Visible*, Linda Williams states that the frenzy of the visible further covers up the true artificiality of pornography. The zombie film's externalizing of the body's interior can be read as a similar attempt to authenticate human subjectivity via corporeal exposure.

"I Eat Brains … or Dick"

Sexual Subjectivity and the Hierarchy of the Undead in Hardcore Film

Laura Helen Marks

Explaining her role as "zombie slut" in the behind-the-scenes featurette for Tommy Pistol's *Beyond Fucked: A Zombie Odyssey* (2013), Annie Cruz remarks "I eat brains." After a pause, she adds, "or dick," as if contemplating for a moment the incongruity of her position as a dick-sucking brain eater. Cruz's remark is reminiscent of the blurb for the 2011 porn movie, *I Can't Believe I Fucked a Zombie*: "'Braaaaaaains.' I mean, 'Peniiiiiiiiiiiis!'" Such confusing motivations capture a key difficulty in creating a cohesive zombie porn narrative. This incongruity between zombie and pornographic narratives also points towards a particular type of pornographic role—the sexually active female subject—that is most desired in porn and that the zombie has difficulty performing. Although abjectness in the form of walking death and rotten flesh might appear to be the biggest obstacle to sexual desire in zombie porn, pornography has historically been quite comfortable with the abject. Rather, I contend that pornography's reluctance to accommodate the zombie in the same way as mainstream media has to do with a pornographic desire for a particular kind of active female sexuality that is both predatory but contained, self-directed yet carefully constructed. By analyzing hardcore pornography that features the living dead, this essay seeks to illuminate how some of these desires relate to abject matter, disgust, and the ideal pornographic subject. Below, I will analyze three films: vampire-zombie hybrid *Dark Angels 2: Bloodline* (2005), and two recent zombie porn films, *Beyond Fucked: A Zombie Odyssey* and *The Walking Dead: A Hardcore Parody* (2013). While I compare zombies to vampires, the focus here is squarely on zombie porn and the problematic nature of presenting the zombie in a pornographic context. These porn texts reveal not only what sexual cultural baggage vampires and zombies bring along with them, but also what vampire and zombie porn can tell us about porn's preferred sexual subjects more broadly.

Porn of the Undead: Zombies and Vampires as Sexual Subjects

Over the past decade, zombies have become one of the most prolific monsters in popular culture. In academia, too, the zombie has attracted attention as an indicator of changing times. For example, its popularity has been attributed to shifts in technology and consumer culture, particularly to a postmodern anxiety around connectivity and subjectivity; as Stephanie Boluk and Wylie Lenz assert, "the zombie is simultaneously a vision of capitalism's fulfillment in the form of a stasis of perpetual desire, as well as a model of proletarian revolution, depicting the emergence of a new classless society" (7). Furthermore, the zombie is highly adaptable, a "figure of contagion" (Boluk and Lenz 3) and self-referentiality that can seemingly merge with (or infect) any other genre. Pornography, itself a postmodern genre concerned with anxieties over subjectivity and desire, as well as a highly self-referential genre that plays with its own relationship to "legitimate" culture, is not impervious to the zombie virus.

In spite of the zombie's ubiquity in popular culture, zombies remain relatively unpopular pornographic subjects. Jamie Russell notes that "sex and zombies have a curiously fertile history in exploitation cinema" (135), adding that after Joe D'Amato's grimy hardcore zombie films of the 1970s, "zombie sex has fallen by the wayside" (135). Russell adds that "[w]hile conventional hardcore pornography revels in [the body's] object status and finds pleasure in exposing the body's traditionally hidden zones (the genitals) to view, these zombie movies offer us something more horrific: a vision of the body's essential emptiness" (136). In contrast, when vampires are depicted in porn, they merely render that which was sexually implicit, explicit (Bosky 217). Accordingly, the vampire has enjoyed a more illustrious career in hardcore, softcore, gay, lesbian, and even transgender porn than their undead zombie counterparts.[1]

While the zombie's abject status might seem to be the primary cause for its difficulty in sexually exciting an audience, disgust alone cannot explain their relative unpopularity in porn. Pornography is and historically has been invested in disgust. Porn consumers are savvy to the grotesque features of the various subgenres of hardcore, and select accordingly. Spit swapping, snowballing, ass-to-mouth, gaping, prolapse, and strings of bile from throat fucking are common in contemporary hardcore pornography, and yet all of these acts would be included in William Ian Miller's framework of "contaminating and disgust-evoking" (96–97). Abject disgust alone does not account for the zombie's unpopularity in hardcore porn.

It is my contention that in addition to the careful navigation of desire and disgust, lack of sexual subjectivity plays an important role in the relative unpopularity of zombie porn in ways that complicate simplistic assumptions about pornographic desire. The hierarchy of the undead found in porn indicates a pornographic desire for, and ambivalence toward gender fluidity, polymorphous sexuality, and an equivocating yet active female sexual subjectivity.[2] Moreover, this female subject serves a more elusive function: soothing the inherent homoerotics of heterosexual pornography that, as in vampire mythology, are instigated but also sublimated. The multi-gendered, queer, and sexually active vampire paradoxically "disclaims for male viewers the solitary 'queerness' of the scene of spectatorship by diffusing the homoerotics of spectatorship" (Shelton 132). The comedic zombie narrative may perform this function to a degree, as I discuss below, but ultimately the zombie's lack of consciousness signals a lack of identity, in contrast to the fully conscious vampire. In this way, fully conscious, and therefore more overtly gendered vampires diffuse the homoerotics of spectatorship more easily than the inarticulate, unconscious zombie can. The zombie is not subject enough to adequately *perform* gender for the pornographic spectator so invested in this performance.

Emily Shelton's point that the profoundly homosocial spectatorship of pornography needs "soothing" can point us in the direction of what exactly is occurring in zombie and vampire porn and what this might tell us about pornography as a whole. "Pornography has a far more complex relationship to displeasure than is commonly acknowledged," Shelton notes in her analysis of Ron Jeremy's stardom, adding that "its investment in laughter, as a neutered redirection of anxiety, delivers rich spectatorial rewards for ... its most preferred consumer: not the male viewer, but male *viewers*" (122). The role that Jeremy and comedy play in this mediation, Shelton argues, is similar to that of the female performer: "she" performs the function of a reassuring alibi for some of the more unruly and disconcerting fluid sexualities that arise from "heterosexual" pornography. Although Shelton is not concerned with the undead, vampires and zombies amplify these issues. Zombies are too abject, too genderless in their deadness to perform this mediatory function as satisfactorily as the vampire or the human. In other words, the disgust elicited by zombies is not the primary problem with zombie porn. Rather, the problem is that the zombie's failure to adhere to customary pornographic roles exposes the careful constructions of gendered performance in hardcore. Zombie porn also exposes that gender fluidity and queerness are inherent to all heterosexual pornography.

Antiporn feminists commonly posit that hardcore pornography objectifies women's bodies in degrading and often violent ways for the scopophilic pleasure of a sadistic, solitary, and anonymous male viewers (see Dworkin; Dines).[3] Furthermore, according to this framework, the women of pornography are "always ready for sex and are enthusiastic to do whatever men want, irrespective of how painful, humiliating, or harmful the act is" (Dines xxiii). Yet, I contend, the popularity of the female vampire and concomitant unpopularity of the female zombie in porn disrupts this understanding of the female pornographic subject's function. The women of pornography are neither perpetual victims of the male objectifying gaze, nor independent whores liberated by unbridled sexuality. Furthermore, the spectator is not necessarily male or sadistic (as presumed) and, whether solitary or not, the spectator is part of an extended network of spectators that function in a similar fashion to the porn theater audiences of the 1970s.[4] Indeed, the pornographic promise of liberated sexuality is not only deceptive, but also carefully constructed as an integral part of the genre. The pleasures of transgression and sexual liberation involve a careful navigation of social norms, rather than fully breaking free of social and sexual categorization or heteronormative boundary-drawing. In this sense, pornography is truly "carnivalesque" in that it pleasurably ruptures social conventions while leaving overarching systems intact (Bakhtin).

But pornography does do political work in its transgressions. Indeed, I agree with Laura Kipnis's contention that pornography enacts a "theatrics of transgression" (164) designed to produce pleasure by violating social norms. Still, it is important to demystify and dispel the illusion that pornography is either liberated or wholly damaging genre of fiction. Pornographic films are carefully constructed texts—consisting of "mediated, performed act[s where] every revelation is also a conceal-ment" (Williams *Screening Sex* 2)—that cater to, challenge, and placate a diverse audience who have complex spectatorial desires.

Despite both being undead, the zombie and the vampire stand for subtly but significantly different things, thereby demonstrating the com-plexity of audience desire. Vampires are able to embody a perverse sex-uality that renders gender fluid and sexuality queer. Furthermore, they reflect immortality, beauty, and reproduction. As Judith Halberstam remarks, "[t]he vampire is not lesbian, homosexual, or heterosexual; the vampire represents the productions of sexuality itself" (*Skin Shows* 100). In pornography, a genre that is as obsessed with sexual categorization as it is with sexual perversity, the vampire inhabits just about every pornographic category there is (Marks). Meanwhile, the hardcore zom-bie is scarce in any category, and while they too reproduce and are immortal, the shape that this immortality and reproduction takes con-notes death rather than life. As Jones notes, "[r]eminders of physiological fragility trigger disgust reactions because they disrupt a seductive fan-tasy: the active denial of mortality.... Zombies are doubly disturbing because they are corpses, and yet are immortal. That is, they are both a reminder of human mortality, and simultaneously do not die them-selves" ("XXXombies," 200). Moreover, Bernadette Lynn Bosky observes that while vampires and zombies may both be undead creatures, in the twentieth and twenty-first centuries the vampire has almost entirely shed its connotations of death and decay and instead taken on conno-tations of immortality. Bosky states, "[i]n fiction, the burden of being dead meat has shifted primarily to the cannibalistic living dead.... Sexual stories of these undead do convey the mixture of eroticism and 'repul-sion' or fear that characterizes vampires in Stoker's novel *Dracula* ... but is often missing from vampire fiction today" (218). In this way, the vam-pire embodies the fear (and allure) of death and transformation, while the zombie embodies the fear of deadness. In short, "while death as escape from consciousness is tempting ... dead meat is not" (Bosky 219).

The presence of the zombie in pornography renders the text "some-thing else." Zombie porn's overt appeal to disgust rather than lust marks it as punk rock, avant-garde, or subversive of the assumed pornographic function. Indeed, a large number of existing zombie porn films are part of a punk rock or "alt-porn" aesthetic. In this sense, it is no surprise that Bruce LaBruce—an troublesome filmmaker who rests uneasily (for con-

sumers and critics) in a grey area between art and porn (Brinkema)—
has made two hardcore zombie films, *Otto: Or Up with Dead People*
(2008) and *L.A. Zombie* (2010), both of which were screened at film festivals (and created some controversy as a result).[5] In these films, LaBruce
uses the zombie as a further marker of subversion; as an integral aspect
of his goal of "offend[ing] everyone" (LaBruce): "I'm often surprised that
there is an audience for my work at all. The art world often ignores me
because they think I'm too pornographic, while the porn world resents
me for being too arty or intellectual and interfering with their precious,
pornographically pure project" (LaBruce).

While LaBruce's "arty" filmmaking style certainly interferes with
generic expectations, the zombie itself interferes with the "pornographically pure project" even when the pornographer attempts to integrate
it. Patricia MacCormack's description of D'Amato's hardcore zombie
films as being "about breakdown and dysfunctions of narrative, body,
society and reality" might equally apply to pornography and its fleshy,
indulgent rupture of traditional narrative. Yet, the "death, corroding,
rotting and disheveled flesh" (116) of the zombie occupies minimal space
in this same pornotopic world due to its failure to embody the ideal
pornographic subject. Pornographic desire revolves around delicate and
carefully managed points of breakdown and containment; of letting go
and holding on; of transgressing and maintaining order.[6] The zombie is
too broken, too voiceless, too devoid of subjectivity to fulfill the narrative
requirements of pornography.

"Zombies are bodies, nothing more and nothing less," MacCormack
argues, asking, "[w]hat gender are zombies?" and concluding that they
are "neuter" (104). In a genre where "[s]ex, in the sense of a natural, biological, and visible 'doing what comes naturally,' is the supreme fiction
... and gender, the social construction of the relations between 'the sexes,'
is what helps constitute that fiction" (*Hard Core* 267), genderless objects
are typically incompatible. Moreover, if gender contributes toward subjectivity (Weeks 212), paradoxically the zombie is not enough of a subject
to be a suitable pornographic object. The vampire, in contrast, is perfect:
beautiful and dependent, intelligent and conscious.

Horror, Porn, and the Victim-Hero

Horror and pornography have enjoyed a complimentary, sometimes
fraught, and perhaps paradoxical relationship in both theory and prac-

tice. Isabel Pinedo asserts that horror trades in the "wet death" while pornography trades in the "wet dream" (61), going on to characterize both types of film as genres that "dar[e] not only to violate taboos but to expose the secrets of the flesh, to spill the contents of the body" (61); both genres "are obsessed with the transgression of bodily boundaries" (61). Linda Williams also made such connections in her influential 1991 essay, "Film Bodies," in which she collectively refers to horror, pornography, and melodrama as "body genres," looked down on as "low" due to "the perception that the body of the spectator is caught up in an almost involuntary mimicry of the emotion or sensation of the body on screen along with the fact that the body displayed is female" (270). Significantly, Williams claims that of these three genres, "pornography is the lowest in cultural esteem, gross-out horror is the next lowest" (269). Williams' evaluation reflects broader concerns over the dangers of such "gratuitous" genres: the more excessive, prurient, and "low" the genre, the greater the threat it poses to its audience, and society at large.

While there are similarities and overlaps in horror and pornography, there are also distinct differences in each genre's appeal. Pinedo notes, "[t]he decisive difference between pornography and horror lies in their disparate claims to facticity" (62). Another crucial difference is that "the viewer of pornography is encouraged, indeed expected, to bring his wet dream to fruition ... whereas the viewer of horror is neither encouraged nor expected to participate in murder, mutilation, or bloodletting" (64). Even this distinction has been blurred in the discourse surrounding "torture porn" films (see Jones, *Torture Porn*). When horror and porn meet, then, which is surprisingly often, something of a pleasurable undermining of each genre occurs, exposing the generic frameworks of each.

Horror, pornography, and melodrama, Williams asserts, can be explored as "genres of gender fantasy" ("Film Bodies" 277), but these genres are also sites of gender—and genre—play. Indeed, traditional psychoanalytic approaches to horror and pornography have become increasingly untenable over the intervening years thanks to shifts in the notion of who exactly is watching and how exactly they might be responding. A combination of radical developments in technology and concomitant changes in the gender, race, and sexual orientation of those in front of and behind the camera has meant a revision of theories surrounding body genres, particularly pornography. In her analysis of Internet porn, Susanna Paasonen argues that theories of the sadistic male gaze are rooted in a cinema studies approach no longer relevant to the complex click and "grab" practices of Internet porn consumption (175–

182). Meanwhile, Pinedo has argued that rather than oppressing and marginalizing female viewers or representing women in sadistic scenarios for the pleasures of a male audience (as is commonly purported), contemporary horror's onscreen violence offers pleasures to female audiences. In porn studies, too, women have spoken about their relationship to pornography with a frankness necessary to rupture the traditionally homosocial networks of porn spectators, filmmakers, and fan communities. Most recently, Jane Ward wrote of the seeming contradiction of her, "a feminist dyke" (130), enjoying and getting off watching college reality porn, concluding, "even within this less-than-liberating genre we can find ideas, gestures, and scenes that unintentionally provide fodder for queer orgasms, and opportunities for queer reflection" (137). With this in mind, I do not make claims for a unified, static viewership—indeed, the very notion of a unified, unisexual spectator is unrealistic. Rather, I ask what pornography presents to its viewers and theorize what this might reveal about spectatorial desire—what pornographic filmmakers deem sexy and suitable for mainstream pornographic representation—in an effort to explore how pornography functions as a genre in Western discourse.

A significant connection between horror and pornography is the female victim-hero, a term coined by Carol J. Clover to describe the female protagonist of the slasher film; a woman who possesses both masculine and feminine traits, who is victim to the violent onslaught of an attacker, but who is resilient, persistent, and resourceful and typically fights back in a heroic finale. More recently, David Greven has argued against such binary reductions, conceptualizing victim-heroes as transformative in nature, closer to the protagonists of the woman's picture, and fighting for a stake in gendered power. Similar work has been done by the female protagonists (and filmmakers) of pornography. Contrary to assumptions of inherent misogyny and backlash, pornography has provided a space for women to contest their sexually oppressed status. Yet, while Linda Williams asserts that "*non*-sadomasochistic pornography has historically been one of the few types of popular film that has not punished women for actively pursuing their sexual pleasure" ("Film Bodies" 274), the reality is more complex. First, distinguishing any genre of film from that which elicits sadomasochistic pleasure is difficult, and second, heterosexual pornographic genres utilize the female object/subject in ways that resemble the victim-hero of horror rather than the unpunished and liberated heroine.[7] In this way the horror-porn film renders explicit what some regard as implicit in all hardcore pornography:

the sadomasochistic use of women's bodies "as the primary *embodiments* of pleasure, fear, and pain," "as both the *moved* and the *moving*" (Williams "Film Bodies" 270).

The nineteenth-century vampire exemplifies Williams's point because she is both desirous and threatening in her active sexuality. Representative of a matrix of feminine Others—the New Woman, the colonized Other, the Jew, to name but a few[8]—this seductive and terrifying monster elicits the pleasure and the fear generated by a sexually active and penetrating woman. Phyllis A. Roth remarks, "[p]erhaps nowhere is the dichotomy of sensual and sexless woman more dramatic than it is in [Bram Stoker's] *Dracula* and nowhere is the suddenly sexual woman more violently and self-righteously persecuted than in Stoker's 'thriller'" (412). Yet Jonathan Harker's encounter with the three vampiric sisters provokes arousal as well as fear: "[t]here was something about them that made me uneasy, some longing and at the same time deadly fear. I felt in my heart a wicked, burning desire that they would kiss me with those red lips…. There was a deliberate voluptuousness which was both thrilling and repulsive" (Stoker 42). Roth remarks that the appeal of these vampire women "is described almost pornographically" (412), a characterization that goes undefined and yet points toward excess desire and disgust, fear and temptation, as core aspects of pornographic appeal.

The vampire, in its nineteenth-century and present day manifestations, embodies a complex navigation of gender and subjectivity. As Sarah Sceats observes, the vampire is in fact in "mutual bondage" with his or her victim: "[t]he vampire is entirely dependent: s/he can only exist in relation to the victim/host; the overwhelming desire is for oneness, figured in the fleeting act of incorporation of the other" (108). In this sense, the vampire is not only desirous, but desires to be desired themselves. In pornography, there could not be a more fitting subject for the actively desiring yet representationally contained subject-object. The ideal woman of pornography, like the vampire, is simultaneously active and passive, masculine and feminine, subject and object, protagonist and antagonist. The zombie, on the other hand, struggles to embody these oscillating positions. Both monsters, however, inhabit the spaces between these simplistic binaries that are obsessively reproduced in culture.

Comparatively ungendered, rotting, and exceptionally malleable, the zombie is not as assertive, not as sexual, not as demanding or aggressive as the vampire. One might ask, where is the fun in a pornographic monster that does not give as good as she or he gets? In short, the zombie does not facilitate the same kind of fluid and oscillating pornographic fantasy that the vampire does; the zombie does not move enough, while the vampire is *moved* and *moving*. In Jones's analysis of *Porn of the Dead*, the issues of necrophilia, consent, and female sexual agency are foremost concerns, prompting him to ask, "[c]an a zombie be sexually violated, and can we utilize terms such as 'misogyny' when dealing with the partially formed zombie-subject?" (40). The answer seems to be yes and no. While Jones is "less than convinced that [*Porn of the Dead*] should be read simply as a misogynistic statement that purely takes pleasure in this hatred [of women]" (55), and even suggests that the film is a critique of pornography and male sexual aggression, he also allows that its

> fantasy (whether intended as radical or not) hinges on sexual difference, and we should not overlook that while the zombie may offer a potential liberation for women (in becoming free to explore and perform aspects of aggression and sexual freedom typically denied from femininity, via the fantasy space of the monster), the males (alive and dead) continually reinscribe a traditional gendered system via overt sexual aggression [55].

Vampire porn offers a more palatable, less overtly aggressive manner of indulging in similar fantasies of sexual difference.

In the following analysis, I explore how pornography navigates undeadness in sexually explicit ways. While zombies are indeed unpopular subject matter in hardcore pornography, some films do depict the living dead. Interrogating these films reveals why the zombie is not as pornographically sexy as the vampire. Furthermore, an understanding of pornographic treatments of zombies, and the living who navigate them, reveals broader implications about the genre as a whole. The following analysis underlines that despite its reputed misogyny, pornography prefers active, thinking, sexual female agents who can serve as focal point for a fantasizing spectator.

Conflicted Asexual Servants: Zombie Hybrids in Dark Angels 2: Bloodline

Dark Angels 2: Bloodline, an ambitious sequel to *Dark Angels* (2000), illustrates the pornographic hierarchy of the undead through the creation of a vampire-zombie hybrid called a "slag." In *Dark Angels 2*, the vampire bloodline has become tainted: when they bite a human, the victim turns into a slag. The slag is a corrupted, abject creature that, unlike the vampire, is mindless and mortal (they die after seven days of gradual decomposition). The slags never fully transition into vampires themselves, and so are treated as lower-order life-forms; they are disposable soldiers who serve the vampires. Moreover, the vampires underline their assumed superiority by seeking to eradicate the infection in their bloodline. The vampires, led by Draken (Barrett Blade), must seek out The One: a human descended from vampires who is pure (uninfected) and can re-fortify the vampire clan's infected bloodline. One key difference between vampire and zombie slag here is that the latter never engage in any sexual activity. In this way, the distinction between zombies (unsexy) and vampires (sexy) is central to the film's plot.

As the film's vampire hunter Jack Cross (Dillon Day) explains, the slags are "not people. They're dead. Or should I say undead.... They're usually vagrants or bums or street people without any family to really miss 'em. But now they've been changed. Now they're the property of a man called Draken. He uses them as soldiers in his own private army." In this way, the regressive slags perform a role similar to that of Count Dracula's wolves—his "children of the night" whom he controls and uses to physically intimidate antagonists—although Draken is more disgusted by his progeny than the Count was by his wolves.[9]

The slags represent the corroding of Draken's aristocratic and beautiful vampire bloodline; not only are the slags visibly decomposing, they are also not immortal. Cross explains:

> They're not real vampires, they're like half breeds. They've been infected; they don't turn into vampires like you might think. They're more like the walking dead. They've got some of the same characteristics as vampires, like superhuman strength, speed, but they've only got a life span of about nine days. They're decaying like real dead bodies; when the body gets too decomposed, they drop. We can kill 'em just like anyone else.

Cross fails to add that these slags also differ from vampires in that they are mindless, passive beings who are ready to follow orders and lack the ability to speak or assert agency. Thus, *Dark Angels 2* literalizes the hierarchy of the undead only suggested by the respective popularity and unpopularity of vampire and zombie porn. The slags are asexual servants. Furthermore, the slags are not gendered; they are repeatedly referred to as "things" and "those." In this sense, even though the slags bear the markings of gender through clothing and hairstyles, their gender is not emphasized either through sexual intercourse or discourse. Therefore, the zombie queers notions of gender performance, exposing gender *as* performance, emptying gendered signifiers of their supposed significance.

The slags invert vampire mythology in other troubling ways. Most notably, they vomit blood rather than drinking it. The abjectness of this feature reflects William Ian Miller's notion that disgust derives from "[t]he magical transformation that happens once any [dangerous bodily excreta] leaves its natural domain" (97). In porn, vampires typically ejaculate semen and drink blood, rendering the vomiting slags particularly repulsive. Yet pornography is rife with bodily fluids leaving their natural domain. Indeed, the emergent popularity of spitting, cum-swapping, ass-to-mouth, and cum swallowing indicate that pornography routinely *trades* in the abject displacement of bodily fluids. But these bodily fluids are often gendered, particularly in mainstream heterosexual pornography. Hetero-males are not customarily depicted consuming even their own semen,[10] and women are rarely fetishized as expelling or ejaculating unless it is part of a pre-labeled film that indulges in such representation. In this way, oral consumption is gendered feminine, while genital ejaculation is gendered masculine. To ejaculate orally—to vomit—is arguably more complex yet is an act typically prompted by oral consumption in porn and therefore coded feminine. The slags' lack of sexual interaction is suggestive of their inability to embody conventional pornographic sexual subject positions, but also the degree to which vampires and humans are preferable as subjects of pornographic action, both in terms of sexual activity and plot development. The status of the slags suggests that zombies are servants rather than agents of the transgressive pornographic discourse.

In many cases, such as in *Erotic Nights of the Living Dead* (1980) and *Dark Angels 2: Bloodline*, zombies merely function as background players, never participating in the sexual activity at all. In films where the zombies do engage sexually, they are rarely in more than one or two scenes, and if they are they customarily engage with a human who is able to direct the zombie's sexual activity, creating a scenario that is by necessity tinged with non-consent. The vampire, on the other hand, requires no such direction. As a result, regardless of its dependent nature, the vampire does not connote non-consent. On the contrary, they connote sexual predation.

Pornography demands an active agent of sexuality that the zombie struggles to perform. In zombie porn, this agent is embodied in the pornographic "assist." An "assist" is a role undertaken in sports, video-games, pornography, and myriad social situations, and involves the assist guiding and enabling the successful completion of a task by a fellow participant. In pornography, this most often occurs in a threesome where one participant is the star of the scene (the woman, in heterosexual porn), and the third party (the other woman in a boy/girl/girl scene) assists by offering physical and verbal encouragement. These roles may fluctuate throughout the course of the scene. In vampire porn, no human or other entity is generally required to direct the vampire's sexual activity; the vampire has agency and so directs herself or actively engages in proceedings. The zombie, however, is passive, and therefore requires direction either from a vampire or a human assist. The zombie's failure as a sexual agent is inextricable from their undesirability in this context, demonstrating the degree to which pornography customarily associates active sexual agency with desirability.

Conflicted Sexual Subjects: Female Zombies in The Walking Dead: A Hardcore Parody *and* Beyond Fucked: A Zombie Odyssey

The Walking Dead: A Hardcore Parody riffs on the popular AMC television series, *The Walking Dead*, itself based on a comic book series by Robert Kirkman. The film covers three seasons of the television show, but with the twist that the "walkers" can be killed with semen. The walkers engage in sex with humans, but also want to destroy those humans. The walkers crave entrails and brains as a traditional zombie does, but simultaneously crave semen, even though it will kill them. These tensions remain unresolved in the narrative, and are in fact played upon as absurd.

In the first scene Rick (Tommy Pistol) awakens from his coma and is promptly attacked by a gory female zombie. After panicking, Rick inquires, "[w]hat are you doing?" asserting, "I'm married!" He evidently understands that the zombie's attack—aimed in the direction of his crotch—is sexual, yet initially the attack is presented as one of violence and brainlust, not sexual desire. A noticeable shift occurs after Rick makes his verbal ejaculations. The zombie no longer scrabbles at Rick's body in directionless fashion; she instead begins assertively unzipping Rick's fly, and promptly sucks on his penis. Rick's warnings and panicked questions also change into moans of pleasure, assurances ("okay"), and apologies to his wife. The distinctive break between (a) zombie aggression with the goal of consuming flesh and (b) zombie aggression in the direction of sexual intercourse are evidence of the pornographic zombie's incoherence. The pornographic zombie must be both mindless and an active sexual agent.

Later, Daryl (Owen Gray) is out on patrol stabbing zombies in the head. Blood-spattered and decomposing, the zombies seek to consume human flesh, including Daryl's. Daryl gets into a van and finds two female zombies pawing at a male zombie. The male zombie stands with his back to the camera, jeans around his ankles, while the female zombies are on their knees gazing up expectantly but not actually performing any sexual acts. Perceiving their position as an opportunity for sexual pleasure, Daryl breaks the male zombie's neck, declaring that he "[m]ight as well have some fun." He then walks toward the two female zombies who are kneeling on the floor, and initiates sex with them.

The lack of sexual action between the three zombies when Daryl discovers them indicates a sort of zombie autopilot. The female zombies are in the position of performing fellatio on their knees, and the male zombie stands in a conventionally appropriate position, but no sex-action ensues. The zombies are in limbo, merely inhabiting (gendered) sexual positions but with no agency or direction. It is only when the human male replaces the inactive male zombie that sexual activity occurs. Notably, Daryl's intervention ignites their sexual aggression. This indicates the female zombies' desire for sexual agency, but also implicitly demonstrates the degree to which pornographic representation attempts to reconcile female desire with that of the male. The female zombies replicate and mirror the level of sexual aggression exhibited by the male. Even so, there is a limit to what level of sexual agency and subjectivity the zombie can embody, and even in this scene the lack of verbal ability (the zombies growl and moan in a guttural fashion but no more) and adherence to a certain lumbering zombie physicality render the human dominant and the zombies mindless recipients.

In order to maintain a coherent narrative, verbal cues are used unconvincingly in an attempt to rationalize the zombies' behaviors. "No biting," Daryl says while throat fucking one zombie. "Cock!" growls the other zombie. "Cum!" they snarl prior to the money shot. Their lack of agency manifests as a lack of sexual focus or aim; these zombies arbi-trarily choose between brains or dick. Before long, the sex scene falls into a standard routine, including a variety of sexual positions expected from a boy/girl/girl threesome (cowgirl, missionary, doggie). The only point of distinction is that the women growl and grunt in deep tones rather than squealing and moaning in higher pitched tones. The zombie women even masturbate during the sex, and assist each other. The performers must necessarily break character—act less like a zombie—in order to adequately perform their gendered porn personas.

Furthermore, the zombies' cries for "dick" and "cum" underlines the impossible position they are caught in. Verbally, they articulate a desire for the conventional objects of heterosexual pornographic desire. Yet, their lack of rational agency results in their inability to reflect on the danger they face: as Daryl reminds us post-cum shot, "[c]um kills you, zombie whores." This narrative conceit seeks to reconcile the tension raised by placing zombies in a pornographic context. In order to depict humans and zombies having sex, *The Walking Dead: A Hardcore Parody* suggests humans have sex with zombies in order to kill them, while zombies crave sex in return. In attempting such a reconciliation of two incongruous concepts, the filmmakers merely reemphasize the incompatibility of the passive, inarticulate zombie and the active, vocal pornographic woman.

Later, too, in the third scene involving a human and a zombie, Carl (Wolf Hudson) is instructed by his father to have sex with the zombie Sofia. The scene is initiated and directed by Carl's parents, Lori and Rick, and the incongruity of the scenario is navigated using humor. At first, Glen thinks it's just another walker, and starts to unbutton his fly, muttering, "[d]on't worry, I've got this one." Rick halts him with a hand: "No Glen, put your dick away. That one's for my boy." As with the earlier scene, the zombie's lack of consciousness and subjectivity requires action and assistance on the part of the human participants, and codes the scene as irretrievably nonconsensual. The humans organize the zombie's sexual activity without the zombie's interjection (which it is by its nature unable to provide).

"It's been a crazy day, hasn't it, son?" Rick counsels Carl on bended knee, "[t]hat's just how life is gonna be from now on. And you gotta be strong. Now Carl, I gotta know, do you have it in you to go over there and fuck that girl? And kill her with your cum?" Carl nods gravely. "Well you go on, boy, and you do what you gotta do." Rick stands with Lori and the others and they proudly watch their son have sex with Sofia, and ejaculate in her mouth to kill her. Throughout the scene, the film cuts to Lori and Rick giving hand signals and thumbs up signs, encouraging and instructing their son. The zombie herself is unable to direct or instruct, despite appearing to take on an active role by participating in the cowgirl position, for example.

As if serving as a reminder of the various inconsistencies, contradictions, and outright absurdities that Joseph Slade has argued are among the primary pleasures of pornographic texts (41), a car horn, the beeping of a reversing delivery truck, and other traffic sounds can be heard during this sex scene, rupturing the notion that the characters occupy a desolate apocalyptic landscape. Yet, subversive, text-rupturing pleasures aside, zombidom is incompatible with active sexual agency. Thus, the female performer resorts to more conventional modes of performance as the sex scene progresses. Sofia's initial passive acceptance, and eventual recourse to a standard, active sexual performance (albeit with zombie make-up and grunting), demonstrates that the zombie is incompatible with conventional pornographic desire. She must eventually break character, ride Carl cowgirl, finger her clit, and enthusiastically perform oral sex, all while staring blankly and grunting repetitively.

The Walking Dead: A Hardcore Parody employs comedy as one way of evading the pitfalls of a nonsensical plot and the abject grotesqueries of growling, decomposing bodies. When Carl realizes Sofia has been left behind at the mercy of the undead, he is upset, asking, "[w]hat if she turned already?" and demanding they go back for her. Rick gives the sobbing Carl a talk, set to amusingly melodramatic music: "Now listen up, big man. All right? There's still a chance she may have turned. Okay? Which means you're gonna have to fuck her mouth and cum in her. To kill her." The performers pull bemused faces during their absurd and melodramatic dialogue, reflecting what Jones regards as horror-porn's particular self-consciousness, which commonly manifests via "self-deprecating jokes about the film's status *as* porn" (*Torture Porn* 161).

Unlike *The Walking Dead*, *Beyond Fucked: A Zombie Odyssey* is not an outright comedy. Rather, it is a post-apocalyptic thriller with satirical elements. The film does not depict any human-zombie sexual interaction, and so does not require comedy to defuse the incongruity of the passive and abject zombie. The film takes place during the zombie apocalypse, brought about by a drug created by the government to control the obesity epidemic. When people take the new wonder drug, they lose weight. Protagonist Bonnie explains in the introductory voice over, "how it worked basically was your body would feed off the fat from the inside. Great right? ... But once you've had no more fat to take off, that's when the hunger would take over." Bonnie is a professional zombie killer hired by Dr. Life (Mark Wood) to search for pure semen that can be used to inseminate a new "mother Mary" and restart a pure human civilization. The majority of the film takes place in an exclusive bar that hosts human/zombie fights, and where Bonnie has a female lover whom she visits during her downtime. The refusal to depict human-zombie sexual interaction, combined with human use of zombies for entertainment and (as we shall see) sexual resolution of emotional wounds, indicates the degree to which zombie sex requires an active human assist in order to be pornographically pleasing.

Beyond Fucked depicts several scenes of gore and abject horror, yet the sex scenes (all between humans but one) are narratively framed as "clean." Indeed, a key aspect of the narrative is the need to stay "clean" and avoid contracting disease from sexual intercourse. On arriving at the club, Bonnie is tested with a device that detects zombie infection. "Looks like you're clean," the owner says after pressing the device to Bonnie's neck. Later, Bonnie and her lover, Lucky Lucy (Nikki Hearts), test each other prior to sex. This plot detail creates a strict separation between human and zombie, narratively refusing any sexual interaction between human and zombie. The film does not hold back on the abject; indeed, it is one of the more consistently grimy and gore-filled porn features, creating a convincingly dark and dirty apocalyptic world. However, the abject and the clean are kept separate.

Later in the film, Bonnie participates in the zombie fights and wins. During this fight, she recognizes one of the zombies as Tommy, and requests that he and another zombie (Annie Cruz) be brought to her room along with "two shots of adrenaline ... I'm gonna say the goodbye I never had the chance to say." One might expect the following scene to involve sexual intercourse between Bonnie and zombified Tommy; certainly that is what Bonnie's verbal transition indicates. Yet, Bonnie does not participate fully. Rather, she orchestrates sex between the two zombies in some sort of vicarious sexual "goodbye." Furthermore, she must shoot both zombies up with adrenaline in order to prompt them to engage sexually. After injecting the zombies, Bonnie grabs the female zombie's hand and places it on Tommy's crotch, pushes their mouths together to instigate a kiss, and then steps back weeping as the two zombies "autonomously" engage in sex. Bonnie sits and watches, crying. Just as in *The Walking Dead: A Hardcore Parody*, zombie sex requires a human assist, ideally a female human assist, indicating that zombies lack sexual desire.

Also like *The Walking Dead: A Hardcore Parody*, the zombie sex performance soon begins to deteriorate into active and articulate pornographic performance. The female zombie, even when shot up with adrenaline, is incapable of the sexual passion expected of the pornographic subject, thus the female performer injects pornographic sexual agency into her zombie performance. As the scene draws closer to the concluding cum shot, the female zombie begins to verbalize stock phrases such as, "[o]h give me that load right now," and "give me that cum." Meanwhile, Tommy maintains zombie-like composure, reflecting Jones's contention that heterosexual male performance in porn is quite zombielike (Jones "Porn of the Dead" 52).[11]

Conclusion: Queer Implications

These films demonstrate the degree to which pornography prefers an active female agent of sexuality, as well as a highly ritualistic performance of femininity. Yet, these performances are juxtaposed with moments of queer sexuality and gender fluidity; slippages that belie the function of the sexually mobile woman in homosocial visual spaces such as pornography. It is my contention that the zombie is not gendered or active enough to provide an alibi for or bypass the homoerotic desire inherent to heterosexual hardcore. Accordingly, when the zombie does appear in hardcore some form of human assistance in the scene is required to diffuse this homoeroticism. With these assists in place, homoeroticism abounds as it does in the notoriously queer vampire narrative.

Much of the humor in the hardcore *The Walking Dead* parody derives from an intimate knowledge of the television show and the various melodramatic relationships. Most notably, the series establishes a love triangle between Lori, Rick (Lori's husband), and Shane (Rick's best friend). The porn film queers their conflict by presenting it as a threesome—a "truce" as Lori calls it—that highlights the television show's homosocial and homoerotic components, particularly when the threesome are united in a double penetration scene. The homoerotic component is made especially clear when, after killing Shane, Lori notices Shane "starting to turn" into a zombie. Rick responds by unbuckling his belt, and tugging on his penis, seeking to kill Shane by ejaculating on him. Lori begins to protest, but Rick stops her, asserting, "I have to ... Shane would want it like that." He continues masturbating, but Lori dispatches Shane "the old-fashioned way" (shooting him) before Rick can reach climax and ejaculate on him. Clearly, comedy displaces the homoerotics created by the homosocial sharing of Lori, yet without the female presence even comedy could not dispel the threat to discourses of heterosexual desire generated within the majority of "straight" porn. While it might be tempting to say that moments such as this subvert the monosexual fantasy customarily offered within heterosexual hardcore, homoerotic jokes are rife in pornography and constitute an important aspect of a genre that spends much of its time focused on the naked, erect bodies of men.

The film also literalizes the implicit homoeroticism of Andrea and Michonne's relationship on the television show. Both Andrea (Kleio) and Michonne (Skin Diamond) "hate zombie dick" and are thrilled to have another lesbian woman to fuck. Of course, in heterosexual porn, which in its most conventional forms has a strict homosexual taboo (Waugh 319),[12] lesbian homoeroticism is more acceptable than male homoeroticism. In keeping with those conventions, the homoerotics of Shane and Rick are merely verbalized and rendered comedic in the porn parody, while Andrea and Michonne are featured in their own sex scene.[13]

Despite these normative restrictions, the recent turn towards zombie-porn may signal several key changes in heterosexual porn's articulations of desire, as well as its consumers' desires. For example, the combinations of porn and horror found in these hardcore zombie films may signal that in some respects pornographic formulae are being relaxed, with the result that accompanying anxieties surrounding gender and sexuality are also less rigid than they once were. Alternatively, zombie porn may reflect a reaction to a cultural interest in zombies that, while unsuitable for pornography, nevertheless offers an opportunity to play with the gender and narrative constructs of pornographic genre. Certainly, the involvement of punk rock alt-porn star Joanna Angel in so many of these zombie-porn endeavors should prompt conversations about the role of women and counterculture in these marginal pornographic trends.

These recent examples of zombie porn prompt such questioning because they are founded on a tension. On the one hand zombies rupture conventional pornographic formulae. On the other, female zombies are necessarily passive, voiceless objects; as such they embody the conventions that many anti-porn feminists have evoked when vilifying porn's depiction of sexuality. However, passive female zombies highlight that women in porn are not conventionally passive as they are typically presumed to be. Perhaps unintentionally, the female zombie and her human female assists provide a refreshing counterpoint to the pornographic woman who is desired for her predatory assertiveness; an assertiveness that belies her dependency and narrative containment, but opens contested fantasy space for myriad spectatorial fantasies that bridge gender and sexuality. How this subject position might change (and is changing) in light of new and newly-revealed audiences and desires is a critical point of discourse for ongoing genre studies.

NOTES

1. See for example, *Gayracula* (1983), *Dragula* (1973), *The Night Boys* (1991), and the many softcore lesbian vampire films produced in the 1970s by Jess Franco and in the twenty-first century by Seduction Cinema. Hustler's decision to simultaneously release the straight *Dracula XXX* and gay *His Dracula* in 2012 indicates the ease with which the vampire adheres to multiple sexualities.

2. While my focus in this essay is on the female subject, my argument can be extended to male performers also, particularly in gay porn and pre–80s porn. Indeed, in a telling coincidence, Steve Jones compares the voiceless and objectified male performers of gonzo porn to zombies ("Porn of the Dead" 50) while male performer Kurt Lockwood compares male performers to vampires. These comparisons would make for a fascinating extension of my argument here; an extension that is beyond the scope of the current project.

3. For a thorough analysis of antiporn radical feminism in the 1970s and 1980s, see Strub 213–255.

4. For an analysis of cross-gender identification in pornographic film, see Wilcox. Loftus' *Watching Sex* demonstrates the variety of motivations, preferences, and responses when it comes to male consumption of pornography. See Schaefer for a discussion of the diverse audiences who attended adult films. See Berenstein for a similar discussion regarding the mixed gender address of classic horror advertising. See Delaney for a description of the ways in which heterosexual film exhibition mobilized queer sexual interactions in the audience.

5. LaBruce's *L.A. Zombie* was banned from the 2010 Melbourne Film Festival. The festival organizers did not seem to feel the need to justify this decision beyond their ruling that the film was "porn."

6. In this way, the prolapse and anal gape are instructive. Gaping, the forerunner of the prolapse, offers a vision of the interior of a man's or woman's body sealed in by a membrane. The prolapse takes it a step further, offering a rosy red "bud" that is as close to the bloody intestines of a zombie victim as one might get while still technically remaining sealed and integrated.

7. See Paasonen for a complication of the notion of objectification and a discussion of pornography's construction of people as "both sexual subjects and objects" (175).

8. For an analysis of vampire fiction as representing a fear of reverse colonization (gendered feminine), see Marilyn Brock; see Christopher Craft for an analysis of gender fluidity and homoerotic displacement in *Dracula*; for the argument that Count Dracula represents a fear of the Jewish Other, see Judith Halberstam's *Skin Shows* (specifically chapter four); finally, for an analysis of *Dracula* as a reaction to the increasingly liberated woman see Carol A. Senf.

9. Towards the end of the film, as their vampire lair comes under attack by Jesse (Sunny Lane) and Cross, Quinn cries, "I'll release the hounds!" in reference to the slags.

10. An important exception to this rule is the femdom pegging subgenre. In the *Strap Attack* series (2004–12), for example, the male performer customarily consumes his own cum shot at the scene's conclusion. In addition, in cuckold films such as *Shane Diesel's Cuckold Stories* (2009–present), the cuckolded husband typically consumes the other man's semen at the end of the scene.

11. It is worth noting that Tommy Pistol is typically one of the more vocal, animated male performers in porn. It is unusual to see him embody a passive character in this way, then, but this merely serves to emphasize the ease with which male performers might embody the zombie role in heteroporn.

12. When looked at from a broad vantage point, however, "straight" porn is incredibly queer. In order to assert that heteroporn has a homosexual taboo, one must filter out the many subgenres that complicate the notion of coherent heterosexuality, hence my reference to "conventional" pornographies. Even "mainstream" heteroporn, as discussed in this chapter, contains instances of homoeroticism if not outright homosexual acts, though there are even exceptions to this such as *The Story of Joanna* (1975) and *The Erotic Adventures of Candy* (1978), both of which depict homosexual acts between men. While such homosexual transgressions were a more common occurrence in 1970s porn, a minimal amount of recent straight hardcore films depict simulated male homosexual acts as part of the narrative, such as in *Southern Hospitality* (2013).

13. In contrast, vampire porn boasts an entire subgenre devoted to lesbian interactions that requires no such staging; rather, vampires are to a degree always-already queer.

Pretty, Dead

Sociosexuality, Rationality and the Transition into Zom-Being

STEVE JONES

Unlike other horror archetypes, zombies have an established presence in philosophical discussion. Following David Chalmers in particular,[1] many philosophers have evoked the undead when hypothesizing about consciousness. In recent years, zombies have been utilized to examine phenomenology and mental knowledge (see Furst; Malatesti; Macpherson), visual processing and intentional action (see Mole; Wayne Wu), and the relationship between consciousness and cognition (Smithies). These are all variations on the explanatory gap problem, which refers to a rift between psycho-physiological explanations of mental function (deriving from neuroscience, for instance) and the intuitive sense that selfhood, agency, and introspective knowledge are metaphysically significant.

Such discussion frequently feels nebulous. Neuroscience is fascinating, but its empirical findings can be difficult to relate to everyday, experiential reality. Indeed, neuroscience habitually seeks to uncover how the mind operates *in spite* of our intuitions. Abstract philosophical discussions about consciousness are just as intangible. Debates over philosophical zombies (hereafter, p-zombies) are commonly rooted in notions about hypothetical twin worlds, ruminations on the impossibility of imagining what it would be like to lack phenomenal experiences, and semantic discussions regarding whether conceivability equates to possibility. Again, it is often hard to comprehend how such discussion relates to personal experiences.

Although p-zombies and movie zombies are regarded as entirely separate entities by key thinkers in the field (for reasons that will become apparent in due course), I propose that movie zombies illuminate these somewhat opaque philosophical debates by offering an accessible route into the issues. Fundamentally, both the p-zombie debates and zombie movies are underpinned by the same focal point: zombies are non-conscious humans. Yet the filmic version of that problem is grounded in an experiential world rather than conceptual theorization. Cinematic storytelling devices—narrative, characterization, dialogue and so forth—allow filmmakers to present characters' experiences in an instinctively accessible manner. Protagonists interact in social worlds that are comparable to our own, and narrative drama is typically driven by social interaction. The characters' interactions are thereby rendered concrete and familiar, regardless of their fictionality. Whereas conjectural debates regarding p-zombies begin with theoretical models of self (seeking to test their legitimacy), zombie movies are rooted in and prioritize an experiential vision of selfhood.

This essay focuses on a particular strand of the subgenre: transition narratives, in which human protagonists gradually turn into zombies. In transition narratives, protagonists are able to articulate their experiences as they undergo their transformation.[2] As such, they directly reflect on changes in their mental states, linking those shifts to the physical and social realms they occupy. The specific case study examined in this essay is *Pretty Dead* (2013). The film is partially constructed from footage shot by lead protagonist Regina, a 24-year-old MD, as she charts her metamorphosis into a zombie. After killing a pizza delivery driver and eventually turning on her fiancé Ryan, Regina is institutionalized. In tandem with Regina's autobiographical footage, *Pretty Dead* is comprised of videotaped interviews with a clinician (Dr. Romera)[3] who is convinced that Regina is suffering from Cotard's syndrome: a delusion in which the patient believes they are dead. The narrative is ambiguous about the legitimacy of Regina's claims throughout, intercutting between her own assertions and Romera's rationalist explanations. The clash between Regina's experiences as a transitional being and Romera' scientific diagnosis is centralized in *Pretty Dead*. That is, the narrative brings two views on the self—intuitive and empirical—into direct conflict. *Pretty Dead* thereby encourages the viewer to question the validity of both, and their compatibility.

As is common among transition narratives, sociality is emphasized as a defining aspect of Regina's life in *Pretty Dead*. Transitional protagonists' metamorphoses are conventionally punctuated by turning points at which they attack living counterparts; usually their closest companions. For example, in *Harold's Going Stiff* (2011) and *Return of the Living Dead Part 3* (1993), full-blown zombies are depicted as inarticulate beasts who violently attack the living. Knowing that the same fate awaits them, the transitional protagonists "live" in fear that they will eventually turn on their loved ones. Both *Harold's Going Stiff* and *Return of the Living Dead Part 3* are stories driven by romantic couplings, meaning that the transitional protagonist's loss of rational control—their inability to halt their transfiguration into zombidom (or zom-being) and the ruination of their bonds with other humans—is accentuated. This theme is ubiquitous in transition narratives, which typically situate metamorphosing protagonists within intimate relationships with living partners. Other examples of this trend include *Zombie Honeymoon* (2004), *Zombie Love* (2008), *Zombie Love Story* (2008), and *True Love Zombie* (2012).[4]

Following this convention, when Regina films her transformation in *Pretty Dead*, she also captures a parallel change in her love life. In particular, the footage charts the detrimental impact her transformation has on her relationship with her fiancé Ryan. As such, Regina's identity and rationality—what she is, how she behaves, even how she experiences the world—are inextricable from her sociality; affiliations and interactions with other beings that give her (human) life meaning. Eventually, Regina loses control. Her romantic attachment to Ryan is replaced by her desire for his flesh. Although both types of desire reach their fullest expression carnally—human love-making or zombie flesh-eating—the former signifies Regina's recognizably human sociality, while the latter denotes Regina's movement into zom-being.

From Regina's anthropocentric view, the latter is monstrous. She understands love, in contrast, as a sign of her humanity. In *Pretty Dead*, Regina's humanity is measured by the self-control she exerts in resisting her urge to harm Ryan. As such, Regina's love for Ryan is characterized as rational agency. Yet that conception of sexual love is counter-intuitive: that kind of passion does not emanate from conscious, rational choice in the first instance. That is not to say that sexual passion is synonymous with complete irrationality. On this point I concur with Nikolay Milkov, although Milkov's subsequent assertion that "sexual experience *proceeds in* acts of reasoning" (159, emphasis added) does not adequately resolve the problem either. Rather, it should be noted that phenomena such as love and sexual passion can be explained or reflected on via rationality, but the *emotional experience* of social kinship cannot be captured via such language. Experiencing and rationalizing are ontologically different. Sex thus illustrates that (a) there is a troubling disjuncture between rationalist-theoretical conceptions of selfhood and selfhood as it is experienced in the real, social realm, and (b) there is a natural bridge between personal, introspective self-knowledge and external social selfhood. Throughout this essay, I use the term "sociosexual" to denote ways in which sexuality epitomizes the relationship between sociality and self-hood as it is experienced in the real, interdependent world.

By emphasizing sociosexuality's role in self-experience, *Pretty Dead* illuminates aspects of consciousness that are neglected in philosophical debates regarding p-zombies. Consciousness sets apart humans from zombies. Ergo, so too does sociosexuality. Insofar as sociosexuality is measurable via behavior, it can be pinned down in a way that conscious-ness and qualia cannot. The p-zombie argument is undercut by the notion that p-zombies might have conscious experiences, but might not be able to articulate them. Similarly, an articulate zombie may lack qualia, but may lay verbal claims to consciousness that could not be proven false. Consciousness is invisible and intangible because it is intro-spective and metaphysical. This is not to suggest that all mental states are manifested in behavior.[5] Rather, when Regina turns on Ryan, that behavior evinces a significant change in her consciousness. The action violates Regina's conscious will to maintain the sociosexual relationship she shares with Ryan, and manifests an ontological shift away from her identity as a human. Although she does not become a full-blown non-conscious zombie before the end credits roll, Regina overtly becomes less human and more akin to a zombie as the text progresses. Killing Ryan is a key indicator that Regina is "pretty dead," but only inasmuch as Regina believes she is a rational being, able to know and control her behaviors via cognition and reflection.

Conscious State[ment]s: A Primer in Zom-Being

Contributors to the p-zombie debates principally seek to test the legitimacy of physicalism (see Lehrer; Garrett; Horowitz) and/or to understand whether qualia—the essential properties of experiences—can be explained by functionalist accounts of selfhood. These debates hinge on the idea that p-zombies are physically identical to living humans, but have no conscious experiences. Consequently, "there is nothing it is like to be a [p-]zombie" (Chalmers "Consciousness and Its Place in Nature" 249). To put it in concrete terms, although p-zombies are physically identical to any conscious person, they do not have qualia.[6] So, a p-zombie can walk hand-in-hand on a beach with another p-zombie, look into their partner's eyes and kiss as the sun sets, but during this interaction neither p-zombie will *experience* anything. The possibility of p-zombies poses a threat to functionalism since it amounts to saying that it is conceivable (and therefore possible)[7] that consciousness is separable from our physical capacity for conscious experience.

As Chalmers notes in his influential argument, p-zombies are not the same as the filmic undead (*The Conscious Mind* 95). Rebecca Roman Hanrahan succinctly summates the reason why: "it would be very difficult to make a movie about [p-]zombies, since they behave just as their qualia-ridden human counterparts do." Therefore, "[t]here would be no way for the filmmakers to depict any ... difference between [p-zombies] and ordinary humans" (303). However, the p-zombie argument's premise—that zombies are identical to living humans but lack phenomenal experience—has become ever more pertinent to zombie fiction over the last thirty years. The lumbering, somnambulistic movie zombies Hanrahan has in mind are relatively uncommon in contemporary zombie narratives. Contemporary movie zombies are beings whose vital organs have ceased to function, and so they externally *appear* to be different to living humans. To answer Hanrahan, *this* is how filmmakers distinguish between living and undead individuals. Zombies also engage in behaviors such as flesh-eating, which are frowned upon by their living counterparts. In many contemporary zombie movies, zombies are akin to pale, cannibalistic humans who suffer from a severe skin condition. That is, their conventional behaviors and appearance do not necessarily evince a lack of cerebral acuity or any essential quality of their mental processes.

Transition narratives such as *Pretty Dead* flag this kinship between living and undead by focusing on protagonists who transform from the former into the latter, thereby linking those states. Transitional protagonists have consciousness at the narrative outset: they do not simply exist in the qualia-less twin-worlds of p-zombie argumentation. Because they begin as conscious entities, transitional protagonists can articulate changes they undergo as they experience them, so long as they remain partially human and conscious. In what follows, I am not concerned with casting doubt over physicalism, so for the sake of clarity let us take for granted that full-blown zombies' mental states *are* different to their living counterparts.[8] This is certainly implied by *Pretty Dead*'s evocation of cordyceps, the fungus Regina cites as the cause of her metamorphosis. Cordyceps is said to "infect" its host's mind, "win[ning] control ... compel[ling]" the host's behavior.[9] Regina's experiential accounts indicate that her zombified mindset is unlike her conscious experiences. When she kills, she proclaims that the fungus "must have taken over ... I don't even remember biting him ... I black out or something." Her defensive assertion "[i]t's not me, it's what's inside me" overtly distinguishes between her conscious awareness and the zombie-state the fungus instills.

Despite this clear delimitation of human consciousness and zombeing, the transition happens gradually, and the boundary between the two states is fuzzy. Regina does not become a full-blown zombie when she first eats human flesh since she exhibits leanings towards such behavior beforehand. She rejects fresh foods (claiming they smell "rotten") and instead eats raw bacon; she bites Ryan; she sucks the blood from a used tampon. None of these transition behaviors is enough to denote that Regina has stopped living and has become undead. It is also unclear precisely when her body dies. Regina's face starts to rot and she craves human flesh while she still has a pulse. Her heart has stopped by the time she is institutionalized, but she remains lucid. Regina's physiological change is on-going, so there is no definitive break between life and death.

These gradual slippages mean that even if we agree that full-blown zombies are non-conscious, it is difficult to measure the difference between human and zombie by referring solely to physical modifications, reported mental experiences, or behavioral changes. Notably, these three elements are indicative of opposing schools within philosophy of self: physicalism/functionalism, phenomenology/consciousness studies, and behaviorism. Regina's transformation reveals that the self cannot be apprehended by just one of these divisive theories, because selfhood is a compound of these elements. For instance, phenomenal experiences are shaped by physical, sensory faculties (see Schechtman). Ergo, without a body, our consciousness would differ in a way that we (as embodied beings) cannot imagine. The reverse is also true: one cannot envision what it would be like to be a conscious-less body, since such imagination *a priori* requires sentient, self-reflective experience. The p-zombie conceivability debate is founded on that impossibility. However, proponents of the p-zombie argument seldom explain embodiment's impact on consciousness in this way. Neither do they typically account for the connections between selfhood and identity. Regina's mutation into zombeing is a shift away from humanity, but her humanity has meaning as an aspect of Regina's social identity.

Zom-Body to Love: Sociosexuality of the Living Dead

Regina's struggle is grounded in concrete social relationships and structures. Contra to Fiona Macpherson's assurance that introspection is enough to validate phenomenal experience, because "introspective knowledge that I have of my own consciousness does not depend for its existence on conditions external to me" (231–2), in *Pretty Dead* it is recognized that human self-experience is always-already dependent on external factors. Identity does not tally with solipsistic asociality. Indeed, practical, social circumstances facilitate the individual's ability to form identity (see Werth 339; Epright 801; Winter 235).

Entirely asocial selfhood is just as unconceivable as disembodied consciousness, because humans are interdependent from birth. The relationalist proposal that "the well-being of each member [of the populace] is interwoven with the well-being of all other members" (Killmister 256) may leave little room for independence, but it underlines how significant social relations are in forging the self. In addition, many pragmatic social tenets stem from essential interconnection, including theories of dignity and moral responsibility (see Ober 832). Thus, sociality impacts directly on how we position ourselves in the world, how we relate to others, how we assess ourselves, and so forth. This cultural-relational account does not supplant physicalism. Indeed, Amy Banks draws on neuroimaging to make an essentialist case that humans are interconnected by default. The cultural-relational paradigm implies that any one exclusory philosophical model (physicalism, behaviorism, functionalism) fails to paint a complete enough picture of selfhood, because these theoretical conceptions of selfhood do not do enough to account for how we actually experience selfhood in the social realm.

Although Regina prizes her social bonds, zombies—who routinely kill and devour—do not (or at least zombies do not express sociality in the way humans do). As she undergoes her transition into zom-being, Regina is torn between two incompatible modes of existence. Her autobiographical accounts are thus conflicted. Even though she does not recall "doing any of the … shit" she is accused of, Regina expresses regret over her actions. For example, she admits liability for those actions as if she were conscious of her behaviors: "I know I did it … I didn't mean to do it." Regina's question "what kind of cure is there for the things I've done? … I don't want to be a monster" is particularly telling in this light. First, she takes ownership over the killings committed ("things I've done"). Second, she assesses those acts according to human values, suggesting that they are incurably monstrous actions. Third, she writes those actions into her identity, dubbing herself "a monster." Regina thereby anchors her liability for the killings in her selfhood. However, this means that she both judges her actions from a human perspective—distancing herself from the perpetrator's monstrosity—and also recognizes that she is the inhuman creature she vilifies. Her discordant assessment is only deepened by her outright denials elsewhere in the film: "I swear I didn't do this ... that wasn't me."

Regina's conflicting statements reveal not a tug of conscience, but a disjuncture in her being. The onset of zom-being impels Regina towards forsaking the values and social bonds that define her humanity. Zom-being necessitates anti-social activity[10]—flesh-eating—and so relinquishing social bonds is a necessary part of zom-becoming. Regina's efforts to resist turning into a zombie are expressed as attempts to maintain her established notion of human sociality. For example, Regina declares, "I don't want to hurt people anymore ... so I stay away from them." Although "stay[ing] away" means negating sociality, her intent is social in orientation since it recognizes her duty to defend others.

Regina's conflict is most notable in her key social relationship: her love for Ryan. Regina wishes to maintain their affiliation, imploring, "I need your help," and angrily accusing Ryan of "ditching [her] when [she] needed [him] most." Simultaneously, by keeping Ryan close, Regina poses a threat to his safety. Although Regina longs to maintain her social links in order to evince her humanity then, in doing so she risks eradicating those bonds. Moreover, Regina's transition into zom-being can be charted via her changing relationship with Ryan, because Ryan's presence underscores her loss of humanity-qua-sociality. The earliest point in the plot is Regina's first date with Ryan, and the bulk of *Pretty Dead* maps their relationship until Ryan's death. Ryan's changing attitudes towards Regina also illuminates her gradual transformation. Ryan initially accepts Regina's behavior. He laughs it off when Regina bites him ("I appreciate your enthusiasm, but Jesus Christ you've got to watch those chompers"), and proclaims that he loves her "despite the fact that [she is] eating raw bacon." Ryan jokingly adapts Kelis' 2003 song *Milkshake*, singing "you like to drink human lard, I'm going to blow my chunks" as Regina consumes a glass of liquidized fat. Ryan admits that such jokes help him "cope." As the film progresses however, Ryan's gags articulate his escalating trepidation. Although light-hearted in tone, Ryan's request "don't eat me if I die" expresses a valid fear. As Regina changes and his doubts intensify, Ryan's jokes are replaced by serious requests—"[l]et me take you to the hospital ... it's not funny"—and eventually outright terror: "you asked me to shoot you ... I'm scared fucking shitless." These shifts chronicle the decline of their relationship.

Ryan provides a constant human presence that throws Regina's changes into relief. The disjuncture between Regina's self-as-experienced and the social world that situates her increases as she transforms. Regina attempts to resolve that tension by embracing death: that is, consciously turning her back on her previous life. After a bleach cocktail ("kill juice") fails to cure her, Regina decides to shoot herself. This suicide attempt is shown twice: once at the outset, and again towards the end of the film. This repeated incident bookends Regina's transition into zom-being and the decline of her union with Ryan. The suicide attempt fails, only scarring her face. Regina then immediately kills Ryan. Although her ontological status remains unclear in the remainder of the film, killing Ryan is a significant marker in Regina's movement towards the "end of her life" as a sociosexual being.

The second most significant turning point in her transformation is presented at the film's conclusion, and again appears to connote the end of Regina's life. In the final frames before the closing credits, Regina's rotting body is carried away on a gurney. A pulsing double-beat redolent of a heartbeat occupies the soundscape, and is eventually replaced by a high-pitched tone reminiscent of a heart-monitor flat-lining. To think of this as a straight-forward physical death is to misread Regina's transformation and the sequence's sociosexual significance. The sound does not indicate that Regina completely "turns" or physiologically dies. Nurse Boyle is unable to find Regina's pulse some time before these closing frames, and so the final soundscape does not denote asystole. Furthermore, Regina already survived flat-lining at a much earlier point in the plot. Before Regina and Ryan are engaged, she overdoses on drugs. In a retrospective voice-over, Regina theorizes that when Ryan resuscitated her, she was brought back as one of the undead: "I died that night, I've been dead ever since." Regina's statement is definitive, as if there was a single moment in which she became a zombie. This distinction is not corroborated by the gradual transition she undergoes. More precisely, when Ryan resuscitated Regina, he started her on the path from humanity to zom-being. The flat-line tone recurs throughout the film. It is heard regularly during Regina's interviews with Dr. Romera, and also sounds in the wake of Ryan's death.

The film's closing sequence underscores that Regina's relationship with Ryan is inextricable from her sociosexual identity. The film's final flat-line tone is another phase in her on-going transition rather than a distinct physiological tipping-point. Indeed, visual cues suggest that the flat-line is metaphysical rather than literal. CCTV shots of Regina's decomposing body being carried from a padded cell are intercut with flashes of Regina and Ryan together before the onset of her transformation. The insert shots are edited to the soundscape's pulsing heartbeat. Intercutting between Regina's lost relationship and images of her putrid body (the state in which she caused Ryan's death) suggests that Regina's *metaphorical* heart—her capacity for love—dies in these climactic moments. Her memories of Ryan pulse like a heartbeat, indicating that Regina's brain functionality (her consciousness) ceases simultaneously. The flat-line tone indicates the death of Regina's humanity-qua-sociality. The cessation of Regina's sociosexuality punctuates the film's closure.

Cumulatively, Regina's overdose, suicide attempts, and gradual putrefaction are inseparable from the metaphoric demise of her sociosexuality, her consciousness, and thus her humanity. However, Regina's subsequent state is not fully realized in the film. Her continuing transition into zom-being does not evoke death as an ending. After all, even full-blown zombies continue to exist. The narrative shape corroborates this theme. The film features two post-credit sequences, further underlining that ostensible endings are instead points of continuation. *Pretty Dead* also opens with Regina's apparent suicide which a) only *appears* to be an ending, and b) happens more than once: it is repeated later in the film. It is beyond the film's capacity to finally elucidate Regina's experience of full-blown zom-being. Instead, *Pretty Dead* de-naturalizes Regina's assumptions about the difference between humanity-qua-rationality and "irrational" zom-being. Despite her desire to control (hinder) her transformation, Regina cannot impede the inexorable change. Regina's behavior is thus at odds with her ability to control or rationalize her conduct, leaving Regina torn between two states of being. *Pretty Dead* thereby flags that rationalizing discourses are unable to capture or wholly explain self-experience.

Zom-Beauty/Zom-Beast: Rationality and the Experiential Hierarchy

Rationality is premised on the idea that humans ought to be able control their behaviors and desires. In this view, the capacity for rationality separates humans from animals, and animal consciousness is implied to be deficient in comparison to human consciousness. An archetypal version of this argument is John Stuart Mill's valorization of human satisfactions (14). Although he has no insight into what it is to be like a pig, Mill presumes that because a pig lacks the human capacity for understanding, a pig's experiences of the world are inferior to a human's. Mill's partiality towards human consciousness is commonplace. Indeed, it is replicated in and legitimated by the authoritative structures of medical science, psychology, law, economics, and so forth. These vast institutions contribute to the existential grand narrative that human consciousness is the standard against which all other experiential viewpoints are tested and found wanting. Experiences of selfhood that contradict that overwhelming grand narrative are consistently invalidated. Indeed, the specter of mental illness underlines that there are "incorrect" ways of experiencing the world. Those who fail to adhere to established "correct" visions of reality and self-experience are routinely institutionalized, for example. Life-forms that "lack" "full" human consciousness—sentience and/or the capacity for rational reflection—are typically treated with disdain (or even destroyed).

On Mill's scale, the zombie would be a lower-life form because the undead lack consciousness. It is clear why zombies are ostensibly incomplete beings: from the living human's perspective, death is the ultimate loss, and so zombies embody deprivation. Yet, undeath does not strictly equate to lifelessness, since zombies continue to exist and remain animate. The zombie's state is incomparable to the human's. As the p-zombie argument elucidates, it is inadequate to think of zombies as subhumans. Zombies do not have phenomenological consciousness, and therefore occupy the world in a way that is unintelligible to the living because human psychology is rooted in experiential awareness. Although zom-being is a fictional state, as a thought-experiment zombies flag how inadequate Mill's hierarchical stance is. The world may be experienced in numerous ways. Since we have no access to alternative modes of experience, the argument that human sentience supplies the "best" experiences is groundless.

Transitional zombie narratives highlight this inadequacy. Regina offers no direct access to what being a zombie is finally like, since full-blown zombies (following the p-zombie paradigm) can no longer verbalize or reflect on their state, since they have no qualia to refer to. However, this does not mean her slippage into zom-being is an experiential "decline." To Regina-qua-human, her relationship with Ryan deteriorates.

However, it does not follow that Regina's transition into zom-being is itself degenerative. To Regina-qua-zombie, the relationship is meaningless; sociality is not relevant to the zombie's state. Human inability to conceive of what zom-being would be like denotes that our conceptual capacity is insufficient for understanding other entities' states, and even the world itself. Regina flags that inadequacy. Regina's autobiographical statements are themed around her social bonds, her identity, her capacity for consciousness, and her physicality. These reflections underline how she conceives of herself, what she values about her existence, and what (as a human) Regina fears she will lose as a result of her metamorphosis.

Her anxieties stem from the degree of control she has over those changes, and her in/ability to comprehend those changes via an anthropocentric understanding of self-experience. Regina reacts by gripping onto the kind of rationalist view Mill venerates. Yet the scientifically credible actions Regina implements to hinder the process only expedite her transformation: "[e]verything I do to fix myself," Regina observes, "just makes things worse." Eventually, Regina's quest to retain control spirals towards irrationality. For example, she announces that she wishes she could turn her "body inside out and scrub [the fungus] off." Regina's grotesque yearning emphasizes her internal, experiential viewpoint at the point when her rational actions and language fail her.

The sovereignty of rational consciousness is bolstered by institutional structures, and *Pretty Dead* undercuts that ostensibly integral position. The second viewpoint offered on Regina's transition is external: having been institutionalized for murdering Ryan and a pizza delivery driver, Regina is observed by Dr. Romera. Here too she reflects upon her experiences, but her report is contested by Romera's diagnoses. Romera is the mouthpiece for a version of rationalist thought that carries disquieting connotations. *Pretty Dead*'s portrayal of a woman (a) whose rationality is called into question, (b) whose carnality is deemed monstrous, and (c) whose liberty is infringed upon by medico-legal apparatuses, is reminiscent of "hysteria": diagnostic rhetoric that carries deeply misogynistic overtones. As Julie Lokis-Adkins observes, "by the end of the [19th century], half of all women were thought to be hysterics" because they resisted the societal limitations imposed on them; "there were two options for young, unmarried women: enter a convent or marry" (40; see also Greer 55). That is, gender-biased socio-sexual norms were implemented via two types of institution—medical and matrimonial—legitimating the broad fear that any woman who did not adhere to their "proper" social place would "become a sexual predator: a monster even" (Lokis-Adkins 40; see also Mesch 107). Ironically, such terror itself smacks of hysteria. This over-wrought reaction implies that female sexuality is enormously potent, even capable of disturbing the entire patriarchal structure. Neither historically rooted gendered oppression nor contemporary gender politics will be dwelt upon in what follows.[11] Of greater pertinence to the discussion in hand are the ways in which a particular view of existence is validated. The legal-medical structure not only confirms but also enforces a vision of reality that stems from scientific rationality. In *Pretty Dead*, that ethos is embodied by Romera, who seeks to "cure" Regina and return her to "normal." That is, Romera imposes his established rationalist view, ignoring Regina's objections to his diagnosis. Romera talks over Regina's protests rather than considering her purported self-experiences, thereby indicating his belief that his explication is incontestable.

Although Regina's and Romera's diagnoses clash, it is not that their appraisals of Regina's situation are entirely dichotomous. Regina's auto-diagnosis shares Romera's judgment that zom-being is unacceptable. Before Regina is arrested, she proclaims "obviously I'm out of control. I'm a monster." Her assessment is directly echoed in Romera's concern that Regina "is out of control." Regina's self-evaluation denotes her devotion to a rational anthropocentric view of existence despite its incongruity with her self-experience. Although Regina apprehends her position via scientific models ("I'm not schizophrenic ... [or] delusional"), she documents her experiences during her transition by referring to how she *feels* ("I can feel it in me," "I feel pretty dead already"). *Pretty Dead* thereby validates her sensations as a mode of understanding her transition rather than rejecting those expressions of self-experience (as Romera does).

The same balance is achieved via *Pretty Dead*'s form. *Pretty Dead* is characterized as a "true story"; on-screen captions posit that the film is "a collection of ... recovered" footage.[12] Yet *Pretty Dead*'s viewer is not encouraged to side with Romera's rational, external view and reject Regina's internal-experiential claim that she is undead. Romera's and Regina's clashing diagnoses are reflected in *Pretty Dead*'s dual formal perspectives. In the asylum, Regina is perceived via a sterile observatory stance. These sequences are shot via three cameras that are aligned with Romera's perspective, thereby implying that his diagnosis is accurate. The first camera is situated alongside Romera, and films Regina front-on. No reverse angle is available (no camera captures Romera front-on).

Regina is clearly inspected in a way that Romera is not, implying that her version of events requires justification, whereas his is unquestioned. The second is a CCTV camera situated behind Romera. Although much of the room is covered in these shots, the camera faces only Regina: Romera remains anonymous. Additionally, this camera captures other figures (orderlies and nurses) who concur with Romera's diagnosis. Their presence corroborates that his clinical opinion is a majority stance. The third camera is less definitive. Placed side on to Romera and Regina, this camera frames their conversation in a more balanced fashion: Regina on screen-right, Romera on screen-left. Romera is scrutinized on the same level as Regina in these shots. This third camera is more broadly indicative of *Pretty Dead*'s methodology. Approximately 60 percent of the movie is captured by Regina and Ryan's camcorder. In much of that footage, Regina expounds her experiences. Even where the content is highly personal in nature, depicting Regina and Ryan's relationship for example, the found-footage mode paints these incidents as empirical fact, equal to Romera's observations. Indeed, the camcorder tape's status as evidence is verified firstly by an on-screen caption stating that the video is "all that remains to tell [Regina's] story," and secondly by Romera's declaration that the camcorder footage would authenticate Regina's self-diagnosis.

Since *Pretty Dead* includes Regina's auto-documentation, her seemingly irrational diagnosis is legitimated for the viewer. In contrast, Romera fails to cure Regina, despite his plausible explanation for her condition. Scientific rationality is incapable of capturing what is happening to Regina. For instance, although Romera states that "it would be easy to prove what you say is true if we do a physical," even the most rudimentary medical methods fail. Nurse Boyle deems that her equipment is "broken" when she cannot find Regina's blood pressure. The sedatives Romera prescribes are ineffective. Regina's own reliance on scientific rationalization is just as flawed. Although she perceives her transition as a "big medical breakthrough," her documentation quickly spirals into an autobiographical mode, focusing on her crumbling sociosexual relationship. There are no discoveries, just personal effects. Her self-shot video is not available to evince her case to Romera. Instead, the tapes serve an intimate social function: they are an extended suicide note to Regina's companions. In Regina's final moments of auto-documentation, she apologizes to her loved ones ("Sorry, Dad, this isn't your fault") and expresses her self-destructive intentions ("I'm already dead already [sic], I just need a little help lying down").

Despite their powerful supporting structures, rationalist medico-scientific understandings of Regina's condition are ultimately subordinate to her personal experiences and social identity in *Pretty Dead*. So, contrary to the commonplace notion that rationality is a pre-condition for forming meaningful social bonds (Anderson 127–8), *Pretty Dead* indicates that (a) phenomenological experience is the foundation of selfhood, and (b) social bonds provide an index for the formation of identity. These are the elements Regina loses during her transition into zombeing. Rationality provides one mode of apprehending self, but here it pales in comparison with experiential understanding of selfhood in the socio-sexual realm.

Zom-Bequeathed: Sociosexual P-Zombies

Although *Pretty Dead* does not answer the question of what it is like to be a zombie, Regina's transition highlights crucial differences between human experience and zom-being. Most notably, *Pretty Dead* probes the role sociality—here, epitomized as sociosexuality—plays in self-conception. The narrative thereby also undercuts the anthropocentric "experiential hierarchy" on which rationalist notions of human consciousness are founded. Thus, transitional zombie narratives such as *Pretty Dead* highlight areas in selfhood philosophy that would benefit from greater critical attention. First, intuitive self-experience should not be neglected. Self-reports are typically viewed as problematic because they are prone to bias and error (see Doucet; Hohwy; Whiting). However, dismissing autobiographical accounts entirely risks privileging rationalism and misses what is useful about such accounts: that they reflect how selfhood is experienced in the social realm. Second, we should not be blind to the impact institutional arrangements of power have both on self-experience and on conceptions of selfhood. In *Pretty Dead*, these structures are embodied by the rationalist medico-legal institution in which Regina is detained. The conflict between Regina and Romera's viewpoints evinces the need for a new discourse that is attuned to Regina's self-experiences rather than one that quashes incompatible reports.

To neglect the social world—in which experiences happen, in which behaviors manifest, in which identity of formed—is to hark back to a Cartesian model of selfhood, which separates interior and exterior. As Andrea Nye observes, René Descartes' dualistic paradigm is flawed because he envisages consciousness as "solipsistic ... removed from passion and imagination," and ultimately drives a wedge "between feeling and knowing" (26). Although dualism is largely rejected in contemporary philosophy, we should take care not to replicate his conceptual flaw: privileging self-experience to the extent that "self" is divorced from social reality. A coherent theory of selfhood must bridge between the personal, internal world of desires, motives, and intentions on one hand and the external social world on the other. Many proponents of the p-zombie debates fail to achieve this balance because they focus on rationalizing paradigms such as "physicalism," and are not attuned to our experiences of self.

It is surprising that interdependent sociality has featured so little in discussions regarding zombies and consciousness to date. Sociality is fundamental to self-conception, and so it impacts on self-experience. Transitional zombie narratives offer an avenue into examining consciousness that is sensitive to an intuitive version of selfhood, one that develops the p-zombie debates by thinking about selfhood in a pragmatic way. In contrast, p-zombie debates are typically hypothetical in nature, and lead to some outlandish assertions about self-experience. For instance, Philip Goff proposes that he cannot imagine what it is to be a zombie, but can readily conceive of being an equally hypothetical "lonely ghost." It is little wonder that some philosophers have rejected p-zombies altogether. Daniel Dennett, for example, has labeled the p-zombie argument "preposterous," elaborating that it is a "strangely attractive" but "unsupportable hypothesis" that ought to be "dropped ... like a hot potato" (171).

Those zombies we *can* apprehend—those represented in popular culture—are of philosophical value in ways that their p-zombie brethren are not. Contemporary movie zombies are becoming ever more akin to humans, and commonly occupy human social situations. Rather than being denizens of apocalyptic wastelands, the undead are now frequently placed in unexceptional "human" scenarios, as titles such as *Zombie Cheerleading Camp* (2007), *Zombie Beach Party* (2003) and *Brunch of the Living Dead* (2006) evince. As they come to inhabit a broader range of everyday social spheres and become increasingly alive to human experiences, movie zombies are becoming progressively valuable conduits for philosophical reflection on the self and ourselves.

As I have argued throughout this essay, *Pretty Dead* is a prototypical example of how zombie movies can be utilized for philosophical enquiry into sociosexual existence. *Pretty Dead* is rooted in reality, both formally (employing found-footage realism), and thematically (focusing on Regina's medico-legal and social conditions). Crucially, *Pretty Dead* underlines Regina's *experience* of transition, and this is what viewers engage with. Rationally, we know Regina's story is fictional, that Regina is performed by an actor (Carly Oates), and that zombies do not genuinely exist. Viewers who engage with *Pretty Dead* as a narrative do so at an intuitive, experiential level. Compared with the cold, dead analysis of p-zombie argumentation, zombie movies are animate and vital. Interaction with Regina's story is closer to a social, emotive experience than it is an intellectual process. That experience is not adequately captured by the rationalist conceptual tools currently at our disposal. Films such as *Pretty Dead* do not just engage its viewers in an intuitive kind of philosophical thinking. By depicting a form of selfhood that defies rationalist logic (zom-being), these films also challenge their viewers into developing new conceptual (theoretical and imaginative) vocabularies via which to describe and engage with both selfhood and sociosexuality.

NOTES

1. The philosophical zombie was evoked earlier by Kripke and Block for example, although Chalmers' contentions (*The Conscious Mind*) have inspired much recent debate.

2. A terminological point requires clarification. The term "transition" carries established meanings in the context of sociosexual identity discourse. Individuals experience sociosexual transformations of all kinds, ranging from pubescence to "coming out" to transsexual transition. My use of "transition" does not seek to draw a comparison between any of these particular shifts and becoming undead.

3. This play on "Romero" evinces that the narrative is clearly staked as a zombie film, despite the ambiguity over Regina's undeadness.

4. There are two notable variations on this theme. First, films such as *Zombie Love* (2007) and *A Zombie Love Song* (2013) depict zombies falling in love with living persons. Zombies are limned as having autonomy in these cases, and so they will not be considered here. Second, *Dating a Zombie* (2012) presents a living protagonist who eschews relationships with the living in favour of partnerships with the undead. In this case, sociality's value is called into question. Anyone interested in the practicalities of sociosexuality in the wake of outbreak may wish to consult *Chip and Bernie's Dating Guide for the Zombie Apocalypse* (2011), which outlines problems associated with "zomance" and offers advice on handling the "opposite" (undead) sex.

5. Indeed, zombies exhibit behaviors, but (presumably) have no underlying mental states.

6. Qualia, in this view, are indicators of consciousness.

7. On the conceivability of p-zombies and epistemic limitations, see Hanrahan; Goff; Diaz-Leon; Majeed.

8. As an aside, some full-blown zombies claim to have experiences and display awareness of their state. One prototypical example is the female zombie torso in *Return of the Living Dead* (1985) who is able to articulate that being undead "hurts"; she explains that zombies eat brains because it temporarily assuages the agony of being dead. This zombie purports to have at least one kind of phenomenal experience

(pain), which signifies self-knowledge: the zombie describes herself as an entity that has undergone an experience. One could argue that the zombie is mistaken and does not really have phenomenal experiences. There is a difference between stating that one has had an experience and actually *having* an experience. However, the same line of thought would give us reason to doubt the veracity of qualia in general. We have no means of knowing whether other living humans' reports of experiencing are as false as the zombies' are. Moreover, if the zombie believes that they are experiencing, there is every chance that one's own claims to experiencing are also false. Incredulity over the zombies' claim to consciousness leaves the living sceptic with no grounds for demonstrating their own claim to consciousness (on this quandary, see Macpherson 231–2).

9. Cordyceps fungus also causes the zombie plague in the recent videogame *The Last of Us* (2013).

10. Flesh eating is anti-social according to Regina's norms. In some cultures cannibalism is a social practice rooted in compassion and interpersonal obligation. For example, see Conklin.

11. For discussion of zombies and gender politics, see Jones "Gender Monstrosity."

12. Moreover, the film-makers have declared that they intended to make a realistic, "scientifically plausible" zombie film. See Wilkins.

Bibliography

Aggrawal, Anil. *Necrophilia: Forensic and Medico-Legal Aspects.* Boca Raton: Taylor and Francis, 2011.

Ahmed, Sara. *Queer Phenomenology: Orientations, Objects, Others.* Durham: Duke University Press, 2006.

Alaimo, Stacy. *Bodily Natures: Science, Environment, and the Material Self.* Bloomington: Indiana University Press, 2010.

Althaus-Reid, Marcella. *Indecent Theology: Theological Perversions in Sex, Gender and Politics.* London: Routledge, 2000.

Anatole, Emily. "Generation Z: Rebels with a Cause." *Forbes.* 28 May 2013.

Anderson, Scott. "On Sexual Obligation and Sexual Autonomy." *Hypatia* 28.1 (2013): 122–41.

Aquilina, Carmelo, and Julian C. Hughes. "The Return of the Living Dead: Agency Lost and Found." In *Dementia: Mind, Meaning, and the Person.* Eds. Julian C. Hughes, Stephen J. Louw, and Steven R. Sabat. Oxford: Oxford University Press, 2006. 143–61.

Attwood, Feona. "Sexed Up: Theorizing the Sexualization of Culture." *Sexualities* 8.5 (2006): 77–94.

_____, and Clarissa Smith. "Extreme Concern: Regulating 'Dangerous Pictures' in the United Kingdom." *Journal of Law and Society* 37.1 (2010): 171–88.

Auerbach, Nina. *Our Vampires, Ourselves.* Chicago: University of Chicago Press, 1995.

Augustine. *City of God.* Trans. Henry Bettenson. London: Penguin, 1972.

Austen, Jane, and Seth Grahame-Smith. *Pride, Prejudice and Zombies.* Philadelphia: Quirk, 2009.

_____, and Ben H. Winters. *Sense and Sensibility and Sea Monsters.* Philadelphia: Quirk, 2009.

Bakhtin, Mikhael. *Rabelais and His World.* Bloomington: Indiana University Press, 1984.

Banks, Amy. "Developing the Capacity to Connect." *Zygon* 46.1 (2011): 168–82.

Barrett, C.K. *A Commentary on the Epistle to the Romans.* London: Adam and Charles Black, 1957.

Barrett Gross, Matthew. *The Last Myth.* New York: Prometheus, 2012.

Barth, Karl. *The Epistle to the Romans.* Trans. Edwyn C. Hoskyns. London: Oxford University Press, 1933.

Bayer, Ronald, and Eric A. Feldman, eds. "Understanding the Blood Feuds." In *Blood Feuds: AIDS, Blood, and the Politics of Medical Disaster.* Eds. Eric A. Feldman and Ronald Bayer. New York: Oxford University Press, 1999. 1–16.

Beaudoin, Tom. *Virtual Faith: The Irreverent Spiritual Quest of Generation X.* San Francisco: Jossey-Bass, 1998.

Behlmer, George K. "Grave Doubts: Victorian Medicine, Moral Panic and the Signs of Death." *Journal of British Studies* 42.2 (2003): 206–35.

Behuniak, Susan. M. "The Living Dead? The Construction of People with

Alzheimer's Disease as Zombies." *Ageing and Society* 31.1 (2011): 70–92.

Benshoff, Harry M. *Monsters in the Closet: Homosexuality and the Horror Film*. Manchester: Manchester University Press, 1997.

Berenstein, Rhona J. "'It Will Thrill You, It May Shock You, It Might Even Horrify You': Gender, Reception, and Classic Horror Cinema." In *The Dread of Difference: Gender and the Horror Film*. Ed. Barry Keith Grant. Austin: University of Texas Press, 1996. 117–142.

Berlant, Lauren. "Intimacy: A Special Issue." In *Intimacy*. Ed. Lauren Berlant. Chicago: University of Chicago Press, 2000. 1–20.

Bersani, Leo. "Is the Rectum a Grave?" *October* 43.1 (1987): 197–222.

Bersani, Leo. *The Freudian Body: Psychoanalysis and Art*. New York: Columbia University Press, 1986.

Bertellini, Giorgio. "*Profundo Rosso/Deep Red*: Dario Argento, Italy, 1975." In *The Cinema of Italy*. Ed. Giorgio Bertellini. London: Wallflower Press, 2004. 213–22.

Bishop, Kyle William. *American Zombie Gothic: The Rise and Fall (and Rise) of the Walking Dead in Popular Culture*. Jefferson: McFarland, 2010.

_____. "Raising the Dead: Unearthing the Non-Literary Origins of Zombie Cinema." *Journal of Popular Film and Television* 33.4 (2006): 196–205.

Block, Ned. "Are Absent Qualia Impossible?" *The Philosophical Review* 89.2 (1980): 257–74.

Bosky, Bernadette Lynn. "Making the Implicit, Explicit: Vampire Erotica and Pornography." In *The Blood is the Life: Vampires in Literature*. Eds. Leonard G. Heldreth and Mary Pharr. Bowling Green: Bowling Green State University Press, 1999. 217–33.

Briggs, Laura. *Reproducing Empire: Race, Sex, Science, and U.S. Imperialism in Puerto Rico*. Berkeley: University of California Press, 2002.

Brinkley, Alan. "The Conquest of the Far West." In *The Unfinished Nation: A Concise History of the American People*. Eds. Alan Brinkley, Harvey Jackson, and Bradley Rice. New York: McGraw Hill, 2004. 176–186.

Brock, Marilyn. "The Vamp and the Good English Mother: Female Roles in Le Fanu's *Carmilla* and Stoker's *Dracula*." In *From Wollstonecraft to Stoker: Essays on Gothic and Victorian Sensation Fiction*. Ed. Marilyn Brock. Jefferson: McFarland, 2009. 120–31.

Brooks, Max. *The Zombie Survival Guide*. New York: Random House, 2003.

Brooks, Max. *World War Z*. London: Gerald Duckworth, 2006.

Brown, Kate E. "Beloved Objects: Mourning, Materiality, and Charlotte Brontë's 'Never-Ending Story.'" *English Literary History* 65.2 (1998): 395–422.

Brown, Norman O. *Love's Body*. Berkeley: University of California Press, 1966.

Brown, Wendy. *Edgework: Critical Essays on Knowledge and Politics*. Princeton: Princeton University Press, 2005.

Browne, Scott G. "Zombie Gigolo." In *The Living Dead 2*. Ed. John Joseph Adams. San Francisco: Night Shade Books, 2010. 265–68.

Bryan, T. J. "It Takes Ballz: Reflections of a Black Attitudinal Femme Vixen in tha Makin.'" In *Brazen Femme: Queering Femininity*. Eds. Chloë Brushwood Rose and Anna Camilleri. Vancouver: Arsenal Press, 2002. 147–59.

Butler, Judith. *Gender Trouble*. New York: Routledge, 1999.

Butler, Judith. *Precarious Life: The Powers of Mourning and Violence*. London: Verso, 2004.

Cacho, Lisa Marie. *Social Death: Racialized Rightlessness and the Criminalization of the Unprotected*. New York: New York University Press, 2012.

Camporesi, Piero. "The Consecrated Host: A Wondrous Excess." In *Fragments for a History of the Human Body*. Ed. Michel Felier. New York: Zone, 1989. 220–37.

Canter, David V., and Natalia Wentink. "An Empirical Test of Holmes and

Holmes's Serial Murder Typology." *Criminal Justice and Behavior* 31.4 (2004): 489–515.

Castillo, Michelle. "Rotten to the Core." *New York Press*. 26 May 2010.

Castronovo, Russ. "Political Necrophilia." *boundary2* 27.2 (2000): 113–148.

Chalmers, David. *The Conscious Mind: In Search of a Fundamental Theory*. Oxford: Oxford University Press, 1996.

_____. "Consciousness and Its Place in Nature." In *Philosophy of Mind: Classical and Contemporary Readings*. Ed. David Chalmers. Oxford: Oxford University Press, 2002. 247–72.

Chen, Mel Y. *Animacies: Biopolitics, Racial Mattering, and Queer Affec*t. Durham: Duke University Press, 2012.

Christie, Deborah, and Sarah Juliet Lauro, eds. *Better Off Dead: The Evolution of the Zombie as Post-Human*. New York: Fordham University Press, 2011.

Ciampa, Roy E., and Brian S. Rosner. *The First Letter to the Corinthians*. Grand Rapids: Wm. B. Eerdmans, 2010.

Clark, Danae. "Commodity Lesbianism." In *The Lesbian and Gay Studies Reader*. Eds. Henry Abelove, Michèle Aina Barale, and David M. Halperin. New York: Routledge, 1993. 186–201.

Clarke, Amy M., and Marijane Osborn. *The Twilight Mystique: Critical Essays on the Novels and Films*. Jefferson: McFarland, 2010.

Click, Melissa A., Jennifer Stevens Aubrey, and Elizabeth Behm-Morawitz, eds. *Bitten by Twilight: Youth Culture, Media, and the Vampire Franchise*. New York: Peter Lang, 2010.

Clover, Carol J. *Men, Women, and Chain Saws: Gender in the Modern Horror Film*. Princeton: Princeton University Press, 1992.

Cohen, Jeffrey Jerome. *Monster Theory*. Minneapolis: Minnesota University Press, 1996.

Comaroff, Jean, and John L. Comaroff. "Alien-Nation: Zombies, Immigrants, and Millennial Capitalism." *The South Atlantic Quarterly* 101.4 (2002): 779–805.

Combs, Mary Beth. "'A Measure of Legal Independence': The 1870 Married Women's Property Act and the Portfolio Allocations of British Wives." *The Journal of Economic History* 65.4 (2005): 1028–57.

Comeau, J. L. "Seminar Z." In *Dead Set: A Zombie Anthology*. Eds. Michelle McCrarym and Joe McKinney. Jefferson, TX: 23 House, 2010. 171–92.

Conklin, Beth. *Consuming Grief: Compassionate Cannibalism in an Amazonian Society*. Austin: University of Texas Press, 2001.

Cornwall, Susannah. *Controversies in Queer Theology*. London: SCM Press, 2011.

Craft, Christopher. "'Kiss Me with Those Red Lips': Gender and Inversion in Bram Stoker's *Dracula*." *Representations* 8.3 (1984): 107–33.

Creed, Barbara. *The Monstrous-Feminine: Film, Feminism, Psychoanalysis*. London: Routledge, 1993.

Davis, Wade. *The Serpent and the Rainbow*. New York: Simon & Schuster, 1985.

Delaney, Samuel R. *Times Square Red, Times Square Blue*. New York: New York University Press, 1999.

Dendle, Peter. "The Zombie as Barometer of Cultural Anxiety." In *Monsters and the Monstrous: Myths and Metaphors of Enduring Evil*. Ed. Niall Scott. New York: Rodopi, 2007. 45–57.

Dendle, Peter. *The Zombie Movie Encyclopedia*. Jefferson: McFarland, 2000.

Dennett, Daniel C. "The Unimagined Preposterousness of Zombies: Commentary on Moody, Flanagan and Polger." *Brainchildren: Essays on Designing Minds*. Ed. Daniel C. Dennett. London: Penguin, 1998. 171–77.

Dennison, Michael J. *Vampirism: Literary Tropes of Decadence and Entropy*. New York: Peter Lang, 2001.

Diaz-Leon, E. "Are Ghosts Scarier Than Zombies?" *Consciousness and Cognition* 21.2 (2012): 747–48.

Dines, Gail. *Pornland: How Porn Has Hijacked Our Sexuality*. Boston: Beacon, 2010.

Doucet, Mathieu. "Can We Be Self-Deceived About What We Believe? Self-Knowledge, Self-Deception, and Rational Agency." *European Journal of Philosophy* 20.1 (2012): 1–25.

Downing, Lisa. "Death and the Maidens: A Century of Necrophilia in Female-Authored Textual Production." *French Cultural Studies* 14.2 (2003): 157–68.

Drezner, Daniel W. *Theories of International Politics and Zombies*. Princeton: Princeton University Press, 2011.

Dudley, Scott. "Conferring with the Dead: Necrophilia and Nostalgia in the Seventeenth Century." *ELH: English Literary History* 66.2 (1999): 277–94.

Duggan, Lisa. "The New Homonormativity: The Sexual Politics of Neoliberalism." In *Materializing Democracy: Toward a Revitalized Cultural Politics*. Eds. Russ Castronovo and Dana D. Nelson. Durham: Duke University Press, 2002. 175–94.

Duggan, Lisa. *The Twilight of Equality? Neoliberalism, Cultural Politics, and the Attack On Democracy*. Boston: Beacon Press, 2003.

Dworkin, Andrea. *Pornography: Men Possessing Women*. New York: Plume, 1989.

Dyer, Richard. "Stereotyping." In *The Columbia Reader on Lesbians and Gay Men in Media, Society, and Politics*. Eds. Larry Gross and James Woods. New York: Columbia University Press, 1999. 297–301.

Edelman, Lee. *No Future: Queer Theory and the Death Drive*. Durham: Duke University Press, 2004.

Elliott-Smith, Darren. "Death is the New Pornography! Gay Zombies, Homonormativity and Consuming Masculinity in Queer Horror." In *Screening the Undead: Vampires and Zombies in Film and Television*. Eds. Leon Hunt, Milly Williamson, and Sharon Lockyer. London: I.B. Tauris, 2013. 148–171.

Episcopal Church. *The Book of Common Prayer*. New York: Church Hymnal Corporation, 1979.

Epright, M. Carmela. "Coercing Future Freedom: Consent and Capacities for Autonomous Choice." *Journal of Law, Medicine & Ethics* 38.4 (2010): 799–806.

Faetopia Crew. "Zombie Christ Haunted House." Zombiechristwww. 29 March 2013.

Farnell, Gary. "Theorizing the Gothic for the Twenty-First Century." In *Twenty-First-Century Gothic*. Eds. Brigid Cherry, Peter Howell, and Caroline Ruddell. Newcastle upon Tyne: Cambridge Scholars, 2010. 7–18.

Foucault, Michel. *The Government of Self and Others: Lectures at the Collège de France 1982–1983*. Ed. Arnold I. Davidson. Trans. Graham Burchell. New York: Palgrave Macmillan, 2010.

Foucault, Michel. *The History of Sexuality Vol. 1*. Trans. Robert Hurley. Harmondsworth: Penguin, 1990.

Freud, Sigmund. *Introductory Lectures on Psychoanalysis*. Trans. James Strachey. Harmondsworth: Penguin, 1975.

_____. "Three Essays on Sexuality." In *On Sexuality*. Trans. James Strachey. London: Penguin, 1991. 45–170.

_____. *Totem and Taboo*. London: Routledge Classics. 2001.

Furst, Martina. "Exemplarization: A Solution to the Problem of Consciousness?" *Philosophical Studies* 161.1 (2012): 141–51.

Fuss, Diana. 'Oral Incorporations: *The Silence of the Lambs*." In *Identification Papers*. New York: Routledge, 1995.

Garland-Thomson, Rosemarie. "Integrating Disability, Transforming Feminist Theory." In *Feminist Disability Studies*. Ed. Kim Q. Hall. Bloomington: Indiana University Press, 2011. 13–47.

Garrett, Brian Jonathan. "Causal Essentialism Versus the Zombie Worlds." *Canadian Journal of Philosophy* 39.1 (2009): 93–112.

Gates, Henry Louis, Jr. *The Signifying Monkey: A Theory of African Ameri-*

can Literary Criticism. New York: Oxford University Press, 1988.

Gaudiosi, John. "Skybound Entertainment Founder Robert Kirkman Talks Comics, videogames And *The Walking Dead.*" *Forbes.* 26 November 2012.

Giddens, Anthony. *The Transformation of Intimacy: Sexuality, Love and Eroticism in Modern Societies.* Stanford: Stanford University Press, 1992.

Gilbert, Sandra M., and Susan Gubar. *The Madwoman in the Attic: The Woman Writer and the Nineteenth-Century Literary Imagination.* New Haven: Yale University Press, 2000.

Giroux, Henry A. *Zombie Politics and Culture in the Age of Casino Capitalism.* New York: Peter Lang, 2011.

Glassner, Barry. *The Culture of Fear: Why Americans Are Afraid of the Wrong Things.* New York: Basic Books. 1999.

Goff, Philip. "A Priori Physicalism, Lonely Ghosts and Cartesian Doubt." *Consciousness and Cognition* 21.2 (2012): 742–46.

Gordon, Henry Laing. *Sir James Young Simpson and Chloroform 1811–1870.* Honolulu: University Press of the Pacific, 2002.

Gordon, Joan, and Veronica Hollinger. *Blood Read: The Vampire as Metaphor in Contemporary Culture.* Philadelphia: University of Pennsylvania Press, 1995.

Grant, Barry Keith. "Taking Back the Night of the Living Dead: George Romero, Feminism, and the Horror Film." In *The Dread of Difference.* Ed. Barry Keith Grant. Austin: University of Texas Press, 1996. 200–12.

Grau, Marion. *Of Divine Economy: Refinancing Redemption.* New York: T&T Clark, 2004.

Gray, Kurt, and Daniel M. Wegner. "Torture and Judgments of Guilt." *Journal of Experimental Social Psychology* 46.1 (2010): 233–35.

Green, Amber. *Dead Kitties Don't Purr.* Atlanta: Noble Romance, 2012.

Greenberg, Harvey. "Reimagining the Gargoyle." In *Close Encounters: Film,* *Feminism and Science Fiction.* Eds. Constance Penley, Elisabeth Lyon, Lynn Spigel, and Janet Bergstrom. Minneapolis: University of Minnesota Press, 1993. 83–106.

Greer, Germaine. *The Female Eunuch.* London: HarperCollins, 2008.

Greven, David. *Representations of Femininity in American Genre Cinema: The Woman's Film, Film Noir, and Modern Horror.* New York: Palgrave, 2011.

Gross, Neil, and Solon Simmons. "Intimacy as a Double-Edged Phenomenon? An Empirical Test of Giddens." *Social Forces* 81.2 (2002): 531–55.

Grosz, Elizabeth. *Space, Time, and Perversion: Essays on the Politics of Bodies.* New York: Routledge, 1995.

Gutierrez, Roberto, and Roger Giner-Sorolla. "Anger, Disgust, and Presumption of Harm as Reactions to Taboo Breaking Behaviors." *Emotion* 7.4 (2007): 853–68.

Guy, Jean-Sebastien. "Rethinking Sexuality with Luhmann and Giddens." Paper presented at the Canadian Sociological Association Annual Meeting, Waterloo. 26 May 2012.

Halberstam, Judith. *Female Masculinity.* Durham: Duke University Press, 1998.

_____. *The Queer Art of Failure.* Durham: Duke University Press, 2011.

_____. *Skin Shows: Gothic Horror and the Technology of Monsters.* Durham: Duke University Press, 1995.

Hall, Kim Q. "Introduction." In *Feminist Disability Studies.* Ed. Kim Q. Hall. Bloomington: Indiana University Press, 2011. 1–10.

Hancock, Philip, Bill Hughes, Elizabeth Jagger, Kevin Paterson, Rachel Russell, Emmanuelle Tulle-Winton, and Melissa Tyler. *The Body, Culture and Society.* Buckingham: Open University Press, 2000.

Hannabach, Cathy. "Technologies of Blood: Asylum, Medicine, and Biopolitics." *Cultural Politics* 9.1 (2013): 22–41.

Hanrahan, Rebecca Roman. "Consciousness and Modal Empiricism." *Philosophia* 37.2 (2009): 281–306.

Hanson, Ellis. "Undead." In *Inside/Out: Lesbian Theories, Gay Theories*. Ed. Diana Fuss. London: Routledge, 1991. 324–26.

Hardy, Ernest. "Zombie Deep Throat." *Blood Beats*. 7 January 2010.

Harman, Chris. *Zombie Capitalism: Global Crisis and the Relevance of Marx*. Chicago: Haymarket Books, 2012.

Harmes, Barbara. *Fin de Siècle: Sexual Crisis and Social Disorder*. University of Southern Queensland PhD, 1999.

_____, and Marcus Harmes. "*My Secret Life* and the Sexual Economy of *Fin-de-Siècle* England." *Australasian Journal of Victorian Studies* 17.1 (2012): 15–26.

Harvey, David. "Neoliberalism as Creative Destruction." *The Annals of the American Academy of Political and Social Science*, 610.1 (2007): 21–44.

Harvey, David. *A Brief History of Neoliberalism*. New York: Oxford University Press, 2005.

Hawkes, Gail. ed. *The Blackwell Encyclopedia of Sociology*. Malden, MA: Blackwell, 2007.

Hays, Matthew. *The View from Here: Interviews with Gay and Lesbian Directors*. Vancouver: Arsenal Pulp Press, 2007.

Heil, John. *From an Ontological Point of View*. New York: Clarendon Press, 2003.

Hodgson, Peter C. *Hegel and Christian Theology: A Reading of the Lectures on the Philosophy of Religion*. London: Oxford University Press, 2005.

Hoffman, Nina Kiriki. "Third Dead Body." In *The Living Dead*. Ed. John Joseph Adams. San Francisco: Night Shade Books, 2008. 83–97.

Hohwy, Jakob. "Phenomenal Variability and Introspective Reliability" *Mind & Language* 20.3 (2011): 261–86.

Horowitz, Amir. "Turning the Zombie on its Head." *Synthese* 170.1 (2009): 191–210.

Howard, John. *Men like That: A Southern Queer History*. Chicago: University of Chicago Press, 1999.

Jameson, Fredric. "Progress versus Utopia; or Can We Imagine the Future?" *Science Fiction Studies* 9.2 (1982): 147–58.

Johnson, E. Patrick. *Sweet Tea: Black Gay Men of the South, an Oral History*. Chapel Hill: University of North Carolina Press, 2008.

Johnson, Paul. "Haunting Heterosexuality: The Homo/Het Binary and Intimate Love." *Sexualities* 7.2 (2004): 183–200.

Jones, Steve. "Gender Monstrosity: Deadgirl and the Sexual Politics of Zombie-Rape." *Feminist Media Studies* 13.4 (2013): 525–39.

_____. "Porn of the Dead: Necrophilia, Feminism, and Gendering the Undead." In *Zombies Are Us: Essays on the Humanity of the Walking Dead*. Eds. Christopher Moreman and Cory Rushton. Jefferson: McFarland, 2011. 40–61.

_____. *Torture Porn: Popular Horror after Saw*. London: Palgrave, 2013.

_____. "XXXombies: Economies of Desire and Disgust." In *Thinking Dead: What the Zombie Apocalypse Means*. Ed. Murali Balaji. New York: Lexington, 2013. 197–214.

Julian of Norwich. *Revelations of Divine Love*. Trans. Elizabeth Spearing. London: Penguin, 1998.

Keesey, Douglas. "Intertwinings of Death and Desire in Michele Soavi's *Dellamorte Dellamore*." *Horror Studies* 2.1 (2011): 105–14.

Killmister, Suzy. "Why Group Membership Matters: A Critical Typology." *Ethnicities* 12.3 (2012): 251–69.

Kinnard, Meg. "Zombie Fads Peak When People Are Unhappy." *Huffington Post*. 11 March 2013.

Kipnis, Laura. *Bound and Gagged: Pornography and the Politics of Fantasy in America*. Durham: Duke University Press, 1999.

Kirk, Robert. *Zombies and Consciousness*. Oxford: Oxford University Press, 2005.

Kirkman, Robert, and Charlie Adlard. *The Walking Dead: Compendium Two*. Berkeley: Image Comics, 2012.

Kirkman, Robert, Tony Moore, and Charlie Adlard. *The Walking Dead: Compendium One.* Berkeley: Image Comics, 2011.

Kirtley, David Barr. "Skull Faced City." In *The Living Dead 2.* Ed. John Joseph Adams. San Francisco: Night Shade Books, 2010. 175–90.

Koplowitz, Howard. "'Miami Zombie' Victim Ronald Poppo Details Recovery One Year After Gruesome Attack." *International Business Times.* 21 May 2013.

Kozlowski, Jan. "First Love Never Dies." In *Hungry for Your Love.* Ed. Lori Perkins. New York: St. Martin's Griffin, 2009. 89–103.

Kripke, Saul. *Naming and Necessity.* Cambridge: Harvard University Press, 1972.

LaBruce, Bruce. "Interview with Bruce LaBruce." *Baader-Meinhoff.* 11 October 2011.

LaCugna, Catherine Mowry. *God for Us: The Trinity and Christian Life.* New York: HarperSanFrancisco, 1992.

Langdridge, Darren, and Trevor Butt. "The Erotic Construction of Power Exchange." *Journal of Constructivist Psychology* 18.1 (2006): 65–73.

Larsen, Kari. "Search for Security." *Infosecurity* 7.1 (2010): 32–35.

Larsen, Lars Bang. "Zombies of Immaterial Labor: The Modern Monster and the Death of Death." *e-flux* 15.1 (2010).

Lauro, Sarah, and Karen Embry. "The Zombie Manifesto: The Nonhuman Condition in the Era of Advanced Capitalism." *boundary2* 35.1 (2008): 85–108.

Lehrer, Keith. "Consciousness, Representation and Knowledge." In *Self-Representational Approaches to Consciousness.* Eds. U. Kriegel and K. Williford. Cambridge: MIT Press, 2006. 409–20.

Liss, David. "What Maisie Knew." In *The New Dead.* Ed. Christopher Golden. New York: St. Martin's Griffin 2010. 9–41

Locke, Don. "Zombies, Schizophrenics, and Purely Physical Objects." *Mind* 85.337 (1976): 97–99.

Lockwood, Kurt. "Vampire Porn: The Top 10 Reasons Why Male Porn Stars Are Like Anne Rice Vampires." *Baltimore City Paper.* 17 July 2013.

Loftus, David. *Watching Sex: How Men Really Respond to Pornography.* New York: Thunder's Mouth, 2002.

Lokis-Adkins, Julie. *Deadly Desires: A Psychoanalytic Study of Female Sexual Perversion and Widowhood in Fin-De-Siecle Women's Writing.* London: Karnac Books, 2013.

Lugones, María. *Pilgrimages=Peregrinajes: Theorizing Coalition Against Multiple Oppressions.* Lanham, MD: Rowman & Littlefield, 2003.

MacCormack, Patricia. *Cinesexuality.* Hampshire: Ashgate, 2008.

MacCulloch, Diarmaid. *A History of Christianity.* London: Penguin, 2009.

Macpherson, Fiona. "A Disjunctive Theory of Introspection: A Reflection on Zombies and Anton's Syndrome." *Philosophical Issues* 20.1 (2010): 226–65.

Majeed, Raamy. "Pleading Ignorance in Response to Experiential Primitivism." *Philosophical Studies* 163.1 (2013): 251–69.

Malatesti, Luca. "Thinking About Phenomenal Concepts." *Synthesis Philosophica* 52.2 (2011): 391–402.

Marion, Isaac. *Warm Bodies.* London: Vintage, 2010.

Marks, Laura Helen. "I Want to Suck Your ... : Dracula in Pornographic Film." In *Dracula in Visual Media: Film, Television, Comic Book and Electronic Game Appearances, 1921–2010.* Eds. John Edgar Browning and Caroline Joan Picart. Jefferson: McFarland, 2011. 193–99.

Martin, George R. R. "Meathouse Man." In *The Living Dead.* Ed. John Joseph Adams. San Francisco: Night Shade Books, 2008. 277–98.

Massumi, Brian, ed. *The Politics of Everyday Fear.* Minneapolis: University of Minnesota Press, 1993.

Matheson, Richard. *I Am Legend.* Greenwich: Gold Medal, 1954.

Mbembe, Achille. "Necropolitics." *Public Culture* 15.1 (2003): 11–40.

McAlister, Elizabeth. "Slaves, Cannibals, and Infected Hyper-Whites: The Race and Religion of Zombies." *Anthropological Quarterly* 85.2 (2012): 457–86.

McElroy, Wendy. *XXX: A Woman's Right to Pornography*. New York: St. Martin's, 1995.

McGlotten, Shaka. "Dead and Live Life: Zombies, Queers, and Online Sociality." In *Generation Zombie: Essays on the Living Dead in Modern Culture*. Eds. Stephanie Boluk, and Wylie Lenz. Jefferson: McFarland, 2011. 182–93.

_____, and Sarah VanGundy. "Zombie Porn 1.0: Or, Some Queer Things Zombie Sex Can Teach Us." *Qui Parle* 21.2 (2013): 101–25.

McIntosh, Shawn. "The Evolution of the Zombie: The Monster that Keeps Coming Back." In *Zombie Culture: Autopsies of the Living Dead*. Eds. Shawn McIntosh and Marc Leverette. Lanham, MD: Scarecrow Press, 2008. 1–17.

McKim, Donald K. *Westminster Dictionary of Theological Terms*. Louisville: Westminster John Knox Press, 1996.

McMillan, Graeme. "Walking Dead Smashed Cable Ratings Records, Beats Broadcast Networks." *Wired*. 12 February 2013.

McNally, David. *Monsters of the Market: Zombies, Vampires and Global Capitalism*. Leiden: Brill, 2011.

McRuer, Robert. *Crip Theory: Cultural Signs of Queerness and Disability*. New York: New York University Press, 2006.

_____, and Abby Wilkerson. "Introduction to Desiring Disability: Queer Theory Meets Disability Studies." *GLQ: A Journal of Lesbian and Gay Studies* 9.1–2 (2003): 1–23.

_____, and Anna Mollow, eds. *Sex and Disability*. Durham: Duke University Press, 2012.

Menninghaus, Winfried. *Disgust: Theory and History of a Strong Sensation*. Albany: State University of New York, 2003.

Merleau-Ponty, Maurice. *Phenomenology of Perception*. Trans. Colin Smith. London: Routledge, 2002.

Mesch, Rachel. *The Hysteric's Revenge: French Women Writers at the Fin De Siècle*. Nashville: Vanderbilt University Press, 2006.

Milkov, Nikolay. "Sexual Experience." In *Sex, Love, and Friendship*. Ed. Adrianne Leigh McEvoy. New York: Rodopi, 2011. 155–66.

Mill, John Stuart. *Utilitarianism*. London: Parker, Son and Bourn, 1863.

Miller, David A. "Anal *Rope*." *Representations* 32.1 (1990): 114–33.

Miller, William Ian. *The Anatomy of Disgust*. Cambridge: Harvard University Press, 2009.

Mogul, Joey L., Andrea J. Ritchie, and Kay Whitlock. *Queer (In)Justice: The Criminalization of LGBT People in the United States*. Boston: Beacon Press, 2011.

Mole, Christopher. "Illusions, Demonstratives, and the Zombie Action Hypothesis." *Mind* 118.472 (2009): 995–1011.

Moreman, Christopher M., and Cory James Rushton, eds. *Race, Oppression and the Zombie: Essays on the Cross-Cultural Appropriations of the Caribbean Tradition*. Jefferson: McFarland, 2011.

Muñoz, José. *Disidentifications: Queers of Color and the Performance of Politics*. Minneapolis: Minnesota University Press, 1999.

Newmahr, Staci. *Playing on the Edge: Sadomasochism, Risk, and Intimacy*. Bloomington: Indiana University Press, 2011.

Nye, Andrea. *Feminism and Modern Philosophy*. London: Routledge, 2013.

Ober, Josiah. "Democracy's Dignity." *American Political Science Review* 106.4 (2012): 827–46.

Ordover, Nancy. *American Eugenics: Race, Queer Anatomy, and the Science of Nationalism*. Minneapolis: University of Minnesota Press, 2003.

Ostherr, Kirsten. *Cinematic Prophylaxis: Globalization and Contagion in the*

Discourse of World Health. Durham: Duke University Press, 2005.

Overstreet, Deborah Wilson. *Not Your Mother's Vampire: Vampires in Young Adult Fiction.* Lanham, MD: Scarecrow Press, 2006.

Paasonen, Susanna. *Carnal Resonance: Affect and Online Pornography.* Cambridge: MIT Press, 2011.

Paffenroth, Kim. *Gospel of the Living Dead: George Romero's Visions of Hell on Earth.* Waco: Baylor University Press, 2006.

Patterson, Natasha. "Cannibalizing Gender and Genre: A Feminist Re-Vision of George Romero's Zombie Films." In *Zombie Culture: Autopsies of the Living Dead.* Eds. Shawn McIntosh and Marc Leverette. Lanham: Scarecrow Press, 2008. 103–18.

Perkins, Lori. *Hungry for Your Love: An Anthology of Zombie Romance.* Boston: Ravenous Romance, 2009.

Phillip, Adam. *On Kissing, Tickling, and Being Bored: Psychoanalytic Essays on the Unexamined Life.* Cambridge: Harvard University Press, 1993.

Pinedo, Isabel Cristina. *Recreational Terror: Women and the Pleasures of Horror Film Viewing.* Albany: State University of New York Press, 1997.

Platt, Carrie Anne. "Cullen Family Values: Gender and Sexual Politics in the *Twilight* Series." In *Bitten by Twilight: Youth Culture, Media, and the Vampire Franchise.* Eds. Melissa A. Click, Jennifer Stevens Aubrey, and Elizabeth Behm-Morawitz. New York: Peter Lang, 2010. 71–86.

Ponder, Justin. "Dawn of the Different: The Mulatto Zombie in Zack Snyder's Dawn of the Dead." *The Journal of Popular Culture* 45.3 (2012): 551–71.

Poole, Daniel. *What Jane Austen Ate and Charles Dickens Knew: From Foxhunting to Whist: The Facts of Daily Life in Nineteenth-Century England.* New York: Touchstone, 1993.

Prothero, Stephen. *American Jesus: How the Son of God Became a National Icon.* New York: Farrar, Straus and Giroux, 2003.

Puar, Jasbir. *Terrorist Assemblages: Homonationalism in Queer Times.* Durham: Duke University Press, 2007.

Read, Benedict. *Victorian Sculpture.* New Haven: Yale University Press, 1982.

Reed, John R. *Victorian Conventions.* Athens: Ohio University Press, 1975.

Richardson, Niall. *Transgressive Bodies: Representations in Film and Popular Culture.* London: Ashgate, 2010.

Ricoeur, Paul. *Interpretation Theory: Discourse and the Surplus of Meaning.* Fort Worth: Texas Christian University Press, 1976.

Robinson, Bruce A. "*The Passion of the Christ*: Assessment by Conservative Christians." *ReligiousTolerance.Org.* 13 March 2005.

Rosch, D. *Chronic Diseases, especially the Nervous Diseases of Women.* Trans. Charles Dummig. New York: Samuel R. Wells, 1870.

Rosin, Hanna. "Can We Really 'Cure' Autism?" *Slate.* 17 January 2013.

Ross, Michael W. "Typing, Doing, and Being: Sexuality and the Internet." *The Journal of Sex Research* 42.4 (2005): 342–52.

Rossetti, Yves, and Antti Revonsuo, eds. *Beyond Dissociation: Interaction between Dissociated Implicit and Explicit Processing.* Philadelphia: John Benjamins, 2000.

Roth, Phyllis A. "Suddenly Sexual Women in Bram Stoker's *Dracula*." In *Dracula.* Eds. Nina Auerbach and David J. Skal. New York: Norton, 1997. 411–21.

Rubin, Edward L. "Sex, Politics and Morality." *William and Mary Law Review* 47.1 (2005): 2–48.

Russell, Jamie. *Book of the Dead: The Complete History of Zombie Cinema.* Surrey: FAB Press, 2005.

Russo, Mary. *The Female Grotesque: Risk, Excess and Modernity.* New York: Routledge, 1994.

Samuels, Ellen. "Critical Divides: Judith Butler's Body Theory and the Question of Disability." In *Feminist Disability Studies.* Ed. Kim Q. Hall.

Bloomington: Indiana University Press, 2011. 48–66.

Sandahl, Carrie. "Queering the Crip or Cripping the Queer? Intersections of Queer and Crip Identities in Solo Autobiographical Performance." *GLQ: A Journal of Lesbian and Gay Studies* 9.1–2 (2003): 25–56.

Sanders, Teela. "Male Sexual Scripts: Intimacy, Sexuality and Pleasure in the Purchase of Commercial Sex." *Sociology* 42.3 (2008): 400–17.

Saunders, Robert A. "Undead Spaces: Fear, Globalization, and the Popular Geopolitics of Zombiism." *Geopolitics* 17.1 (2012): 80–104.

Sceats, Sarah. "Oral Sex: Vampiric Transgression and the Writing of Angela Carter." *Tulsa Studies in Women's Literature* 20.1 (2001): 107–21.

Schaefer, Eric. "Gauging a Revolution: 16 mm Film and the Rise of the Pornographic Feature." In *Porn Studies*. Ed. Linda Williams. Durham: Duke University Press, 2004. 370–400.

Schechtman, Marya. "The Brain/Body Problem." *Philosophical Psychology* 10.2 (1997): 149–64.

Schwartz, Barry. "Mourning and the Making of a Sacred Symbol: Durkheim and the Lincoln Assassination." *Social Forces* 70.2 (1991): 343–64.

Schweik, Susan. *The Ugly Laws: Disability in Public.* New York: New York University Press, 2010.

Sender, Katherine. *Business Not Politics: The Making of the Gay Market.* New York: Columbia University Press, 2004.

Senf, Carol A. "*Dracula*: Stoker's Response to the New Woman." *Victorian Studies* 26.1 (1982): 33–49.

Serlin, David. *Replaceable You: Engineering the Body in Postwar America.* Chicago: University of Chicago Press, 2004.

Shaviro, Steven. *The Cinematic Body.* Minneapolis: University of Minnesota Press. 1993.

Sheets-Johnstone, Maxine. "The Corporeal Turn: Reflections on Awareness and Gnostic Tactility and Kinaesthesia." *Journal of Consciousness Studies* 18.7 (2011): 145–68.

Slade, Joseph W. "Eroticism and Technological Regression: The Stag Film." *History and Technology* 22.1 (2006): 27–52.

Smith, Angela M. *Hideous Progeny: Disability, Eugenics, and Classic Horror Cinema.* New York: Columbia University Press, 2011.

Smithies, Declan. "The Mental Lives of Zombies." *Philosophical Perspectives* 26.1 (2012): 343–72.

Somerville, Siobhan. *Queering the Color Line: Race and the Invention of Homosexuality in American Culture.* Durham: Duke University Press, 2000.

Spade, Dean. *Normal Life: Administrative Violence, Critical Trans Politics, and the Limits of Law.* Brooklyn: South End Press, 2011.

Staskiewicz, Keith. "Grab the shotgun and cover your cranium: We talk to Max Brooks about selling 1 million copies of *The Zombie Survival Guide*." *Entertainment Weekly.* 6 July 2010.

Stoker, Bram. *Dracula.* New York: Norton, 1997.

Strub, Whitney. *Perversion for Profit: The Politics of Pornography and the Rise of the New Right.* New York: Columbia University Press, 2011.

Swanwick, Michael. "The Dead." In *The Living Dead.* Ed. John Joseph Adams. San Francisco: Night Shade Books, 2008. 99–107.

Thomas, Kette. "Haitian Zombie, Myth, and Modern Identity." *Comparative Literature and Culture* 12.2 (2010): 1–9.

Thompson, Kirsten Thompson. *Apocalyptic Dread.* Albany: New York University Press, 2007.

Treichler, Paula A. *How to Have Theory in an Epidemic: Cultural Chronicles of AIDS.* Durham: Duke University Press, 1999.

Trumble, Angus. "Love and Death: Art in the Age of Queen Victoria." In *Love and Death: Art in the Age of Queen Victoria.* Ed. Angus Trumble. Adelaide: Art Gallery of South Australia, 2001. 17–54.

Twitchell, James. *Dreadful Pleasures: An Anatomy of Modern Horror*. New York: Oxford University Press, 1987.

van der Zee, James. *The Harlem Book of the Dead*. New York: Morgan and Morgan, 1978.

Wagner, Brooke. "Becoming a Sexual Being: Overcoming Constraints of Female Sexuality." *Sexualities* 12.3 (2009): 289–311.

Wald, Priscilla. *Contagious: Cultures, Carriers, and the Outbreak Narrative*. Durham: Duke University Press, 2008.

Walker, Tim. "Lena Dunham: Could she be the Voice of a Generation?" *The Independent*. 6 October 2012.

Waller, Gregory A. *The Living and the Undead: From Stoker's* Dracula *to Romero's* Dawn of the Dead. Urbana: University of Illinois Press, 1986.

Ward, Graham. *Cities of God*. London: Routledge, 2000.

Ward, Jane. "Queer Feminist Pigs: A Spectator's Manifesta." In *The Feminist Porn Book*. Eds. Tristan Taormino, Celine Parrenas Shimizu, Constance Penley, Mireille Miller-Young. New York: Feminist Press, 2013. 130–39.

Warr, Deborah J. "The Importance of Love and Understanding: Speculation of Romance in Safe Sex Health Promotion." *Women's Studies International Forum* 24.2 (2001): 241–52.

Waugh, Thomas. "Men's Pornography: Gay vs. Straight." In *Out in Culture: Gay, Lesbian, and Queer Essays on Popular Culture*. Eds. Corey K. Creekmur and Alexander Doty. Durham: Duke University Press, 1995. 307–27.

Webb, Jen, and Sam Byrnand. "Some Kind of Virus: The Zombie as Body and as Trope." *Body and Society* 14.2 (2008): 83–98.

Webster, Jane S. *Ingesting Jesus: Eating and Drinking in the Gospel of John*. Atlanta: Society of Biblical Literature, 2003.

Weeks, Jeffrey. *The Languages of Sexuality*. London: Routledge, 2011.

Werth, Robert. "I Do What I'm Told, Sort Of: Reformed Subjects, Unruly Citizens, and Parole." *Theoretical Criminology* 16.3 (2012): 329–46.

Whiting, Demian. "Are Emotions Perceptual Experiences of Value?" *Ratio* 25.1 (2012): 93–107.

Wilcox, Russell. "Cross-Gender Identification in Commercial Pornographic Films." In *Porn 101: Eroticism, Pornography, and the First Amendment*. Eds. James Elias, Vern L. Bullough, Gwen Brewer, Jeffrey J. Douglas, Veronica Diehl Elias, and Will Jarvis. New York: Prometheus, 1999. 479–91.

Wilkerson, Abby. "Disability, Sex Radicalism, and Political Agency." In *Feminist Disability Studies*. Ed. Kim Q. Hall. Bloomington: Indiana University Press, 2011. 193–217.

Wilkins, Ben. "Director's Statement." Prettydeadwww. N.d.

Williams, Linda. "Film Bodies: Gender, Genre and Excess." In *Feminist Film Theory: A Reader*. Ed. Sue Thornham. New York: New York University Press, 1999. 267–81.

Williams, Linda. *Hard Core: Power, Pleasure, and the "Frenzy of the Visible."* Berkeley: University of California Press, 1989.

Williams, Linda. *Screening Sex*. Durham: Duke University Press, 2008.

Williams, Tony. *The Cinema of George A. Romero: Knight of the Living Dead*. London: Wallflower Press, 2003.

Winter, Steven. "Reimagining Democratic Theory for Social Individuals." *Zygon* 46.1 (2011): 224–45.

Wood, Robin. "An Introduction to the American Horror Film." In *Movies and Methods Vol.2*. Ed. Bill Nichols. Los Angeles: University of California Press, 1985. 195–220.

Wu, Huei-Hsia. "Gender, Romance Novels and Plastic Sexuality in the United States: a Focus on Female College Students." *Journal of International Women's Studies* 8.1 (2006): 125–34.

Wu, Wayne. "The Case for Zombie Agency." *Mind* 122.485 (2013): 217–30.

York, Rafiel, and Chris York, eds. *Comic Books and the Cold War*. Jefferson: McFarland, 2012.

Films, Television Shows and Videogames

At Twilight Come the Flesh Eaters (1998, dir. Vidkid Timo, USA)

Beyond Fucked: A Zombie Odyssey (2013, dir. Tommy Pistol, USA)

Bloodlust Zombies (2011, dir. Len Kabasinski, USA)

Braindead (Dead-Alive) (1992, dir. Peter Jackson, New Zealand)

Bride of Frankenstein (1935, dir. James Whale, USA)

Brunch of the Living Dead (2006, dir. Dan Dujnic, USA)

Call of Duty: Modern Warfare 2 (2009, dir. Jason West, USA)

Chip and Bernie's Dating Guide for the Zombie Apocalypse (2011, dir. Pasquale Murena, USA)

Cockneys vs Zombies (2012, dir. Matthias Hoene, UK)

Corpus Delecti (The Passion of Zombie Jesus) (2009, dir. Ira Hunter, Canada)

Creatures from the Pink Lagoon (2006, dir. Chris Diana, USA)

Cupcake: A Zombie Lesbian Musical (2012, dir. Rebecca Thomson, Australia)

Dance of the Dead (2008, dir. Greg Bishop, USA)

Dark Angels (2000, dir. Nic Andrews, USA)

Dark Angels 2: Bloodline (2005, dir. Nic Andrews, USA)

Dating a Zombie (2012, dir. Jack Abele, USA)

Dawn of the Dead (1978, dir. George Romero, Italy/USA)

Dawn of the Dead (2004, dir. Zack Snyder, USA/Canada/Japan/France)

Dawna of the Dead (2008, dir. Laume Conroy, USA)

Day of the Dead (1985, dir. George Romero, USA)

Dead Island (2011, dir. Pawei Marchewka, Poland)

Deadgirl (2008, dirs. Marcel Sarmiento and Gadi Harel, USA)

Dellamorte Dellamore (1994, dir. Michele Soavi, Italy/Frace/Germany)

Doghouse (2009, dir. Jake West, UK)

Dracula (1931, dir. Tod Browning, USA)

Dracula XXX (2011, dir. Axel Braun, USA)

Dragula (1973, dir. Jim Moss, USA)

The Erotic Adventures of Candy (1978, dir. Gail Palmer, USA)

Erotic Nights of the Living Dead (Le Notti Erotiche dei Morti Viventi) (1980, dir. Joe D'Amato, Italy)

The Fall of the House of Usher (1960, dir. Roger Corman, USA)

Fido (2006, dir. Andrew Currie, USA/Canada)

Flaming Gay Zombies (2007, dirs. Sadya Lashua and Aaron Mace, USA)

Frankenstein (1931, dir. James Whale, USA)

Fury of the Wolfman (La Furia del Hombre Lobo) (1972, dir. J.M. Zabalza, Spain)

Gay Zombie (2007, dir. Michael Simon, USA)

Gayracula (1983, dir. Roger Earl, USA)

Generation Jobless (2013, dirs. Sharon Bartlett and Maria LeRose, Canada)

Girls, "Vagina Panic" (2012, dir. Lena Dunham, USA)

GrubGirl (2005, dir. Craven Moorehead, USA)

Harold's Going Stiff (2011, dir. Keith Wright, UK)

His Dracula (2012, dir. Bobby Drake, USA)

Horno (2009, dir. Terence Williams, USA)

House of the Dead (2003, dir. Uwe Boll, Germany/Canada/USA)

The House of the Dead (1997, dir. Takashi Oda, Japan/Canada)

I Am Legend (2007, dir. Francis Lawrence, USA)

I Can't Believe I Fucked a Zombie (2011, dir. Rodney Moore, USA)

I Walked with a Zombie (1943, dir. Jacques Tourneur, USA)

I, Zombie: The Chronicles of Pain (1998, dir. Andrew Parkinson, UK)

In the Flesh (2012, dir. Jonny Campbell, UK)

Jesus H. Zombie (2006, dir. Daniel Heisel, USA)

Juan of the Dead (Juan de los Muertos, 2011, dir. Alejandro Brugués, Spain/Cuba)

L.A. Zombie (2010, dir. Bruce LaBruce, USA/Germany)

Last Man on Earth (1964, dir. Ubaldo B. Ragona, Italy/USA)

The Last of Us (2013, dirs. Bruce Straley and Neil Druckmann, USA)

Left 4 Dead (2008, dir. Mike Booth, USA)

Lesbian Zombies from Outer Space (2013, dir. Jave Galt-Miller, USA)

Martin (1976, dir. George A. Romero, USA)

The Masque of the Red Death (1964, dir. Roger Corman, USA/UK)

The Mummy (1932, dir. Karl Freund, USA)

The Nature of Nicholas (2002, dir. Jeff Erbbach, Canada)

The Necro Files (1997, dir. Matt Jaissle, USA)

The Necro Files 2 (2003, dir. Ron Carlo, USA)

The Nerdist "Zombies!" (2013, Dir. Alan Wu, USA)

The Night Boys (1991, dir. Gino Colbert, USA)

Night of the Giving Head (2008, dir. Rodney Moore, USA)

Night of the Howling Beast (*La Maldicion de la Bestia*) (1974, dir. M.I. Bonns, Spain)

Night of the Living Dead (1968, dir. George A. Romero, USA)

Night of the Living Dead: Reanimated (2009, dir. Mike Schneider, USA)

Night of the Living Dorks (*Die Nacht der Lebenden Loser*) (2004, dir. Mathias Dinter, Germany)

The Omega Man (1971, dir. Boris Sagal, USA)

The Orgy of the Dead (*La Orgia de los Muerto*) (1973, dir. José Luis Merino, Spain/Italy)

Osombie (2012, dir. John Lyde, USA)

Otto; or, Up with Dead People (2008, dir. Bruce LaBruce, Germany/Canada)

ParaNorman (2012, dirs. Chris Butler and Sam Fell, USA)

The Passion of the Christ (2004, dir. Mel Gibson, USA)

The Pit and the Pendulum (1961, dir. Roger Corman, USA)

The Plague of the Zombies (1966, dir. John Gilling, UK)

Poison (1991, dir. Todd Haynes, USA)

Porn of the Dead (2006, dir. Rob Rotten, USA)

Porn Star Zombies (2009, dir. Keith Emerson, USA)

Pretty Dead (2013, dir. Benjamin Wilkins, USA)

Rape Zombie: Lust of the Dead (*Reipu zonbi*) (2012, dir. Naoyuki Tomomatsu, Japan)

Resident Evil (*Bio Hazard*) (1996, dirs. Mikami Shinji and Hosoki Mtsuhisa, Japan)

Resident Evil (2002, dir. Paul W. S. Anderson, USA)

Return of the Living Dead (1985, dir. Dan O'Bannon, USA)

Return of the Living Dead Part 3 (1993, dir. Brian Yuzna, USA/Japan)

Seven Murders for Scotland Yard (*Jack el Destripador de Londres*) (1971, dir. José Luis Madrid, Italy/Spain)

Shane Diesel's Cuckold Stories (2009-present, dir. Paul Woodcrest, USA)

Shaun of the Dead (2004, dir. Edgar Wright, UK)

Southern Hospitality (2013, dir. B. Skow, USA)

Story of Joanna, The (1975, dir. Gerard Damiano, USA)

Strap Attack (2004–12, dir. Joey Silvera, USA)

Stripperland (2011, dir. Sean Skelding, USA)

Survival of the Dead (2009, dir. George A. Romero, USA/Canada)

Swamp Zombies (2005, dir. Dan Lantz, USA)

The Terrible Secret of Dr Hichcock (*L'orrible Segreto del Dr Hichcock*) (1962, dir. Riccardo Freda, Italy)

Tomb of Ligeia, The (1964, dir. Roger Corman, UK).

True Blood (2008-Present, dirs. Alan Ball et al., USA)

True Love Zombie (2012, dir. Paul Blevins, USA)

28 Days Later (2002, dir. Danny Boyle, UK)

28 Weeks Later (2007, dir. Juan Carlos Fresnadillo, UK/Spain)

Twilight (2008, dir. Catherine Hardwicke, USA)

The Vampire Diaries (2009-Present, dirs. Marcos Siega et al., USA)

The Walking Dead (2010-Present, dirs. Frank Darabont et al., USA)

Walking Dead: A Hardcore Parody, The (2013, dirs. Tommy Pistol and Joanna Angel, USA)

Walking Dead: The Videogame (2012, dirs. Sean Vanaman et al. USA)

Warm Bodies (2013, dir. Jonathan Levine, USA)

White Zombie (1932, dir. Victor Halperin, USA)

Wild Zero (1999, dir. Tetsuro Takeuchi, Japan)

World War Z (2013, dir. Mark Forster, USA/Malta)

Zombie Beach Party (2003, dir. Stacey Case, Canada)

Zombie Cheerleading Camp (2007, dir. Jon Fabris, USA)

The Zombie Christ (2012, dir. Christopher Bryan, USA)

Zombie Creeping Flesh (Virus) (1980, dir. Bruno Mattei, Italy/Spain)

Zombie Flesheaters (Zombi 2) (1979, dir. Lucio Fulci, Italy)

Zombie Holocaust (1980, dir. Marino Girolami, Italy)

Zombie Honeymoon (2004, dir. David Gebroe, USA)

Zombie Love (2007, dir. Yfke Van Berckelaer, USA/Netherlands)

Zombie Love (2008, dir. Ken Morris, USA)

A Zombie Love Song (2013, dir. William Morrison, Canada)

Zombie Love Story (2008, dir. Marcus Slabine, USA)

Zombie Marriage Counselling: I'm a Lesbian (2009, dir. Alex Ferrari, USA)

Zombie Strippers! (2008, dir. Jay Lee, USA)

Zombiechrist (2010, dir. Bill Zebub, USA)

Zombieland (2009, dir. Ruben Fleischer, USA)

Zombies vs Strippers (2012, dir. Alex Nicolaou, USA)

Zombies! Zombies! Zombies! (2008, dir. Jason Murphy, USA)

ZombiU (2012, dirs. Jean Philippe Caro and Florent Sacré, France)

About the Contributors

Sasha **Cocarla** is a PhD candidate with the Institute of Women's Studies at the University of Ottawa. Her research is on popular culture representations of bisexuality and the ways in which they work to act as a counter to homonationalist articulations. She focuses especially on popular culture understandings of queerness, fatness, and monstrosity.

Denise N. **Cook** is a PhD student of sociology at the University of Nevada–Las Vegas. Her interests include the study of culture, social strata, and sexuality. Her MA thesis examined world attitudes pertaining to prostitution as an expression of materialist or postmaterialist attitudes.

Darren **Elliott-Smith** is a lecturer in film and television at University of Hertfordshire. He has published several essays on LGBT horror film and television, and also studies gender and sexuality in film, psychoanalysis and cinema, the consumption of cult/trash television and film, and adaptation/appropriation in the moving image.

Trevor **Grizzell** is a PhD student in women, gender, and sexuality studies at the University of Kansas. His research uses a queer lens to examine interactions of time, embodiment, and power through visual and digital cultures.

Cathy **Hannabach** is an independent scholar and the founder and director of Philly Queer Media, which fosters new creative work at the intersections of queer activism and queer media production. She has taught courses on film/media studies, feminism, queer theory, and American studies at five universities across the U.S.

Marcus **Harmes** is a lecturer at the University of Southern Queensland who specializes in both early modern history and the cultural history of science fiction and horror films. He is the author of *Bishops and Power in Early Modern England* (Bloomsbury, 2013) and numerous articles and essays on topics ranging from Roman history to seventeenth century religious history.

Steve **Jones** is a senior lecturer in media at Northumbria University. His research is principally focused on representations of sex and violence, the philosophy of self, gender politics, and ethics. His monograph *Torture Porn: Popular Horror After Saw* was published in 2013 by Palgrave-Macmillan.

Laura Helen **Marks** is a postdoctoral fellow in the English department at Louisiana State University. Her research concerns gender, genre and sexual representation, specifically in pornographic film and literature and hardcore film adaptations of Victorian literature and the various ways pornography makes use of "the Victorian" as a canvas on which to construct erotic appeal.

Shaka **McGlotten** is an anthropologist and an associate professor of media, society, and the arts at Purchase College-SUNY. Much of his research is ethnographically based, although he also draws on the humanities and arts. His essays on affect, anthropology, race, media, and technology have appeared in journals and books.

Max **Thornton** studied classics at University College London and theology at Graduate Theological Union in Berkeley, California. He is a doctoral candidate in theology and philosophy at Drew University in Madison, New Jersey. His research interests include new media studies, gender and queer theory, deaf and disability studies, and the intersection of Christian theology with the above.

Emma **Vossen** is a comics and sexuality scholar completing her PhD at the University of Waterloo and writing a dissertation about pornographic comics. Her publications cover a variety of topics including Superman's co-creator Joe Shuster, *The Walking Dead* comic and videogame, and the *Fifty Shades of Grey* trilogy.

Index